About this Book

BUSINESSES build and grow and change. Downsizing, upsizing, mergers and acquisitions never cease, and as a result, people face the challenge of learning SAP - often in hectic and fast paced environments, with minimal or no help. This book is written for these people. It is intended as a basic primer for those needing a quick understanding of the key transactions in an SAP ECC (ERP Central Component) 6.0 system, as this software is normally used in small to medium sized manufacturing companies.

We tried to focus this book on a core set of ECC business actions (in SAP speak, 'transactions') that customer service, purchasing, receiving, production planning and shipping personnel perform on a daily basis. *All the topics we cover in this book are covered in other books in greater detail.* Our goal was to provide, in a single reference, the key conceptual information that would help people new to SAP, understand an SAP ECC prototype of *their company*. We believe that it is in these prototype environments, that the real learning of SAP takes place.

We hope to write further works in this area - to cover additional aspects of SAP projects. Specifically, in the areas of configuration, data loading, testing and project management, we have more we would like to share. But those topics are not for this book. Here our focus is restricted to the needs of business users (to us, the SAP operator) and the transactions they execute on a daily basis to run their businesses on SAP.

We hope you buy this book and find it useful in your first SAP project / learning experience. If a friend gave you this book, we hope it came with a good recommendation.

Thank You and Good Luck !

Mike Wangler & Saad Siddiqi

June, 2012

This book represents the technical opinions and research of its authors in regards to the optimal business practices for the use of the SAP ERP Central Component (ECC) software in a general manufacturing environment. As such, it is original work and its copyright is pending.

The authors are independent consultants with over 20 years of practical SAP experience through dozens of R/3 and ECC 6.0 implementations. The authors are not associated with SAP AG. The technical opinions presented in this book represent their best independent assessment of how SAP ERP Central Component capabilities can (and usually are configured to) work in a manufacturing enterprise.

SAP, SAP ERP, ERP Central Component, ECC, R/3, mySAP.com and other SAP products and services mentioned are registered trademarks of SAP AG Germany. Other product and service names mentioned herein are the trademarks of their respective companies.

The screenshots contained in this book originated from a licensed and functional SAP ECC system hosted by Software Lab Access.

The authors wish to thank the following individuals who gave much to us in our careers – helping us learn the capabilities of SAP. To us, they are the true definition of expert business consultants – and we are indebted to them for their time, their patience and their knowledge that they freely shared with us.

Rainer Hoepfler, **Francisco Herrera** and **Kevin Thompson** for many ideas in the areas of Master Data, Materials Requirements Planning and Production Order Management.

Rudolf Schauerte for his help in all aspects of Sales and Distribution (SD) Module – including Inquiries, Quotes, Sales Orders and Pricing Procedures.

Carlos Sousa and **Ken Picarel** for their help in understanding many SD aspects, especially availability processing and sales reporting.

And most of all, **Dirk Salzsaeuler**, CEAG Soest Germany, a true gentleman and scholar, and a ready source of information on nearly every aspect of an SAP ECC System from ABAP programming to Z-Transactions. Dirk was our mentor and our coach and always a good friend.

We also wish to thank dozens of Cooper Industries employees (too many to name here) that we had the opportunity to work with on a series of challenging SAP projects in Canada, Mexico, Europe, India and the United States. We enjoyed working with you and hope you enjoyed, at least in some part, learning SAP with us.

Mike Wangler: I wish to thank Saad for his steadfastness in seeing this book through to its completion.

Saad Siddiqi: I would like to thank my father, **Haroon Siddiqi**, and my mother, **Sabiha Siddiqi**, for the love and guidance they have provided me throughout my career. Without their effort and belief in me, writing this book would not have been possible. I would also like to thank my mentor and friend, **Mike Wangler**, whose leadership and direction has had a major impact, not only on this project, but also on my job, and for it, I am extremely grateful.

S & W

SAP will tell you that the best run businesses run on SAP and we agree, but we think it is also important to recognize the people that *run* SAP in these enterprises. We find that these people — we refer to them as *SAP Operators* — are often taken for granted and their training and proficiency goes under-valued. We do not refer to these people as 'users' — Facebook and AOL have users. To function effectively, SAP needs Operators; and we think it is important to recognize the SAP Operator for their proficiency and skill.

When beginning basic operator SAP training, we present a map of key business transactions (like the one on the next page) and ask our students to focus on these transactions - and we say this:

'It's OK to get lost in SAP, just don't lose the map…'

It's hard for us to say anything more than that.

It is easy to get lost in SAP, because the options it presents are nearly endless. We hope that you find the transaction map useful as one way towards understanding how to run your business on SAP.

We also hope that you can keep your focus on the basic things that make SAP work.

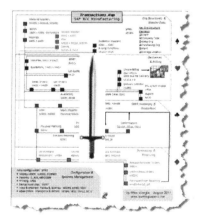

Don't forget the Operators

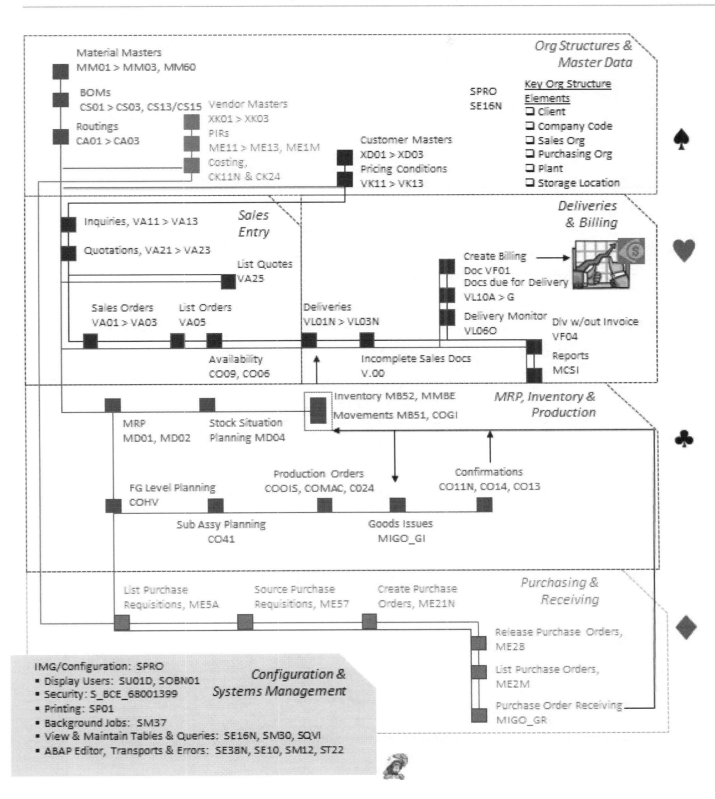

Org Structures & Master Data

Material Masters
MM01 > MM03, MM60

BOMs
CS01 > CS03, CS13/CS15

Routings
CA01 > CA03

Vendor Masters
XK01 > XK03

PIRs
ME11 > ME13, ME1M

Costing,
CK11N & CK24

Customer Masters
XD01 > XD03
Pricing Conditions
VK11 > VK13

SPRO
SE16N

Key Org Structure
Elements
❑ Client
❑ Company Code
❑ Sales Org
❑ Purchasing Org
❑ Plant
❑ Storage Location

♠

Sales Entry

Inquiries, VA11 > VA13

Quotations, VA21 > VA23

List Quotes
VA25

Sales Orders
VA01 > VA03

List Orders
VA05

Deliveries
VL01N > VL03N

Availability
CO09, CO06

Incomplete Sales Docs
V.00

Deliveries & Billing

Create Billing
Doc VF01
Docs due for Delivery
VL10A > G

Delivery Monitor
VL06O

Dlv w/out Invoice
VF04

Reports
MCSI

♥

MRP, Inventory & Production

Inventory MB52, MMBE
Movements MB51, COGI

MRP
MD01, MD02

Stock Situation
Planning MD04

Production Orders
COOIS, COMAC, CO24

Confirmations
CO11N, CO14, CO13

FG Level Planning
COHV

Sub Assy Planning
CO41

Goods Issues
MIGO_GI

♣

Purchasing & Receiving

List Purchase
Requisitions, ME5A

Source Purchase
Requisitions, ME57

Create Purchase
Orders, ME21N

Release Purchase Orders,
ME28

List Purchase Orders,
ME2M

Purchase Order Receiving
MIGO_GR

♦

IMG/Configuration: SPRO
- Display Users: SU01D, SOBN01
- Security: S_BCE_68001399
- Printing: SP01
- Background Jobs: SM37
- View & Maintain Tables & Queries: SE16N, SM30, SQVI
- ABAP Editor, Transports & Errors: SE38N, SE10, SM12, ST22

Configuration & Systems Management

SAP ECC Manufacturing Transaction Map Legend

The map depicts 6 functional areas, each assigned a playing card symbol:

✓ Org Structures & Master Data (Spades) ♠

✓ Sales Entry (Hearts 'A') ♥ A

✓ Deliveries & Billings (Hearts 'B') ♥ B

✓ MRP, Inventory & Production (Clubs) ♣

✓ Purchasing & Receiving (Diamonds) ♦

✓ Configuration & Systems Management (Jokers) 🃏

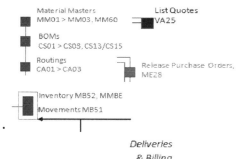

page 72

Org Structures & Master Data ♠

The card symbols also indicate page – area assignment.

A Transaction (or group of transactions) are displayed as a box – e.g. the Material Master series of transactions includes MM01, MM02, MM03 & MM60 and is depicted like this:

Material Masters
MM01 > MM03, MM60

Data flows between transactions are displayed as lines with 3 master data types indicated:

✓ Material Master/Production Line

✓ Vendor Master/Purchasing Line

✓ Customer Master/Pricing Line

Material Masters
MM01 > MM03, MM60

List Quotes
VA25

BOMs
CS01 > CS03, CS13/CS15

Routings
CA01 > CA03

Release Purchase Orders,
ME28

Inventory MB52, MMBE
Movements MB51

A Solid line is used to depict Inventory related data.

A chart symbol indicates the final destination and essential goal of all the transactions included on the map – to increase on time customer deliveries and raise the profits for the enterprise.

Deliveries
& Billing

Create Billing
Doc VF01N
Docs due for Delivery
VL10A > G

This book is organized into 4 sections.

The first section provides an **executive level overview** of SAP, the company, and some needed background on the ERP Central Component. This is done in the fewest pages possible.

The second section covers **User Interface basics** of the ERP Central Component. Here you will find information on how to logon to SAP, how to open and close windows, execute transactions, load Menu favorites, set default parameters, perform field level searches and printing, and how to export your business data into other business applications such as Excel. We organized this section around a **'First 40 List'** of topics that we believe all SAP operators should know in order to gain the maximum utility from an SAP ECC system.

The third (and largest) section of the book presents a **Transaction Map** of SAP ECC application. This map identifies 45 transaction 'groups' that we have found essential in understanding how SAP is normally deployed in a manufacturing environment. The map is divided into 6 functional areas – and in each of these areas, screen level transactional summaries and concept briefings on key subjects are presented.

The last section is a glossary of SAP terminology. We call this an 'It's a…' summary of the key SAP ECC transactions, tables and terms that are included in the book.

SAP / ERP FAQS Background

Operator Interface Basics 'First 40' List

Transaction Map and Screen Surveys

'It's a… ' Table

SAP ERP Central Component in Manufacturing an Operator's Guide

Table of Contents

Section/Topic	Page
Section 1: ECC Background	13
SAP AG	15
SAP AG Market Size / Compare	16
SAP ERP Central Component ("ECC")	17
ECC means Sales, Purchasing and Production Orders	18
ECC Order Process Flows	19
SAP means Configuration	20
IMG Configuration Tool (SPRO)	21
SAP means Master and Transactional data	22
SAP Data and the Client Server Concept	23
SAP provides Security	24
Section 2: ECC Operator Basics	25
The Sandbox (find one)	27
SAP Logon Pad	28
Adding a New System to SAP Logon Pad	29
SAP Initial Logon and Change Password Dialog	30
SAP Main Menu Window Controls	31
System Menu Line and Display Technical Names	32
SAP Green Check & Command Field	33
SAP System Icons	34
Main Menu Icons	35
SAP Easy Access Window – User Favorites	36
SAP Easy Access Window – SAP menu	37
SAP menu – Logistics key areas	38
System Notification & Status Bar	39
Window and Transaction Controls	40
Transaction Codes	41
Finding Transactions	43
Starting a Transaction	45
Getting Help	46
Getting Help – Field Level Example	49
Opening & Closing Windows	51
Field Level Selections	53
Printing	57
Exporting Data to Excel	59
Setting User Parameters	61
Maintaining User Favorites	65
SAP ECC Operator 'First Forty' List	66

SAP ERP Central Component in Manufacturing an Operator's Guide
Table of Contents

Section/Topic	Page
Section 3 Transaction Map & Screen Surveys	68
ECC 6.0 Transactions Map (Manufacturing)	70
Map Area 1 Org Structures and Master Data	71
Org Structures	73
The SAP Client	76
Company Codes	77
Plants	78
Storage Locations	80
Sales Organizations	81
Purchasing Organizations	82
Transaction Notes: SPRO	83
Transaction SPRO	84
Transaction Notes: SE16N Table Viewer	86
Key SAP Tables	88
Transaction Group Overview: Material Master Data	89
Material Masters in BOMs, Routings & PIRs	90
Material Master Data Types a Summary	91
Material Master Example Views	92
Material Master Views Concept Diagram	93
Material Master Views Summary	94
Material Master Views Examples	96
Material Master Key Fields	109
Transaction Notes: MM03, Display Material Master	112
Transaction Notes: MM02, Change Material Master	115
Transaction Notes: MM01, Create Material Master	117
Transaction Group Overview: Bills of Material (BOMs)	120
Transaction Notes: CS03, Display BOM	122
Transaction Group Overview: Routings	126
Transaction Notes: CA03, Display Routing	129
Transaction Group Overview: Vendor Master	133
Transaction Group Overview: Purchasing Info Records	135
Transaction Notes: ME1M, Display PIR Report	136
Transaction Group Overview: Material Costing	139
Transaction Group Overview: Customer Master	141
Transaction Group Overview: Pricing	143

SAP ERP Central Component in Manufacturing an Operator's Guide
Table of Contents

Section/Topic	Page
Map Area 2A: Customer Service Sales Order Entry	145
Section Overview	146
Transaction Group Overview: Inquiries	147
Transaction Group Overview: Quotations	148
Transaction Group Overview: Sales Orders	149
Sales Orders: Additional Key Concepts	15`
Transaction Overview: Availability Check	152
Transaction Notes: CO09, Material Availability	153
Transaction Notes: CO06, Back Order Processing	154
Sales Order Incompleteness Procedure Overview	155
Transaction Notes: V.00, Incomplete Sales Documents	156
Map Area 2B: Deliveries and Billing	157
Transaction Group Overview: Deliveries	158
Transaction Overview VL01N, Create delivery	159
Transaction Notes: VL10 Create Deliveries	160
Transaction Notes: VL060, Outbound Delivery Monitor	161
Transaction Notes: VT01N-VT03N, Shipments	162
Transaction Group Notes: VF01-VF04, Billing	164
Reporting	166
Map Area 3: MRP, Production and Inventory	167
MRP, Production & Inventory Transaction Summary	169
MRP Concept: What happens when MRP runs	170
MRP Concept Diagram	171
SAP Production Order Basics	172
Production Order Overview	173
Collective Planned Order Processing Strategy	174
Concept Overview Finished Goods Planning, COHV	175
Example Copy/Paste between VA05 and COHV	176
Transaction Notes: COHV, Mass Processing	177
COHV Mass processing	178
COHV Mass Processing Report Display	179
Transaction Notes: CO41, Mass Processing	180
Transaction Notes: COOIS, Order Reporting	182
COOIS Report Display	183
Transaction Notes: COMAC, Missing Parts Update	184
COMAC Report Display	185

SAP ERP Central Component in Manufacturing an Operator's Guide
Table of Contents

Map Area 3: MRP, Production and Inventory (Continued)	Page
Transaction Notes: CO24, Missing Parts Report	186
CO24 Report Display	187
Transaction Notes: MIGO_GI, Goods Issues	188
Transaction Notes: CO11N, Confirmation	190
Transaction Overview: CO14, Display Confirmations	192
Transaction Overview: CO13 Cancel Order Confirmation	193
Transaction Notes: COGI, Production Order Errors	194
Transaction Notes: Run MRP at Plant Level, MD01	196
Transaction Notes: MD02, Single Item / Multilevel MRP	198
Transaction Notes: MD04, Display Stock Situation	200
Transaction Overview: MMBE, Stock Overview	204
Transaction Overview: MB51, Material Movements	205
Transaction Overview: MB52, Stock Report	207

Map Area 4: Purchasing and Receiving	209
Procurement Cycle and Types	210
Internal vs. External Procurement	211
Subcontracting Scenarios	212
Outside Processing Purchasing Concept	213
Procurement Scenario Summary	214
Transaction Notes: ME5A, List Requisitions	215
Transaction Overview: ME53N, Display Requisition	217
Transaction Notes: ME57, Process Requisitions	218
Transaction Notes: ME21N, Create Purchase Order	221
Transaction Notes: ME28, Release Purchase Order	223
Transaction Notes: ME2M List Purchase Orders	226
Transaction Notes: MIGO_GR Receive PO Materials	228

SAP ERP Central Component in Manufacturing an Operator's Guide
Table of Contents

Section/Topic	Page
Map Area 5: Configuration and Systems Management	230
ABAP Related Transactions	232
Transaction SM37, Background Jobs	236
Configuration Tool, SPRO	238
Table Viewer Transactions	240
Transaction Notes: SPO1, Printing	247
User Info/Security Transactions	249
Display User Info/User Security	251
Appendix	254
ITSA Table Summary	255
Transactions Summary	266
Index	267

Section 1
ECC Background

Section Overview.

We provide in this section a very brief overview of SAP the Company and the SAP ERP Central Component (ECC) software in general.

We understand that you did not buy this book for this section – still there are some things here that need to be said. We try to explain these concepts in the fewest words possible.

Background section topics

SAP AG (the company)

SAP ECC (the software)

SAP is Orders (Sales, Purchasing & Production Order Types)

SAP means Configuration (System Setup)

SAP means Data - Master Data & Transactional Data

SAP means Security

SAP is a company selling ERP (Enterprise Requirement Planning), other business applications software and services:

✓ The company was founded in 1972 and has its headquarters in Walldorf, Germany.

✓ SAP describes itself as the world's largest business software company, with more than 50 000 employees and major offices in more than 50 countries.

✓ SAP's customer base includes over 95 000 companies in over 120 countries.

✓ SAP's certified partner base includes more than 2 400 vendors providing add on software components, services and support.

✓ The company's total revenues in 2010 were approximately 11 Billion Euros.

✓ The company is traded on several exchanges in Europe and the Americas under the symbol 'SAP'.

www.sap.com

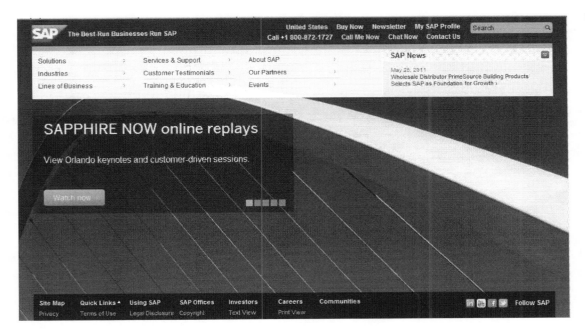

Size Matters (but so does performance and market share).

Comparison of Select Computer Services Sector companies June, 2011.

SAP has a market value of over 75 Billion USD; and it holds the largest share among ERP Software Providers.

Company Name	Symbol	Exchange	Currency	Price	Earnings/ share	P/E ratio	Price-to-book	Price-to-sales	Market Cap ($B)	Employees	Net income	EBITDA
Apple Inc.	AAPL	NASDAQ	USD	344.7	20.98	16.42	6.67	4.93	317.37	46,600	14,013.00	19,317.00
Microsoft Corporation	MSFT	NASDAQ	USD	24.05	2.52	9.54	4.69	3.38	203.06	89,000	18,760.00	26,674.00
Intl. Business Machines	IBM	NYSE	USD	165.3	11.92	13.87	9	2.05	201.53	426,751	14,833.00	22,981.00
Oracle Corporation	ORCL	NASDAQ	USD	32.7	1.51	21.67	5.58	6.46	165.28	107,870	6,135.00	11,360.00
Intel Corporation	INTC	NASDAQ	USD	22.08	2.15	10.29	2.51	2.74	117.12	93,500	11,464.00	20,101.00
Cisco Systems, Inc.	CSCO	NASDAQ	USD	16.11	1.27	12.66	2.15	2.31	88.61	70,700	7,767.00	11,194.00
Hewlett-Packard Company	HPQ	NYSE	USD	36.27	4.08	8.89	2.04	0.64	78.38	324,600	8,761.00	12,963.00
SAP AG	SAP	NYSE	USD	61.35	2.23	27.52	5.23	4.22	75.22	53,872	2,609.65	4,498.15
EMC Corporation	EMC	NYSE	USD	28.25	0.91	30.89	3.38	3.44	58.19	48,500	1,969.69	3,563.89
Dell Inc.	DELL	NASDAQ	USD	15.75	1.67	9.43	3.97	0.49	29.72	100,300	2,635.00	4,403.00
Red Hat, Inc.	RHT	NYSE	USD	42.63	0.55	77.67	6.52	9.26	8.22	3,700	107.28	193.67

Source: Google Finance, 2 June 2011

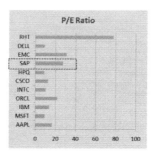

SAP ERP Market Share

Market Cap ($B)

P/E Ratio

SAP HOLDS TOP RANKINGS IN WORLDWIDE MARKET SHARE FOR SAP® BUSINESS SUITE APPLICATIONS

Renowned Independent Research Firm Ranks SAP® Business Suite Applications Number One in CRM, ERP and SCM Markets

WALLDORF, Germany - July 30, 2008 - SAP AG (NYSE: SAP) today announced that it has been named the worldwide market share leader based on total software revenue for business solutions in the customer relationship management (CRM), enterprise resource planning (ERP) and supply chain management (SCM) markets, according to 2007 market share reports published by renowned independent research firm Gartner, Inc.

The following is an overview of the Gartner rankings, measured by total software revenues for 2007:

- SAP leads the CRM market, with a total market share of 25.35 percent, placing nine percentage points over its closest competitor.[1]
- SAP leads the SCM market, with a total market share of 22.% percent, a sizeable lead over second-ranked competitor at 16 percent.[2]
- SAP leads the ERP market, with a total market share of 27.5 percent, far surpassing the second-ranked competitor at 13.9 percent.[3]

"We believe SAP's top leadership position throughout the Gartner Market Share reports is a shining confirmation of the value and continued trust companies place in the SAP Business Suite family of applications," said Jim Hagemann Snabe, member of the Executive Board, SAP AG. "Customers around the world consistently turn to the unmatched end-to-end integration capabilities of the SAP Business Suite to help solve complex business challenges while driving top and bottom line growth."

Within the ERP market, SAP is also further noted as the leader in several relevant categories, including financials and human capital management solutions. SAP also surpassed a major ERP milestone recently (see July 1, 2008 press release, titled "SAP Surpasses Milestone in Product Strategy as 10,000 Customers Run Latest ERP Release"), whereby SAP® ERP 6.0 has become the fastest adopted SAP ERP release in the company's history. Combined with the powerful functionality found in the most current versions of the SAP® CRM 2007 (see December 4, 2007 press release, titled "SAP Unveils Next-Generation Customer Relationship Management Solution") and SAP®

Source: SAP AG Press Release

The Central Component. SAP launched it as ERP Central Component (ECC 6.0) solution in 2005. ECC 6.0 includes several modules supporting Financials, Logistics and Human Resource Management. (Our focus here is on the subset of these modules – as they are normally used in a typical mid-size manufacturing company.)

ECC was developed from earlier releases of SAP ERP software - most notably, R/3, that gained worldwide usage from the 1990s. Release 3 (or 'R3' for short) was the first client/server version of SAP ERP software and it quickly became a defacto standard in the business world. R/3 was the successor to even earlier versions of the SAP ERP software, including the R/2 (mainframe version) which dates from the 1970s.

For more on SAP ERP software history, checkout:

http://www.sapdesignguild.org/index1.asp

SAP's ERP Solutions Map. (circa 2005)

*Comment: A **great** graphic for anyone needing to justify the purchase of SAP - but not much help to those trying to understand SAP at the tactical operator level.*

What's important:
✓ SAP ECC = SAP ERP Central Component.
✓ ERP = Enterprise Requirements Planning (Software).
✓ ECC is a software application for managing Sales, Purchase and Production Orders and their related documents.

We describe the SAP ECC application as an *order processing engine* for the business. We use this description to get to a key concept in all ERP applications - and that is this: It is the **creation, processing and closure of Sales, Purchasing and Production orders** that is the **core function** of any ERP application.

An overview of the relationships, process flows, and the predecessor and successor business objects associated with these three order types are briefly described below.

We note that our interpretation of what the ECC (or any ERP system) is comes from a customer service and operations perspective. Others (Accountants and Auditors), see things differently. To them, the ability to enforce a common set of business standards, and to state clearly the *profits and losses* for an enterprise, are what ERP systems are all about.

We see these differing viewpoints as the opposite sides of the same coin. From either the operations or the accounting perspective, the best run businesses will run some type of ERP software – and ERP software success is based on the efficient processing of Sales, Purchase and Production Orders.

PURCHASE ORDER

This is the triggering document for the creation of a sales order – it is the promise to pay for a product or service that is delivered according to a set of specifications.

*PO's are preceded by **Purchase Requisitions**, usually generated by the **Material Requirements Planning (MRP)** process; PO's are received into inventory via a **Goods Receipt**; the generation of the **Goods Receipt**, in turn, allows the payment of the supplier Invoice.*

SALES ORDER

This is the agreement between a supplier (seller) and a customer to provide a product or a service under terms agreed to by both parties to include technical specifications for the product or service, and its delivery location, date and price.

*In SAP, Sales Orders are preceded by **Inquiries** and **Quotations** and followed by **Delivery Documents**. The **Post Goods Issue** of the Delivery (or completion of the Shipment) allows for Customer **Invoicing**.*

PRODUCTION ORDER

This is an internal order document for the use of materials, labor and equipment in one place to produce a product or product component.

*Production Orders are preceded by **Planned Orders** (also generated by MRP).*

The concept diagram below is a summary of the three main ECC Order Documents and their related predecessor and successor documents. This is how – at a very high level, businesses run on SAP.

SAP ECC Order Overview

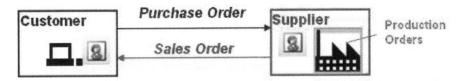

Purchase Order Flow

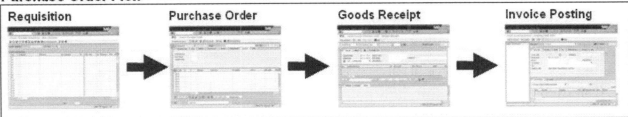

Sales Order Flow

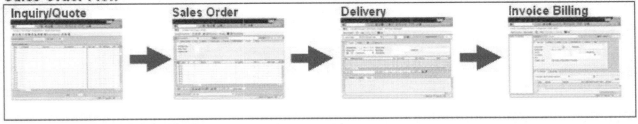

Production Order Flow

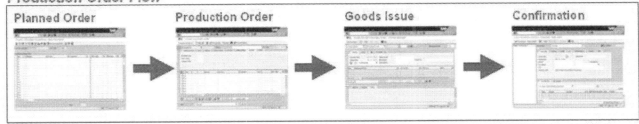

A key aspect of SAP ECC software is that it is configurable – it comes with built in functionality that supports a series of predefined, *standardized* business processes. At the same time, it can be tailored (configured) to specific needs of each enterprise/installation. SAP can be (and is intended to be) set up to run any business – quickly. Typical ECC Configuration tasks include the following:

✓ **Basic System Settings** include languages, clients (complete system environments), communications and transport settings.

✓ **Company Code Setup.** Company Codes are organizational structures representing the basic financial accounting units for an enterprise. Each company code represents a complete chart of accounts.

✓ **Plant Setup.** Plants are physical locations where materials are procured, produced, stored or shipped to customers. Plants are subdivided into **Storage Locations** for Inventory Management purposes.

✓ **Sales Organization set up.** Sales Orgs provide a linkage between customers, delivering plants, materials and pricing conditions.

✓ **Purchase Organization set up.** Purchase Orgs provide a structure for establishing pricing relationships between Vendors, Plants and Materials.

✓ **Master Data Settings.** This category includes field level settings; Material, Vendor and Customer Master related data.

✓ **Sales, Purchase and Production Order Settings** include defining the specific types of orders (and their output form) that will be processed in the system.

Configuration settings are maintained by SAP Analysts/Consultants using a system configuration tool called the **Implementation Management Guide** (**IMG**). The IMG is often referred to by its transaction technical name "**SPRO**".

Author's Note. In this book, we will visit the topic of SAP configuration only briefly. A second book in this series is intended to cover SAP ECC Configuration tasks in a more thorough manner. Our focus in this book, is on Business Operator/End User Transactions.

Selected Key Config Areas in SPRO

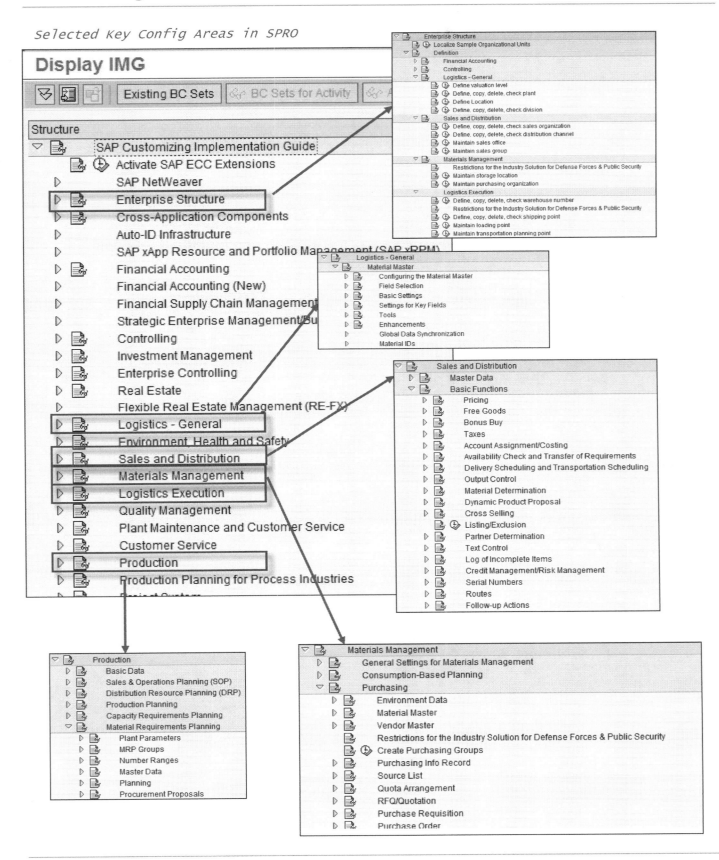

An SAP ECC system (or any ERP system) can be described by the data it contains. Three general data categories are discussed below:
- ✓ Transactional Data
- ✓ Master Data
- ✓ Configuration & Other System Data

Sales, Purchase and Production Orders are examples of **Transactional Data**. Transactional Data changes with each instance (order).   Example ECC transactional data objects include:
- ✓ Sales Inquiries, Quotations and Orders
- ✓ Sales Order Deliveries and Shipping Documents
- ✓ Purchase Requisitions, Purchase Orders and Goods Receipts
- ✓ Planned Orders, Production Orders, Goods Issues and Confirmations

SAP **Master Data** can be described as data pertaining to Customers, Vendors or Materials, and is relatively static and *re-useable* over time.   ECC Master Data objects include:
- ✓ Material Masters, Bills of Materials (BOMs) and Routings
- ✓ Customer Masters and Pricing records
- ✓ Vendor Masters and Purchasing records

In an SAP ECC system, Transaction and Master data are stored in a series of tables maintained in an external Database Management System (DBMS) like Oracle or MS SQL Server.

You may hear the phrase that SAP is, *running on top of the DBMS.*   By this, we mean to say that business users interact with SAP as an application (and not directly) with the tables that hold Master or Transactional data. There are exceptions though; and especially during the initial phases of an SAP project, it is not uncommon for the Business team to view SAP Master Data at the table level for data load validation and testing purposes.

Master and Transactional Data are the main data types stored in an SAP system – but there is another much smaller category of 'Other' data objects. Included in this category are Organizational Structures and System User related data.

Simplified SAP ECC Client Server Model

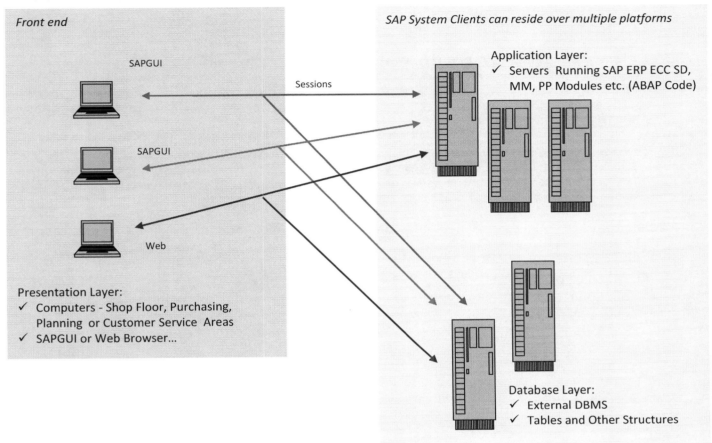

Front end

SAPGUI

SAPGUI

Web

Sessions

SAP System Clients can reside over multiple platforms

Application Layer:
✓ Servers Running SAP ERP ECC SD, MM, PP Modules etc. (ABAP Code)

Presentation Layer:
✓ Computers - Shop Floor, Purchasing, Planning or Customer Service Areas
✓ SAPGUI or Web Browser...

Database Layer:
✓ External DBMS
✓ Tables and Other Structures

SAP Data Objects stored in a commercial DBMS like Oracle

Configuration & 'Other' Data	Master Data	Transactional Data
✓ Org Structures	✓ Material Masters	✓ Sales Orders
✓ Order types	✓ Bills of Materials	✓ Purchase Orders
✓ User Authorizations, Parameters & Favorites	✓ Routings	✓ Production Orders
	✓ Customers	✓ Deliveries
	✓ Vendors	✓ Goods Receipts
	✓ Purchasing Records	✓ Goods Issues
	✓ Pricing Conditions	✓ Inventory

Secure information processing has always been an essential aspect of the SAP's product and services. ECC software is generally considered one of the most secure (if not the most secure) ERP software applications on the market today.

ECC addresses security requirements in three basic ways:

People – All users are assigned security roles. Security roles control access to transactions and data sets; and various monitoring procedures can be invoked at any time.

Processes – Process security is enabled in SAP at both the application and table (data) level. Objects cannot be saved, released or forwarded without passing through a series of rigorous checks designed to verify the integrity of the data being maintained.

Technology – SAP security extends into network and communications layer monitoring and other infrastructure level controls, to include Secure Store & Forward Mechanisms (SSF), Digital Signatures and various kinds internal and external virus checks.

One example of SAP Security and Controls
User Role Transaction Assignments in the ECC.

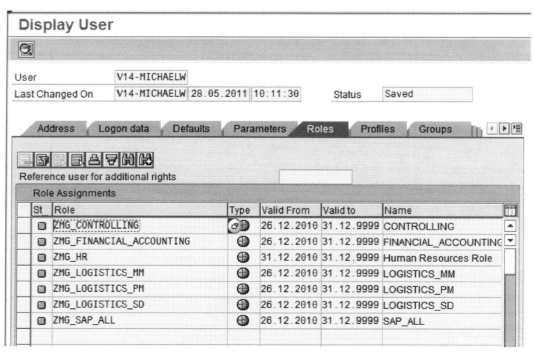

Section 2
SAP ECC Operator Basics

Section Overview. In this section, we describe the key aspects of the SAP Operator System Interface. This information is applicable to all the transactions and functional areas that are described in the remaining sections of this document.

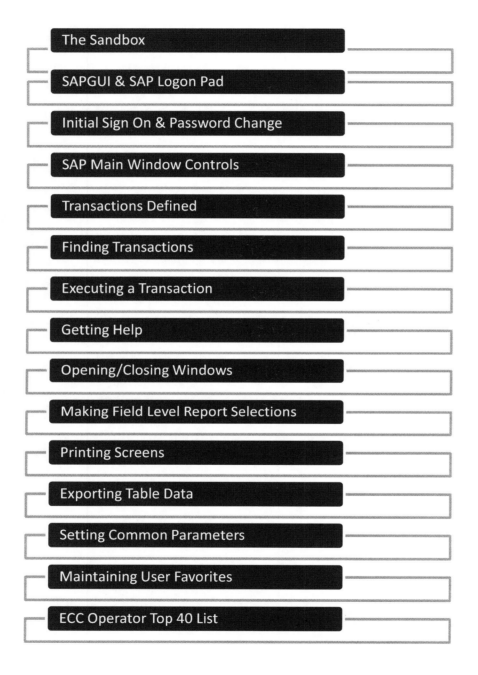

Section Topics
ECC Operator/User Interface
Basics

Sandbox environments are complete, functional SAP systems provided for the purpose of hands on training and learning. Sandbox systems are intentionally separate from the other environments (like Development, Quality and Production) that an SAP project will require and build over its duration.

Most projects choose to maintain their own Sandbox clients on an internal company network. Smaller projects (and individuals learning SAP on their own) may connect to a variety of SAP ECC Sandbox systems via the internet.

The screen captures in this document are taken from an SAP ECC 6.0 Sandbox system hosted by a Canadian company - Software Lab Access. For more information on Sandbox training environments, check out their web site:

http://www.softwarelabaccess.com/index.php

Example SAP Sandbox Service Provider
- SoftwareLabAccess web site

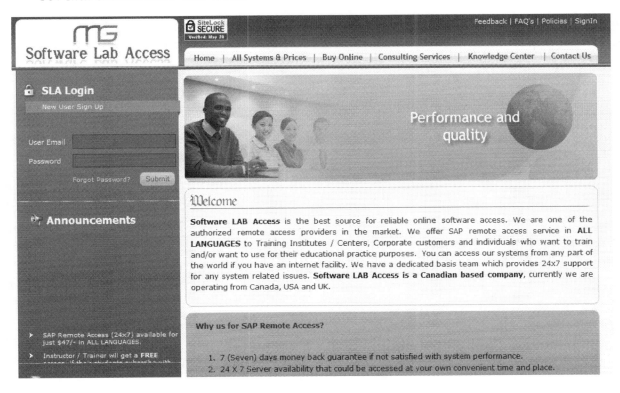

SAPGUI (SAP Graphical User Interface) is a software application installed on the SAP user/operator's workstation. The SAPGUI provides a network connection from the workstation to the servers hosting SAP data and applications.

The SAPGUI may be downloaded from the internet via sap.com or from one of the many other SAP service provider/partner sites.

Once the SAPGUI is installed on your PC, an SAP Logon icon will appear on your desktop.

SAP Logon icon

Double clicking on this icon opens your SAP Logon window. The list of SAP systems that you see in this window will vary and are defined in your **saplogon.ini** file.

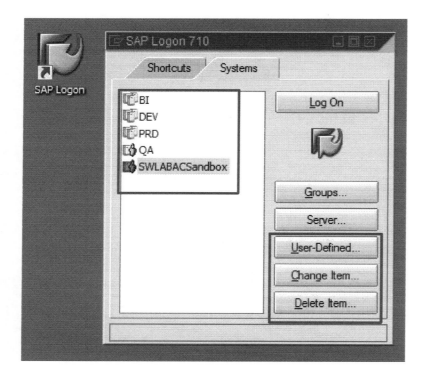

SAP Logon Window / Systems List

✓ Each System requires a User ID and Password.

✓ Systems can be added, changed or deleted from the list using the User Defined, Change or Delete Item buttons.

✓ Double clicking on a System icon opens a connection to that system, beginning the Logon process.

In cases where your sandbox system changes (is built or refreshed etc…), you may need to make a SAP Logon Pad *System/Server* change.

The steps to Add a new system to the Logon Pad are described below.

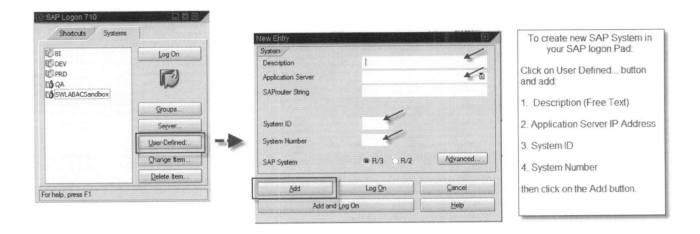

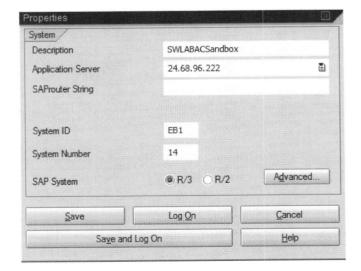

SAP System Properties example.

Your Application Server, System ID and System Number will be provided by the Sandbox System Administrator.

The first time you logon to an SAP ECC system, you will see a screen like this.

SAP Logon Window with Initial Logon Change Password dialog.

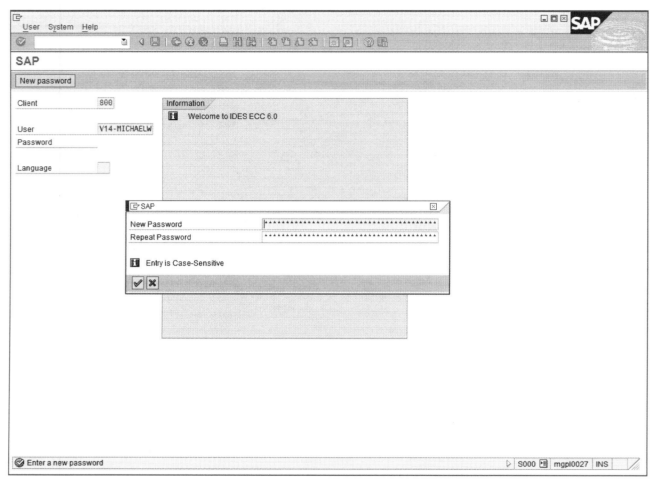

Notes:
- ✓ System Client Number, User ID and Initial Password will be provided the Sandbox System Administrator.

- ✓ Use the keyboard **Tab key** to move between data fields.

- ✓ After the Client Number, User ID and Password are entered, press the **Enter key** – You will be prompted to enter a new Password (twice).

- ✓ Passwords are case sensitive.

- ✓ **Pressing the Enter Key** performs an SAP screen data check – if all data is entered correctly – SAP Easy Access Menu will appear; if not, you will be prompted to change one or more field entries.

The initial SAP Easy Access window that is displayed when you sign on to SAP is show below. This window consists of a series of menus, icons and controls.   The Key functions associated with each control group are described on the following pages.

SAP Main Menu Window.

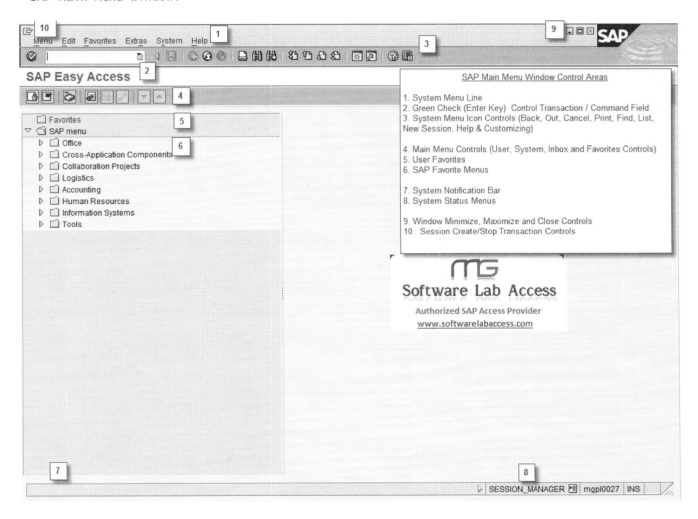

SAP Main Menu Window Control Areas

1. System Menu Line
2. Green Check (Enter Key) Control Transaction / Command Field
3. System Menu Icon Controls (Back, Out, Cancel, Print, Find, List, New Session, Help & Customizing)

4. Main Menu Controls (User, System, Inbox and Favorites Controls)
5. User Favorites
6. SAP Favorite Menus

7. System Notification Bar
8. System Status Menus

9. Window Minimize, Maximize and Close Controls
10. Session Create/Stop Transaction Controls

| 1 | <u>M</u>enu <u>E</u>dit <u>F</u>avorites Ext<u>r</u>as S<u>y</u>stem <u>H</u>elp |

The **System Menu line** provides menu item selections organized by functional area.

Under the Extras menu, there is a setting we recommend making during your first log on – this is the **Extras > Settings Display technical names** setting.

The **Extra > Settings** menu selection opens a settings dialog that controls the display of Transaction Codes in SAP System Menus.

The Display Technical Names checkbox must be checked to display transaction code values in SAP Favorites Menus. Making this settings change early in Navigation Training can eliminate much confusion later on.

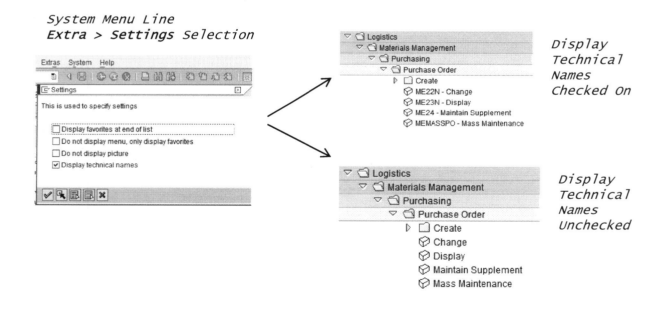

System Menu Line
Extra > Settings Selection

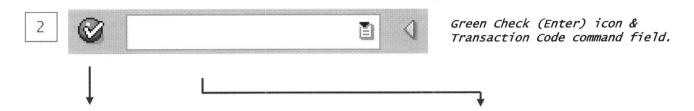

Green Check (Enter) icon & Transaction Code command field.

Green Check button.

Has the same function as the Keyboard Enter Key.

Pressing this button starts a *data entry error check.*

If all required field entries are correct – the next screen in the transaction series appears.

If a field entry error is found – the field is highlighted and an error message is displayed.

Transaction Command Field.

Use this field to type in a Transaction code and press the Enter Key or click on the Green Check icon to execute the transaction.

Although SAP is completely menu driven, many users/operators still find the use of the Transaction Code command field a preferred method for executing transactions.

Transaction Command Field History control.
Displays transactions entered in previous sessions.

Hide Field button. When clicked, Command Field is hidden and the Show Field button is displayed

Hide / Unhide control function

3   **SAP System icons.**

These icons provide access to the most common functions in SAP and appear almost universally across all ECC windows. They may be active or inactive (grayed out) based on the system context/function being performed.

Save

Back

Exit

Cancel

Print

Find/Find Again

List Controls

New Session / Shortcut

Help

User Customizing

4   **Main Menu Icons.**

These icons are specific to the SAP Easy Access Main Menu only (they are not found on other screens).

SAP User Menu

SAP System Menu

Business Workplace Inbox

Favorites - Add

Favorites – Delete

Favorites – Change

Favorites – Move Item Down/Up

5 | **User Favorites.**

▽ 🗀 Favorites
   ▽ 🗀 ECC Key Transactions Guide Favorites
      ▷ 🗀 Org Structures & Master Data
      ▽ 🗀 Sales Entry
          ※ VA11 - Create Inquiry
          ※ VA21 - Create Quotation
          ※ VA01 - Create Sales Order
          ※ VA25 - Quotations List
          ※ VA05 - List of Sales Orders
          ※ CO06 - Backorder Processing
          ※ CO09 - Availability Overview
      ▷ 🗀 Deliveries & Billing
      ▷ 🗀 MRP, Inventory & Production
      ▷ 🗀 Purchasing & Receiving
      ▷ 🗀 Systems Management

User Favorites Example.

✓ *Users Favorites can be Uploaded or Downloaded, allowing Business Teams to develop highly specific menu structures tailored to their work scenarios and processes.*

✓ *Shown here, Favorites File for this book.*

SAP ECC provides a Favorites menu structure that the User/Operator can control.

Operators can store their most commonly used transactions here and can create their own folders as required. User Favorites are not stored on the local computer, but rather in the ECC Database itself. This means that the User Favorites you define on one PC are available from any other machine that that you use to sign on to SAP.

Favorites can also be created to provide links to other documents and web sites.

Later in this section, we provide you with more information on creating and sharing User Favorites.

Favorites functionality in SAP is a power tool for organizing Operator Business Tasks and the supporting documentation for those tasks – yet many SAP implementations fail to take full advantage of Favorites capabilities.

| 6 | **SAP Menu (folder structure).** |

All SAP ECC services are listed in the menu structure. The number of items (folders and transactions) in the menu is over 100 000. The menu structure itself, however, is well organized and it is easy to find transactions if you know where to look and how the SAP Menu Find functionality works.

On the next page, we show some of the most 'high traffic' areas of the SAP menu structure. Later in this section, we describe how to find menus and transactions on your own.

For everyday usage – most SAP users will choose to work from either their Favorites Folders or from the SAP User menu - which contains only the transactions authorized in the security roles attached to the User ID.

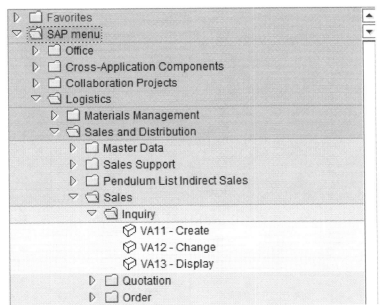

SAP ECC Standard Menu.

Selected SAP menu 'High Traffic' areas.

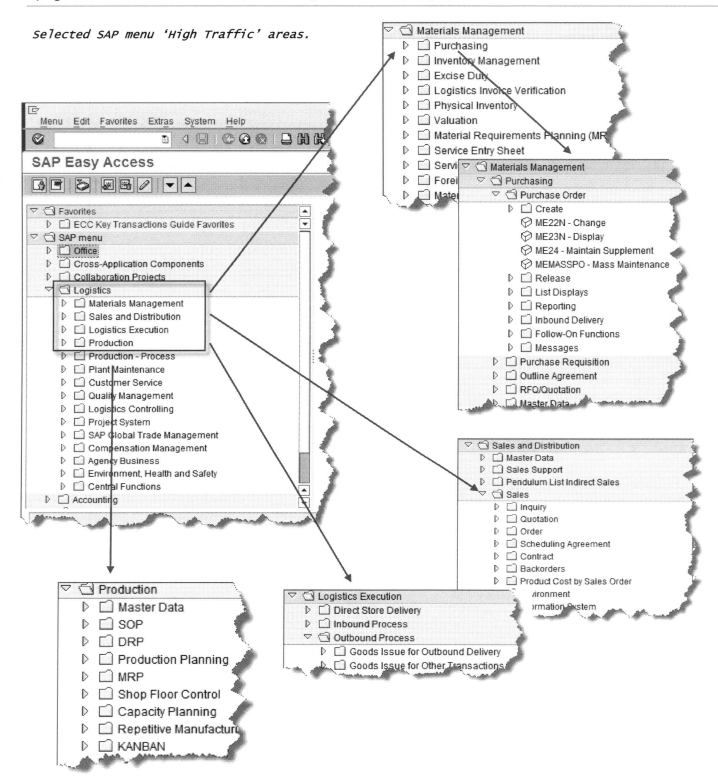

7   **System Notification Area & Status Bar Control.**

System Notification Area   *System Status Bar*
Bottom Left side SAP Window   *Bottom Right side SAP Window*

These control areas are found at the bottom left and right hand side of each
SAP Window.

The **Notification Area** is used to display System Messages:

✓   SAP System Messages include Informational (green √), Warning (Yellow !)
     or Error (Red X) messages.

✓   A setting on the customize Local Layout Menu 🖳 enables further
     message/dialog options…

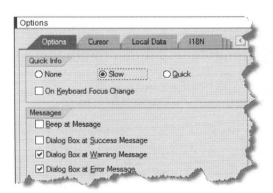

8   **System Status Bar.**

This control is menu driven. A good
initial setting here is the
'Transaction' selection. This allows
the transaction name of the active
screen to be displayed.

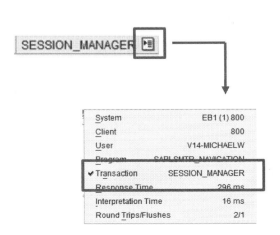

9   **Window Minimize, Maximize and Close Controls.**

 This control group provides the standard windows minimize, maximize and close functions.

10   **Session Create/Stop Transaction Controls.**

This control group, located in the Upper Left Corner of the SAP Window, is useful because it enables new session windows to be opened, or existing sessions (long running transactions) to be stopped.

Transactions Defined.

We define Transactions in two ways:

1. Transactions are the way things get done in SAP. (Action)

2. Transactions are also the way to display if things *are* getting done in SAP. (Reporting)

Examples of Transactions that fall into the first category include:
- ✓ MM01 - Creating a Material Master
- ✓ VA01 - Creating a Sales Order
- ✓ CO02 - Changing Production Order Finish Date

Examples of Transactions that fall into the second category include:
- ✓ MM03 - Displaying a Material Master
- ✓ VA05 - Displaying a list Sales Orders
- ✓ COOIS - Production Order Information Systems Report

SAP ECC comes standard with tens of thousands of transactions.

In addition, by using the ABAP programming Language (the native programming language of SAP), companies (or more precisely, ABAP Developers/Programmers the company pays for) can develop their own *custom* transactions.

Custom Transactions are developed specifically for a project implementation and are not technically supported by SAP.

Custom transactions always begin with the letters Y or Z.

Standard SAP Transactions can begin with any letter *other than* Y or Z. More importantly, Standard SAP Transactions are ruthlessly tested by SAP. If SAP detects an error or possible error condition with a Standard Transaction, it releases an *OSS* (Online Service System) *Note* and Fix for the transaction that is available free of charge to its customers.

Lastly, a transaction or technical name is not the same as the SAP program file name. Transaction Codes are assigned to a program after it has been developed.

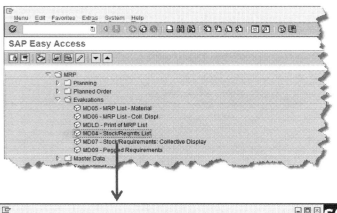

A Transaction Code is way to call an SAP program. To see the actual program name for a Transaction Code, you need to select the System > Status menu selection.

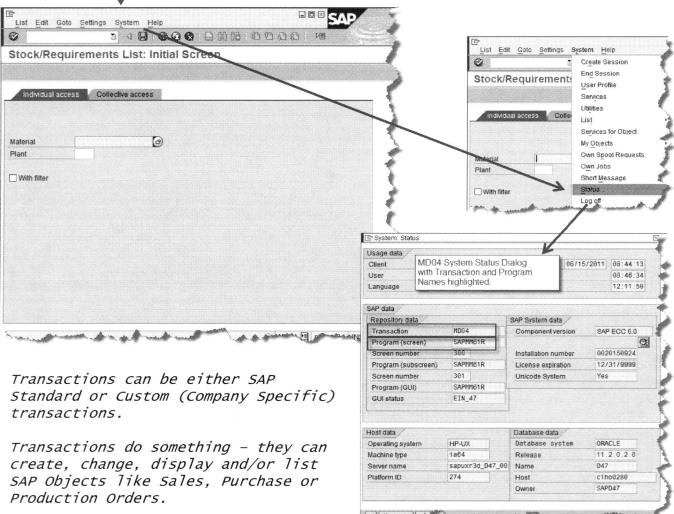

MD04 System Status Dialog with Transaction and Program Names highlighted.

Transactions can be either SAP Standard or Custom (Company Specific) transactions.

Transactions do something – they can create, change, display and/or list SAP Objects like Sales, Purchase or Production Orders.

Find and Find Again Icons.

One the easiest ways for new Operators to find transactions in SAP is by using
these icons. Provided below is a screen sequence/example for finding a
transaction named MM03.

**Before executing this example - make sure the technical names setting
mentioned previously is turned on.** To do this, go to the menu line and select
Extra > Settings, and if not already checked - check the checkbox setting for
Display Technical Names.

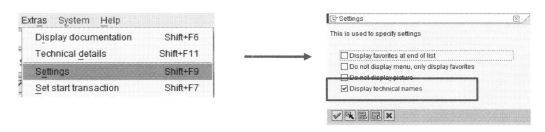

1.   Click on Find Icon.

2.   In the Search Dialog box, enter the text, MM03

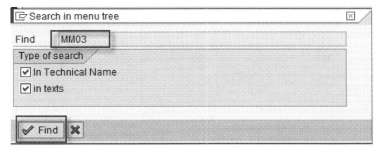

3.   Click on the Find button

4.   In the System Notification pane, a message will appear

Search for Unloaded Menu Sections...

5.   When Search finds the Transaction, its position in the Menu Structure will be displayed...

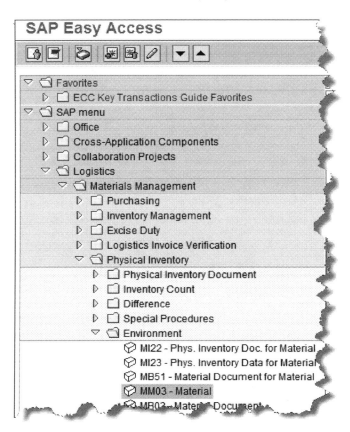

6.   The Find Next button 🔍 can be used to continue the search through the rest of the Menu hierarchy.

There are two basic methods for starting a transaction:

Double clicking on a transaction anywhere it is found in the SAP Favorites, User or System Menus
-or -
Typing the transaction code into the Command Field and pressing the enter key.

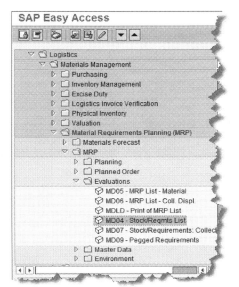

Starting Transactions - Double clicking on a transaction starts the transaction.

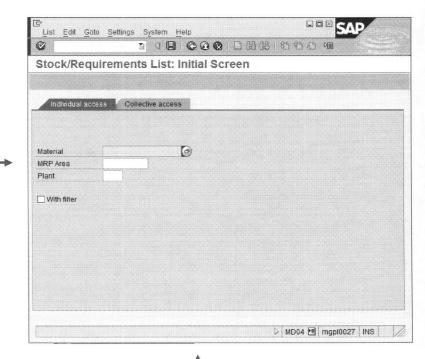

Transactions can also be started by typing the transaction into the Transaction Command Field and pressing the enter key or Green Check button.

Transaction and Field Level Help. In SAP, Help on the standard transactions in is available in three ways:

✓   By highlighting the transaction and clicking on the F1 function key.

✓   By highlighting the transaction and clicking on the System Menu Help icon.

✓   By selecting a transaction and clicking on the Right Mouse Menu Display Document selection.

The first two methods listed above – the F1 function key and System Menu Help icon – also work to display context sensitive help from inside SAP Screen fields (i.e. Field Level Help).

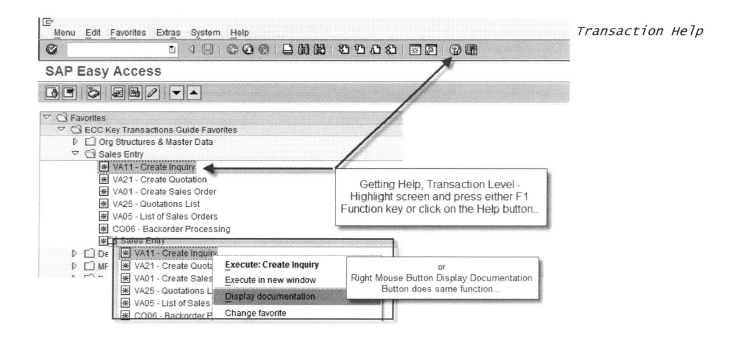

Transaction Help

Example of Help Search Functionality in SAP ECC Help Documentation.

SAP ECC Help Documentation Main.

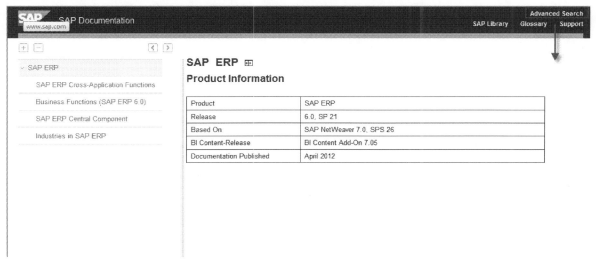

Advanced Help Search Display.

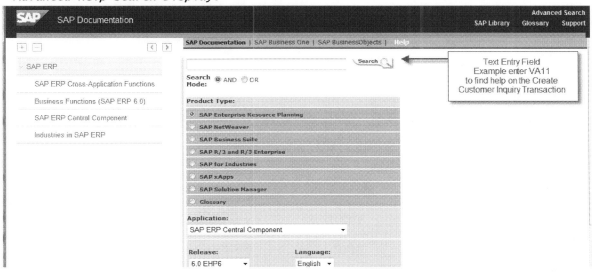

SAP Help can be accessed from any internet connection by going to
http://help.sap.com/

SAP Help Search Results.

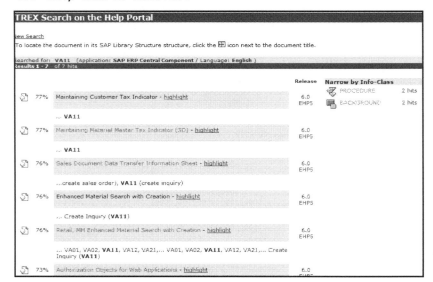

VA11 Search Results - Click on an entry to see the topic.

SAP Help Sample Content.

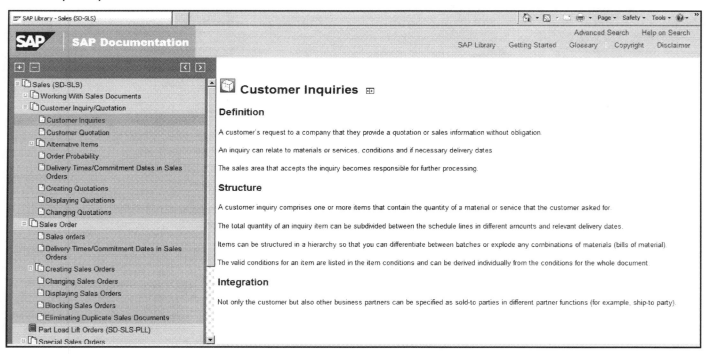

http://help.sap.com/

Field Level Help. The F1 function key also works to display field level help.
In the example below, the MD04 transaction has been executed.

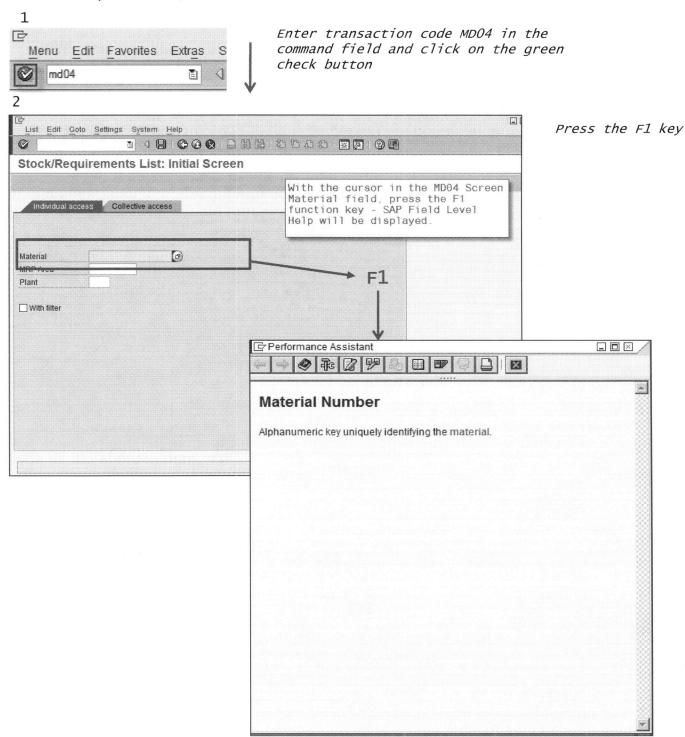

Enter transaction code MD04 in the command field and click on the green check button

Press the F1 key

With the cursor in the MD04 Screen Material field, press the F1 function key - SAP Field Level Help will be displayed.

Material Number

Alphanumeric key uniquely identifying the material.

Field Level Help Icons. A description of the icons displayed in the Field Level Help Window is provided below. Note that it is possible to navigate through Field level help topics and access additional SAP Application documentation from this dialog.

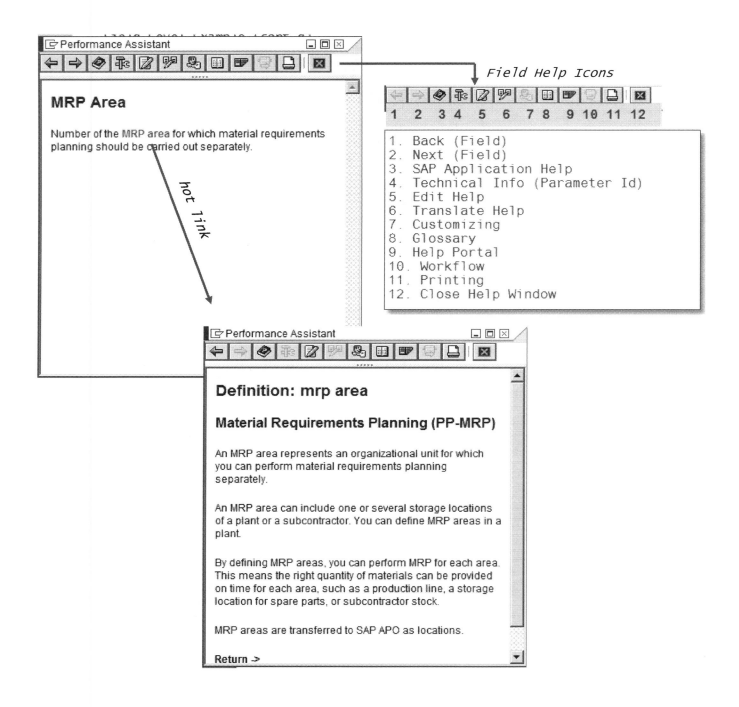

Windows (or in SAP speak, 'sessions') can be closed using the Upper Right Hand **X** or the System Menu **Log off** selection.

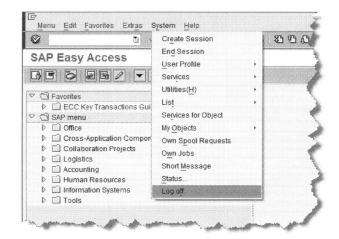

✓   The X Close window control closes the active window.

✓   The System Menu Log off selection closes all windows started by a user.

The System Log Off menu pick generates another dialog asking you to confirm the Log Off Option – **Yes** on this dialog logs you off SAP, **No** returns you to your session.

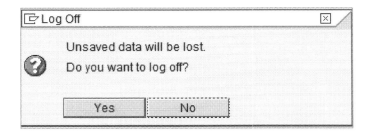

SAP Log Off Confirmation Dialog.

SAP Windows can be opened in several ways:

✓   Double Clicking on a Transaction from the SAP Easy Access Menu opens
    a new window (for the transaction selected) – but closes the original
    window (in effect switching from one window to another).

✓   From the transaction command field, entering the /n prefix before a
    Transaction Code performs the same action – opens a new window for
    the transaction at same time as it closes the previous window.

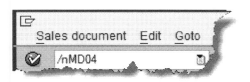

Opens new window, closing existing active window

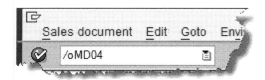

Opens new window, without closing existing active window

Opens new SAP Main Easy Access window, without closing existing active window

Selection Dialog and Required Field Indicator icons.

One of the most frustrating tasks business people who are new to SAP face is finding the data (material numbers, orders, customers, etc) they need in the system. Some basic training in making field level selections goes a long way in easing the pain associated with this task and in increasing business confidence with the system.

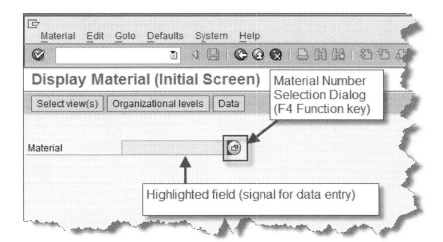

Transaction MM03 - Display a Material Master - initial screen entry view...

Moving the cursor and clicking inside Command Field will change the Material Field appearance - displaying the Required Field Indicator.

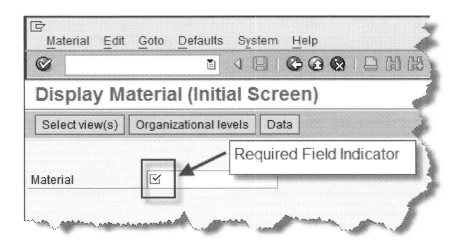

Required Field Indicator - indicates this field is mandatory...

Field Selection Dialog - indicates a search dialog is available to help you find field values.

Selection Dialog.

Clicking on a Field Selection icon brings up a Search Dialog - here you can perform Wild Card searches etc... In addition, most Search Dialogs in SAP offer multiple views - meaning you can select for more than one dialog to find what you are looking for.

Clicking on Field Selection Dialog (or pressing the F4 key) - brings up a Search dialog.

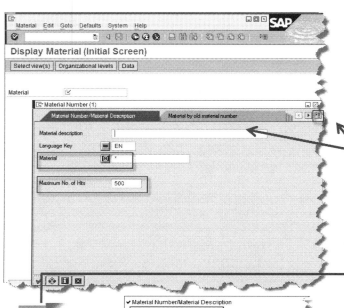

Material Number/Material Description Search Dialog.

Using the * in the Material Number field will bring up the first 500 materials in the system - the number of values displayed is limited by Maximum Number of Hits...

Multiple search dialogs are available - meaning there are multiple ways to find material masters.

Search Dialogs Available for MM03 Material Number field.

✓ Searches can be done by Legacy Material Number, Bill of Material, Routing, Material Type or by Plant Values.

✓ Selecting right search dialog saves Operator time - e.g. restricting a search to your Plant can save considerable time in large systems with hundreds of thousands or millions of material masters.

✓ *Clicking on a Search Dialog selection makes it the active search.*

Making a Selection.

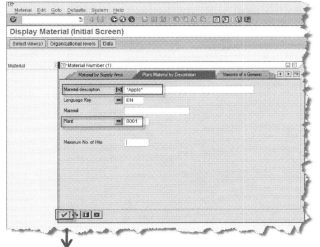

Material Selection by Plant and Material Description Values.

Pressing the Green Check Arrow – executes the search, returning a list of values.

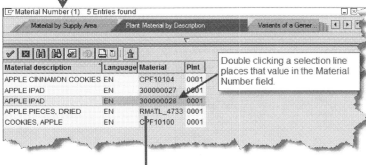

Double clicking on a list item – selects that Material and places its Material Number in the MM03 Material Number Field.

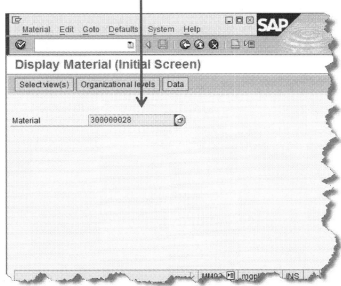

MM03 Transaction with selection value.

Selection Dialog - Final Points.

SAP Search Dialogs are powerful tools, but are often under-utilized because of inadequate end-user training. SAP Operators should know that Find, Print, Revised Selection and Download Options are available on most Search Dialogs. The screenshot below provides an overview of these functions.

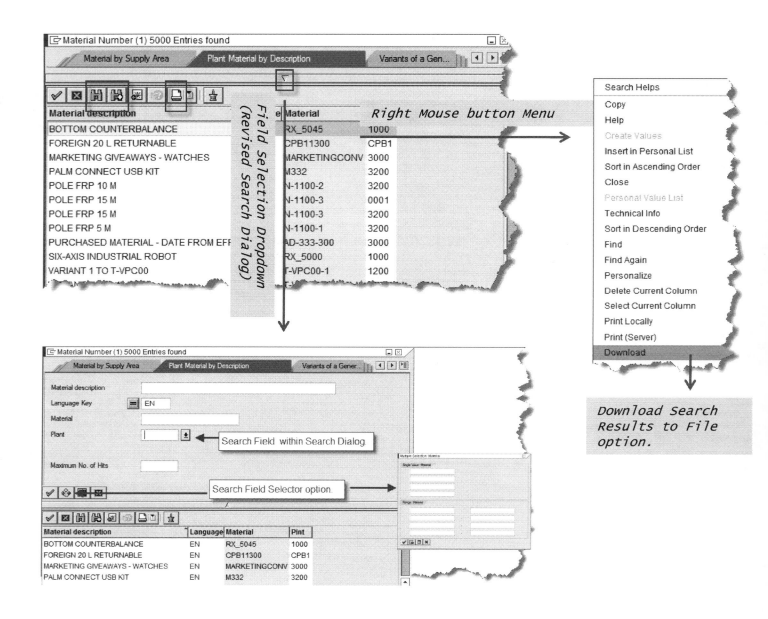

Printing in SAP.

Printing services are available in any SAP screen where the Print icon is not grayed out.

To test print from the SAP Easy Access Main Menu, follow these steps.

1

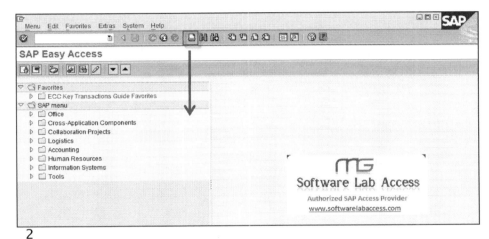

From the SAP Easy Access Menu, click on the Print icon – The SAP Print Area Menu will display.

2

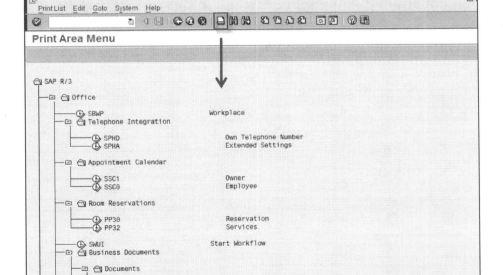

Click on the Print Icon again. This time the Print Dialog box will appear.

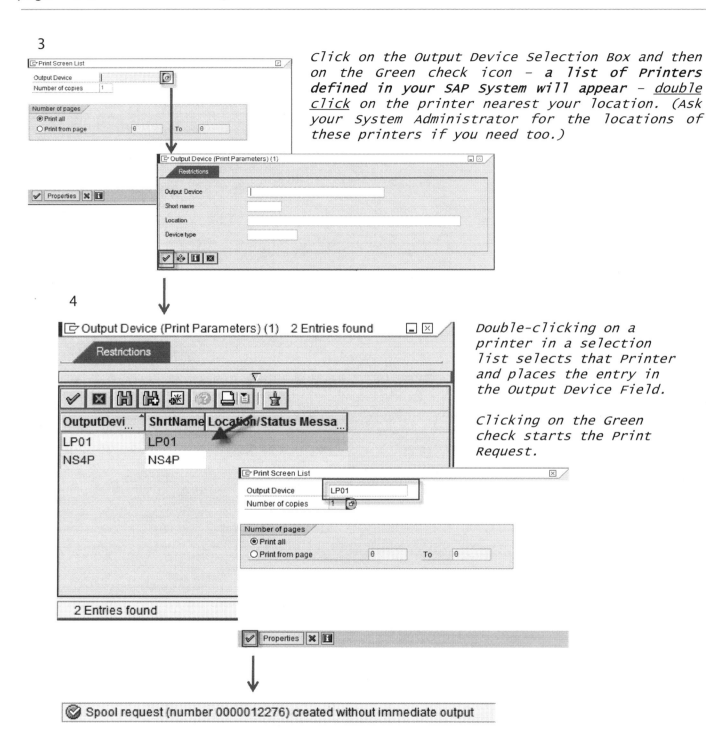

3

Click on the Output Device Selection Box and then on the Green check icon – a list of Printers defined in your SAP System will appear – double click on the printer nearest your location. (Ask your System Administrator for the locations of these printers if you need too.)

4

Double-clicking on a printer in a selection list selects that Printer and places the entry in the Output Device Field.

Clicking on the Green check starts the Print Request.

Spool request (number 0000012276) created without immediate output

The Transaction **SP01**, can be used to view print requests and re-direct output to other printers. In many SAP implementations, the Printer **LOCL** is defined as an output device and if it is available, it can be used to send output to your default Windows printer, but this is not always done; printers must be defined in both SAP and Windows domains.

SAP ERP implementations contain hundreds of reports that can be exported to Excel and other Windows applications. A common option for creating exports, using the **List menu Save > File** command, is outlined below.

1

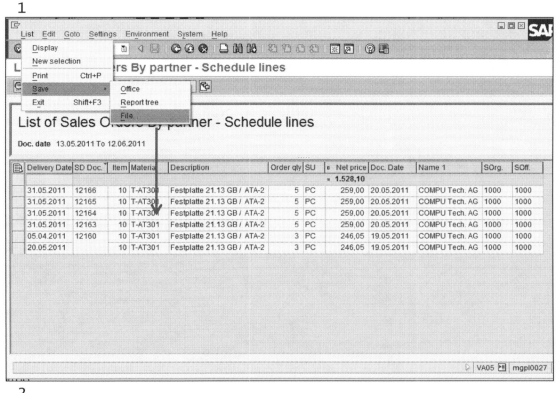

Example SAP Report, VA05 - List of Sales Orders - that can be exported to Excel.

2

3

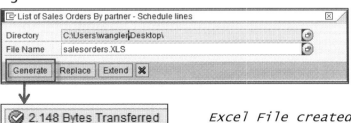

Excel File created on the Windows Desktop.

4

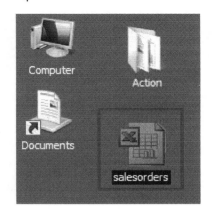

*Windows Desktop - Excel Sales Order
Report file (exported from SAP).*

5

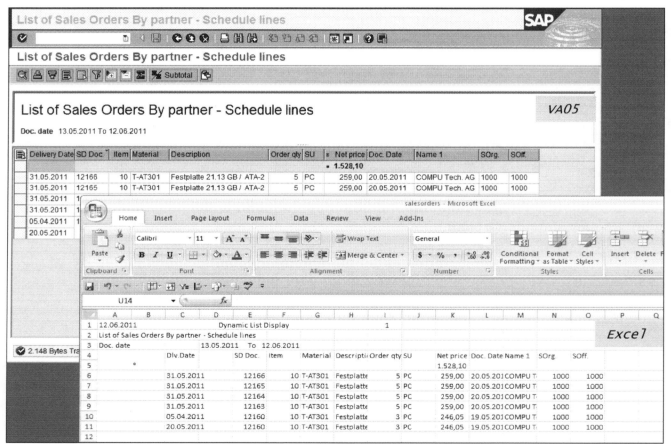

*Note: on many SAP Report screens, this icon provides one click access
to the SAP Export to Windows function.*

User Parameters. SAP allows the maintenance of the default settings and Parameter IDs (field entries) by User ID. This saves operator time – by eliminating the need to re-enter frequently used settings and selections. Default Settings are maintained via the System Menu **Systems > User Profile > Own Data** selection.

1

To maintain User parameters click on System menu, System > User Profile > Own Data selection

2

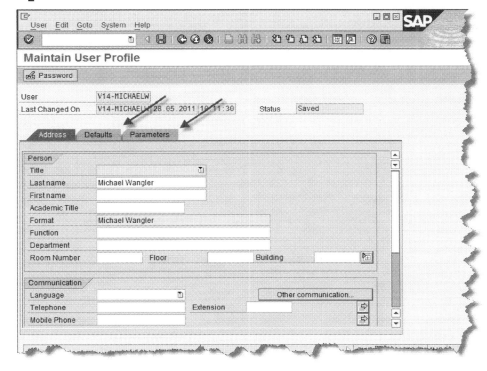

Click on Defaults Tab to set Printer, Decimal Notation and Date default settings.

Click on Parameters tab to maintain Parameter ID defaults.

Maintain User Profile - Defaults Tab Settings.

3

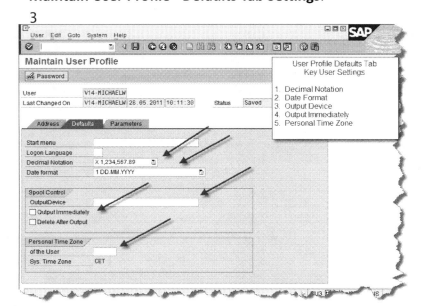

User Profile Defaults Key Settings.

Parameter IDs are default field values entered by SAP anytime a transaction using that field is called.

Maintain User Profile – Parameters Tab Settings.

4

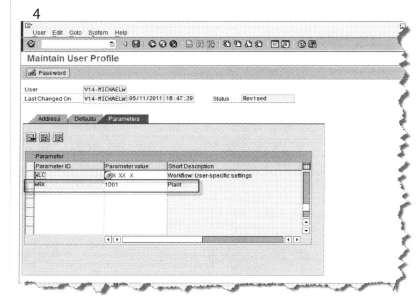

The Parameter ID for the field **Plant** *is 'WRK' – setting WRK to the value 0001 has the effect of defaulting the Plant Field value to 0001 anytime a transaction requiring a Plant is called.*

Default field values can always be changed on the transaction itself.

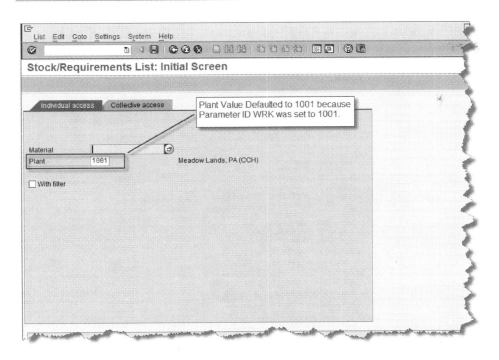

A question many new SAP Operators ask, is how to find a Parameter ID for a field – this can be done by selecting the **Field Level Help (F1 key)** in the field and then clicking on the Technical Information icon.

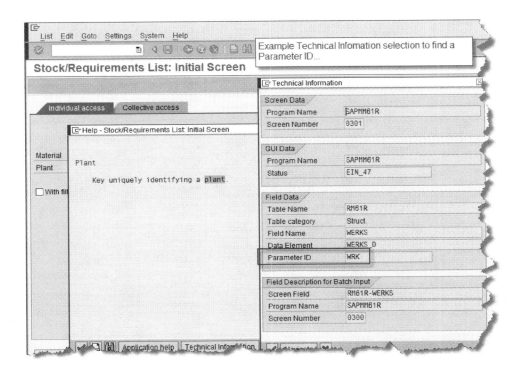

Below is a List of Parameters IDs we think all SAP Logistics Operators should set. We have provided two value columns (left blank) for each ID:

✓   A Typical Sandbox Training Value.

✓   Your Company's Value - as provided by your project team.

Parameter ID	Description	IDES Example	Your Value
BUK	Company code	1000	
DGR	MRP controller		
EKG	Purchasing group		
EKO	Purchasing Organization		
SPA	Division		
VKB	Sales office		
VKG	Sales group		
VKO	Sales organization		
VTW	Distribution channel		
WRK	Plant	0001	
NDR	MM Printing		

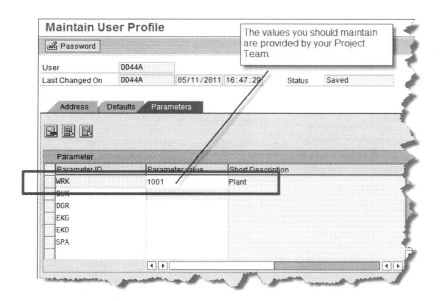

User Favorites.

User Favorites are a special area of the SAP Easy Access Menu that can be tailored specifically to individual operator, department or project needs. Favorites allow quick access to the most commonly used transactions.

- ✓ Users can drag transactions from SAP or the User System Menu Areas to create their own favorites.

- ✓ Groups of Favorites can be organized into Folders.

- ✓ Transaction Descriptions can be edited in Favorites Folders.

- ✓ Favorites can be Uploaded and Downloaded – and shared by Departments.

- ✓ Web Links and other external documents, reports and files can be added to favorites.

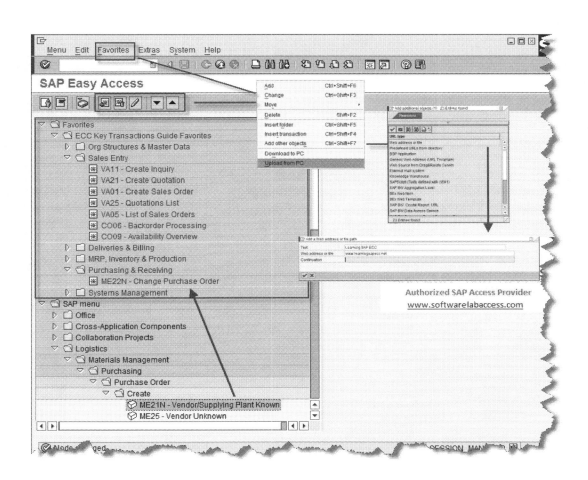

Section Summary / Learning Points.

In the table below, we have listed the key learning points covered in the first two sections of this book. To us, these topics provide fundamental knowledge applicable to all SAP Operators – this knowledge is intended to help the operator gain the most from SAP.

#	Item	Section - Area
1	Sandbox System purpose	2 - Operator Interface Basics
2	SAPGUI software function	2 - SAPGUI
3	SAPLOGON.INI file function	2 - SAPGUI
4	SAP System Properties (needed to create a SAP system in the Logon Pad) > Application Server > System ID > System Number	2 - SAPGUI
5	Tab & Enter Key functions in SAP	2 - SAPGUI
6	System Menu Line function	2 - Window Elements & Controls
7	Function Extras > Settings > Display Technical Names menu selection	2 - Window Elements & Controls
8	Transaction Command Field operation	2 - Window Elements & Controls
9	Green Check Icon function	2 - Window Elements & Controls
10	Transaction Command Field History function	2 - Window Elements & Controls
11	Transaction Command Field Hide/Unhide Controls	2 - Window Elements & Controls
12	SAP Icons > System Icons > Main Menu Icons	2 - Window Elements & Controls
13	User Favorites function	2 - Window Elements & Controls
14	SAP Menu Folder Structure organization	2 - Window Elements & Controls
15	System Notifications Area function	2 - Window Elements & Controls
16	System Status Bar Control Area function	2 - Window Elements & Controls
17	System Message Types – Success, Info/Warning, Error	2 - Window Elements & Controls
18	Window Controls - Min, Max, Close function	2 - Window Elements & Controls
19	SAP Create/Stop Session Controls operation	2 - Window Elements & Controls
20	Transaction Types - Action vs. Reporting	2 - Transactions
21	Transaction Types - Custom vs. Standard	2 - Transactions

#	Item	Area
22	Finding a Transaction Program Name	2 - Transactions
23	Finding Transactions with Find / Find Again icons	2 - Transactions
24	Executing a Transaction	2 - Transactions
25	How to access Transaction Help	2 - Transactions
26	Sample SAP Help Content	2 - SAP Help
27	How Field Level Help works	2 - Field Help
28	Opening/Closing Windows (Transactions)	2 - Transactions
29	Making Field Level Dialog Selections	2 - Field Selections
30	Printing in SAP	2 - Printing
31	Downloading SAP Reports	2 - Download
32	Maintaining User Parameters	2 - Users Parameters
33	SAP Parameter IDs function	2 - Users Parameters
34	Sample Parameter IDs for Plant and Company Code	2 - Users Parameters
35	F1, F4, F8 Function Key Controls in SAP	2 - Various
36	Master Data Types in SAP	1 – Client/Server Concept
37	Transactional Data Types in SAP	1 – Client/Server Concept
38	Predecessor & Successor Documents to a Sales Order in SAP	1 - SAP is Orders
39	Predecessor & Successor Documents to a Purchase Order in SAP	1 - SAP is Orders
40	Predecessor & Successor Documents to a Production Order in SAP	1 - SAP is Orders

Section 3
Advance Operator Training Notes
ECC Transaction Map & Screen Surveys

Section Overview. We present a map of Key ECC Transactions as we have deployed the application in medium sized manufacturing enterprises. The map is followed by Transaction screen summaries organized by the functional areas shown.

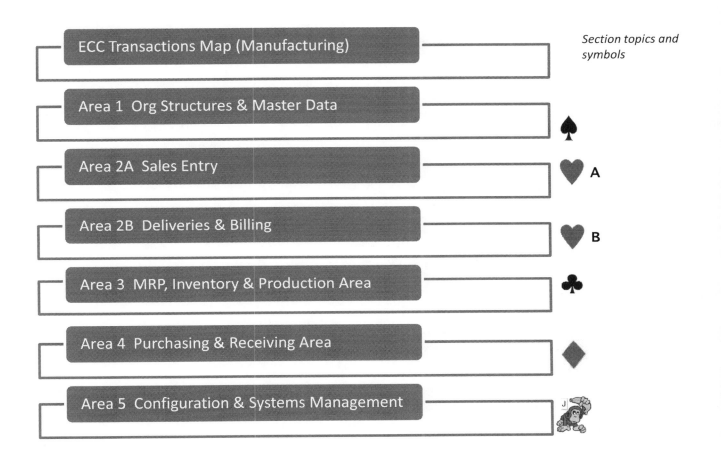

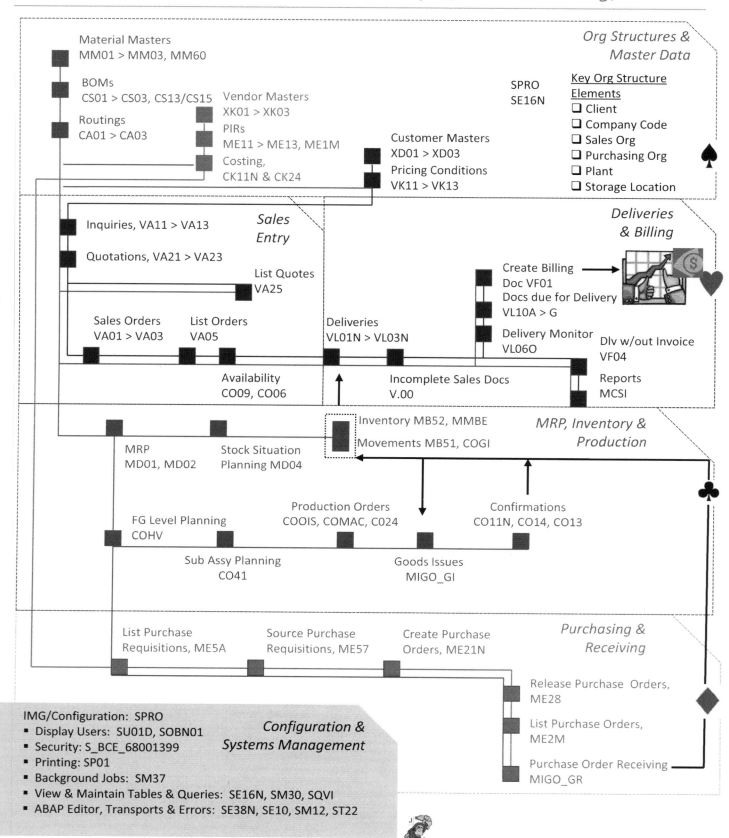

Map Area 1
Org Structures and Master Data

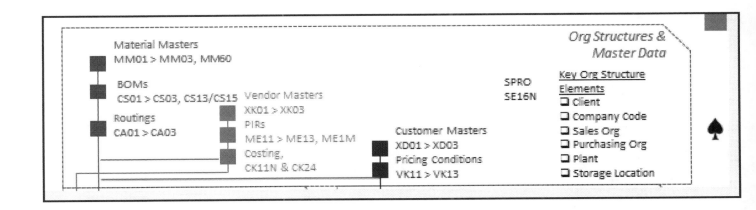

Our map begins with a discussion of Org Structures which impact the Master Data in an SAP ECC system. Overviews of approximately 20 Master Data related transactions are presented.

Three Master Data transaction categories are discussed – Materials, Vendors, and Customers. Two additional transactions, SPRO and SE16N, are introduced because of their use in maintaining and viewing Org Structure and Master Data.

This section is important, because along with Basic Operator Training, Master Data is usually found to be a critical factor in determining the success of an SAP implementation.

Org Structures	*Section*
Org Structure Configuration – SPRO	*Topics*
Viewing Org Structures - SE16N Table Viewer	
Material Master Transaction Series	
Bill of Material (BOMs)	
Routings	
Vendor Masters	
Purchasing info Records	
Costing	
Customer Masters	
Pricing Condition Records	

We find the concept of Org Structures to be one of the most misunderstood areas in all of SAP. Maybe this is because business people, heavily engaged in making SAP work at the Sales, Purchasing or Production Order level, have little time to remember what they were trained on (or in many cases, *were not trained on)* regarding Org Structures in the first place.

Our basic message is three-fold:
- ✓ SAP Org Structures *drive* Master Data requirements.
- ✓ Master Data *drives* Sales, Purchasing and Production Order processing.
- ✓ Order processing errors *drive* people crazy because they have forgotten (or never understood) the underlying SAP Org Structures in the first place.

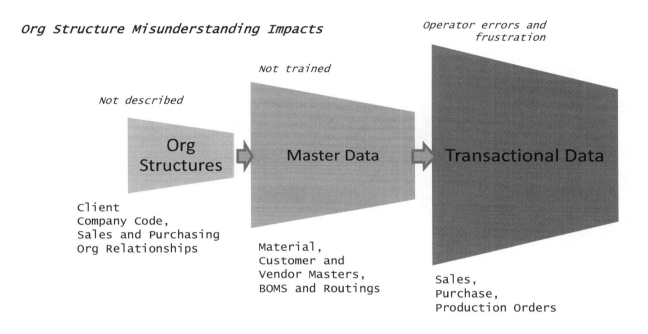

Org Structure Misunderstanding Impacts

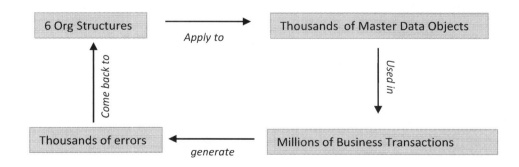

Below we identify some of the most common error conditions that users encounter in SAP and relate these errors to the Org Structure/Master Data relationship that is the root cause of the error.

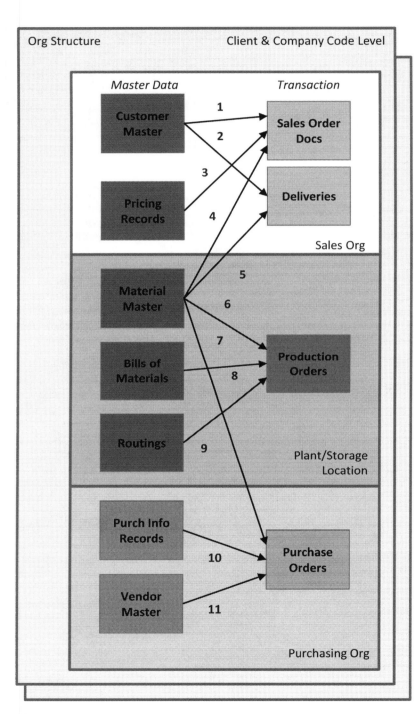

#	Possible Error Sources
1	Customer Master not extended to Sales Org.
2	Delivery Complete Indicator incorrectly set.
3	Missing Pricing Condition.
4	Material Master not extended to Sales Org.
5	Material not extended to Delivery Storage Location.
6	Material MRP/Prod Plng Params incorrect or not set.
7	Material Purchasing Params not set.
8	No/Incorrect BOM; Validity Date Range Errors.
9	No/Incorrect Routing; Control Key, Work Center Error.
10	No PIR; PIR Validity Date Range Errors.
11	Vendor Master not extended to Purchasing Org.

The message here is that Org Structures and Master Data enforce controls on the business.

To auditors, this is a good thing.

We describe an Org Structure as a container, binder or mold that organizes and holds SAP data together.

And when we say this in training – it's almost immediately and universally forgotten. So, we came up with another definition and memory-wise, it works better. So here goes…

ORG Structure =

Meet Fred (the <u>*ERP Bunny)*</u>

An SAP system can support many Org Structures…

Meet Fred's family.

And if we were producers of fine chocolate, we could say that the *molds* into which we pour our chocolate, **the Chocolate Bunny molds**, are **Org Structures.**

So our message here is this:

An Org Structure is a mold (or container) that hold things together.

(it's not the bunny or the chocolate, it's the mold – and it shapes things)

Provided on the next pages are some basic definitions (and concept diagrams) for six key Org Structures that are used in almost all SAP ERP systems.

1 **The client.**

A client is a *complete, standalone system* with its own set of data. The data in a client can be either client-specific or non-specific (i.e. 'cross-client').

- ✓ **Client-specific data** resides in and impacts only one client – examples include: User profile data such as user IDs, parameters and authorizations; **Organizational Structures** and document types; and business Transactional and Master data.

- ✓ **Non-specific** or Cross-client data is shared across multiple clients. Examples include *some* customizing data and all ABAP (code) objects.

- ✓ A client can have *many* **Company Codes, Sales** and **Purchasing Organizations.**

Client Concept Diagram.

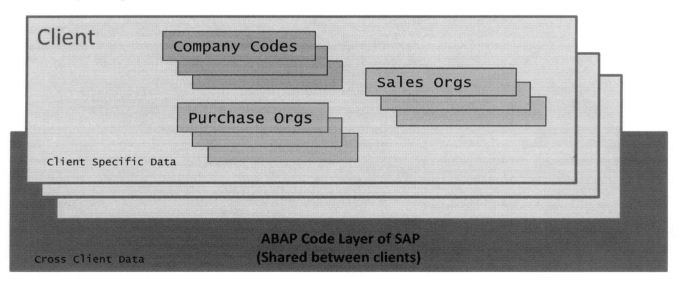

2 **A Company Code** is a Legal Entity providing a complete Chart of Accounts (Balance Sheet / Profit & Loss statement) for a business.

✓ For taxation purposes, a company with Plants in different countries may be split into different company codes.

✓ A company code can have *many* **plants, profit centers** and **cost centers.**

✓ If materials are moved (**bought or sold**) between Plants in different company codes, some kind of financial settlement document is required.

✓ For materials transferred between Plants in the same Company Code, no financial settlement document is required.

Company Code Concept Diagram.

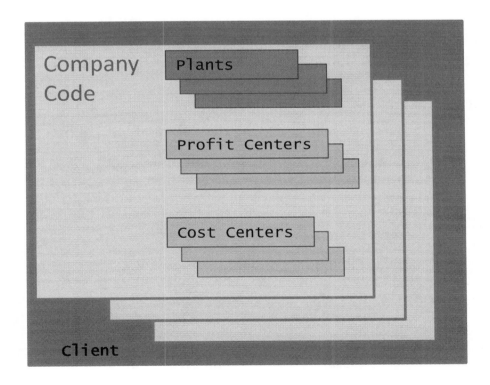

3 A **Plant** is a physical location where we buy, build, store or ship materials.

- ✓ Every plant must be **assigned to one** (and only one) **company code**.

- ✓ A Plant may be assigned to *multiple Sales Organizations* using a **Delivering Plant** in these organizations.

- ✓ Each plant must have a **physical street address** where materials can be delivered to or shipped from.

- ✓ Plants have **Storage Locations** - areas inside the plant where Inventory is stored.

- ✓ Plants have **Work Centers** - places where Manufacturing/Assembly occurs.

- ✓ *Plant - Material Rules.* For selling, buying or manufacturing purposes, Materials are **extended** to a Plant (a single Material can be extended to many plants).

  - ➤ Materials are moved between plants or to customers via **Delivery Documents**. A delivery document can be created for either an STO (Stock Transfer Order, delivery to a Plant) or a Sales Order (delivery to a Customer).

  - ➤ If Materials are sold or moved between plants in different company codes, a financial invoice/settlement is required.

  - ➤ If materials are moved between two plants in same company code, no financial invoice/settlement is required.

  - ➤ Materials can move between Plants on Sales Orders (if the Plants are in different company codes) or via Stock Transport Orders (in the same or different company codes).

  - ➤ Materials are costed at the plant level, based on **Bill of Materials** (Components), **Routings** (Work Center/Labor Rates) and **Purchasing Info Records** (Raw material Costs).

  - ➤ The Material Master Sales Plant View identifies the Profit Center assignment for a Material.

  - ➤ A Material at a plant can be assigned to only one Profit Center.

The Plant Org Structure Concept Diagram.

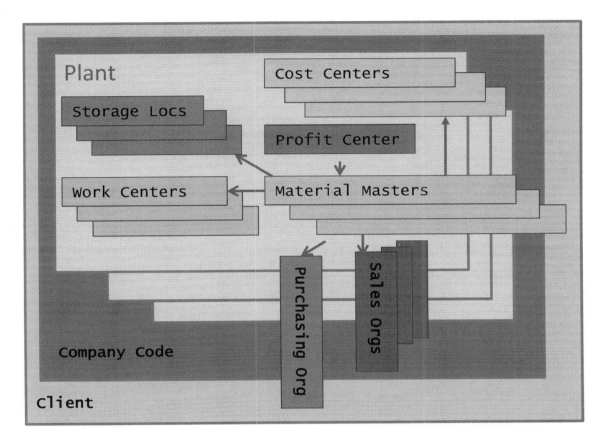

Notes:
- ✓ Because Storage Locations and Work Centers are Plant Specific, they are drawn inside the Plant area;
- ✓ Because Materials can be extended between Plants, they are drawn to extend outside the Plant boundary.
- ✓ The same concept applies to Cost Centers, Sales and Purchasing Organizations – they can extend beyond the Plant level (which gets to the utility of Org Structures).

4   **Storage Locations** are areas inside a Plant where inventory is maintained (and reported on) in SAP.

✓   Inventory is moved in (added to) a storage Location using a **MIGO_GR Goods Receipt** or similar (CO11N, Production Order Confirmation) transaction.

✓   Inventory is moved out of (subtracted from) a Storage Location to a Production Order or Cost Center using a **MIGO_GI Goods Issue** transaction.

✓   Inventory is moved between Storage Locations in a Plant using a **MIGO_TR Transfer** transaction.

✓   Within a Storage Location, a material can have **only one** Storage Bin assignment.

There is an additional inventory Org Structure called, the **Warehouse,** that is used when a material must be stored in multiple bin locations inside a storage location.

✓   In terms of inventory handling, SAP distinguishes between these two options – using the terms 'IM' (Inventory Management) and 'WM' (Warehouse Management).

✓   WM implementations require an additional level of transaction complexity, because inventory is managed at the Storage Location and Storage Bin Level.

For many small to medium size Manufacturing companies, IM – Storage Location based inventory solutions are sufficient – and WM based solutions are not deployed because of their additional complexity and cost.

Example IM based solution for a Plant using 4 Storage Locations.

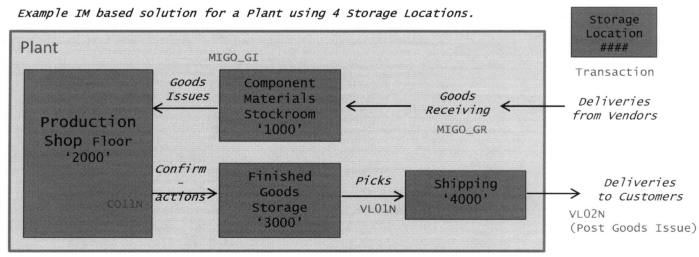

5 **Sales Organizations** are created to link Customers, Materials, Pricing Conditions and Delivering Plant Assignments together.

✓   A sales organization is attached to one company code.

✓   Plants can be assigned to multiple sales organizations.

✓   The plants in a sales organization can be assigned to different company codes.

✓   For selling purposes, materials can be extended to multiple sales organizations.

✓   Mainly for reporting purposes, Sales Organizations are further sub-divided into **Distribution Channels.**

Sales Organization Concept Diagram.

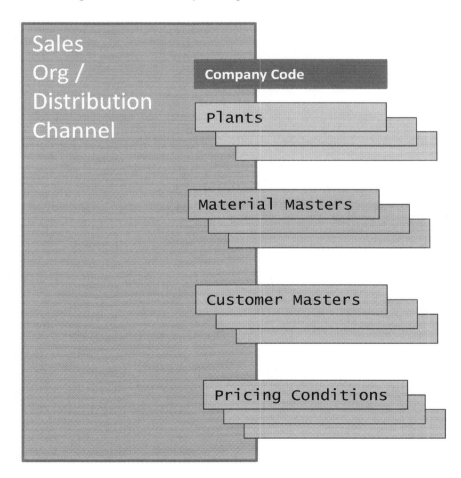

6   Purchasing Organizations are created to link Vendors, Materials and Purchase Price Conditions together.

✓ A purchase organization can have a company code assignment.

✓ Purchasing Organizations can be created by region. (e.g. Purchase Organizations North America, Latin America, Europe, Asia, etc.)

✓ The plants in a purchasing organization can be assigned to different company codes.

✓ Within a Purchasing Organization, a Purchasing Info Record (PIR) establishes the costs of a purchased Part by a Plant and a Vendor.

Purchasing Organization Concept Diagram.

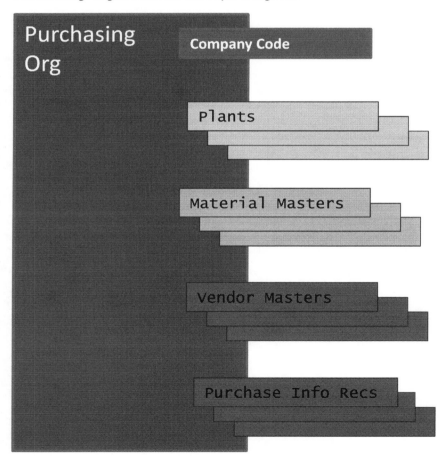

ECC Org Structures are created and maintained in a portion of SAP called the IMG (Implementation Management Guide). The transaction **SPRO** provides access to the IMG. *Most business operators will never utilize this transaction* (configuration changes are usually made by the SAP Consultants working on the Project team), but as an example of how SPRO can be used - we describe here a screen sequence to display a Company Code Address.

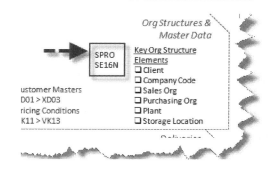

Transaction Flow.

1

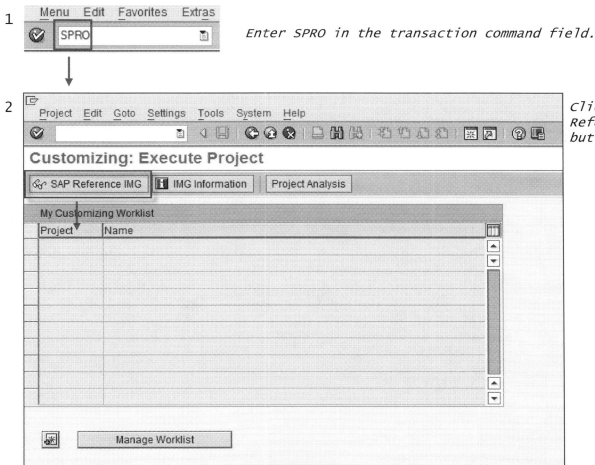

Enter SPRO in the transaction command field.

2

Click on SAP Reference IMG button.

3

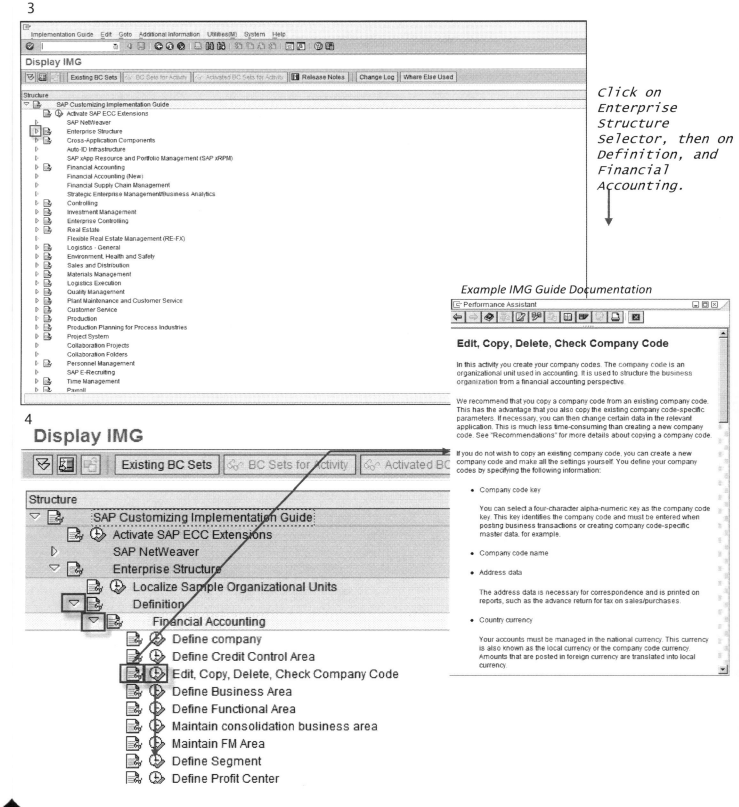

*Click on
Enterprise
Structure
Selector, then on
Definition, and
Financial
Accounting.*

5

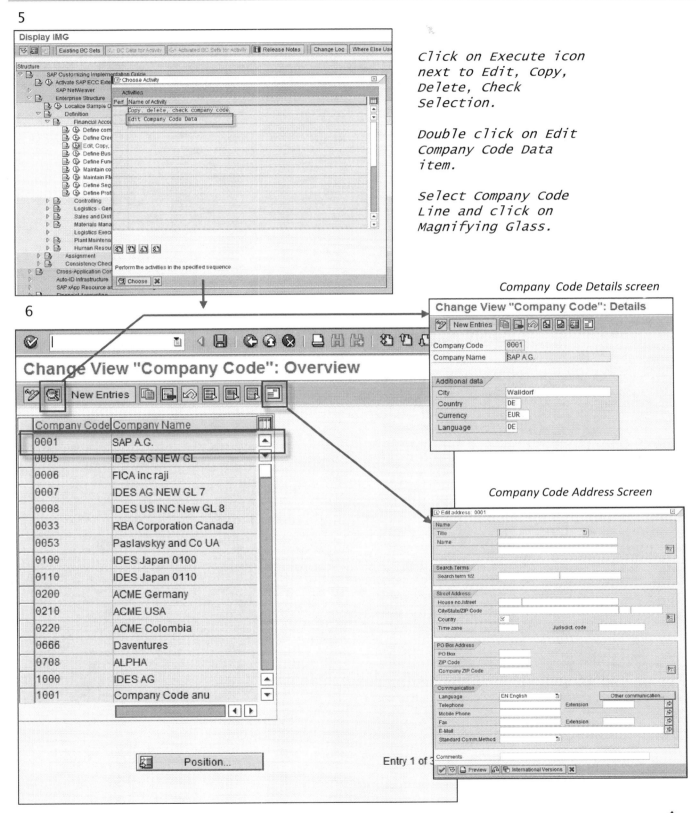

Click on Execute icon
next to Edit, Copy,
Delete, Check
Selection.

Double click on Edit
Company Code Data
item.

Select Company Code
Line and click on
Magnifying Glass.

Company Code Details screen

Company Code Address Screen

6

SE16N is the table viewer in the SAP ECC System. It is described here, because it is often used in looking at the Org Structure Master Data assignments that are configured in your ECC system. To use SE16N, you need to know a table name. A list of key table names is provided at the end of this section.

Shown below is a sequence to display a table view named V_T001. This table view contains all the company codes in a system client.

Transaction Flow.

1

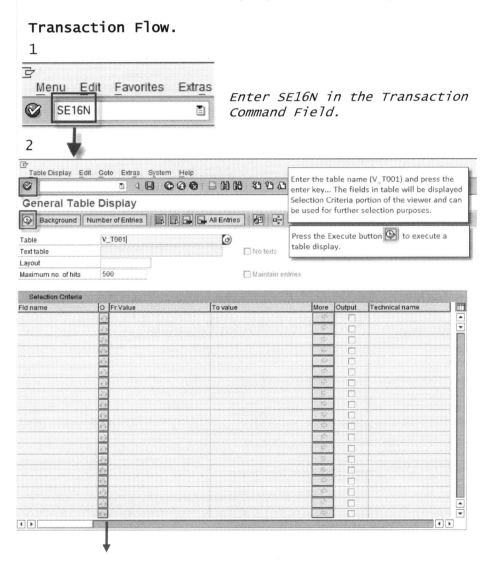

Enter SE16N in the Transaction Command Field.

Enter the table name (V_T001) and press the enter key... The fields in table will be displayed Selection Criteria portion of the viewer and can be used for further selection purposes.

Press the Execute button to execute a table display.

3
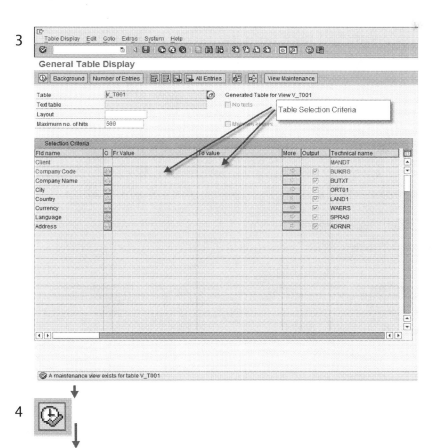

4

5
Display View "Company Code": Overview

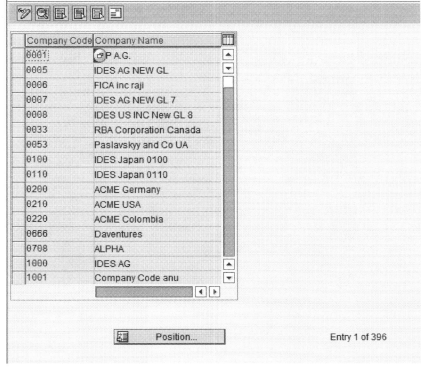

To use SE16N, you will need to know a table name. Provided below is a short list of some frequently searched for SAP ECC tables.

Short List of key
SAP ECC Tables

No	Table Name	Function
1	AUFK	(Production) Order Master Data
2	DD02VV	List of Tables (useful to find tables)
3	DD03M	List of Fields (useful to find a list of tables for a field)
4	EKKO	Purchasing Document Header
5	EKPO	Purchasing Document Line Item
6	LIKP	Delivery Header
7	LIPS	Delivery Item
8	MAPL	Task List to Materials (Materials Routings)
9	MARA	Material Master General Data
10	MARC	Material Plant Data
11	MARD	Stock Storage Location/Plant
12	MAST	Material BOM Link
13	MVKE	Material Master Sales Data
14	STPO	BOM Item
15	T024E	Purchasing Org - Company Code
16	T024W	Plant - Purchasing Org
17	TSTCT	List of Transaction Codes
18	V_MAT_ROUT_BOM	Materials Routings & BOMs (Table View)
19	V_T001	List of Company Codes (Table View)
20	V_T001K_LK	Assignment of Plants to Company Codes (Table View)
21	V_T001L	List of Storage Locations (Table View)
22	V_T001W	List of Plants (Table View)
23	V_T024E	List of Purchasing Orgs (Table View)
24	V_TVKO	List of Sales Orgs (Table View)
25	V_TVKO_LK	Assignments Co Codes to Sales Orgs (Table View)
26	VBAK	Sales Document Header
27	VBAP	Sales Document Line Item

Display	Change	Create	Object
MM03	MM02	MM01	Materials
CS03	CS02	CS01	BOMs
CA03	CA03	CA01	Routings
ME13	ME12	ME11	PIRs

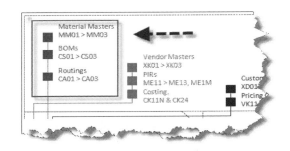

Material Masters. Material Masters are a key Master Data object containing the basic information necessary to buy, build or sell materials, goods and services in SAP. In a manufacturing environment, Materials are organized by an **Industry Sector** (usually **Mechanical Engineering**) and by **Material Type**.

Key Material Types. Some 25 Material Types are supported in standard SAP; our focus here is on the three most widely used: **FERTs**, **HALBs** & **ROHs**.

✓ **FERTs** are the Finished Goods Material Type. These are the sellable end items; *normally* FERTS are manufactured (but can be purchased). To be manufactured, FERTs require (in addition to a Material Master) a **Bill of Material (BOM)** and **Routing**. (If they are procured, FERT materials must have the necessary MM Purchasing Views and be assigned a **Special Procurement Key** indicating procurement source from another plant or a **PIR (Purchasing Info Record)** if procurement is from an outside vendor.)

✓ **HALBS** are the sub assembly material type. A series of HALBs (as specified in BOM), are used to create a FERT. HALBs themselves can have a BOM - composed of other HALBs, FERTS and/or ROH Materials. HALBs are normally not sold (but can be, by adding necessary sales views) and can manufactured in house or procured internally or externally. To be manufactured internally, HALBs (like FERTs) require BOMs and Routings. To be procured, they require either a Special Procurement Key or PIR.

✓ **ROHS** are the Raw Material Type. ROH materials are never manufactured, are always procured – either internally (by Special Procurement Key setting) or externally from a Vendor (with a PIR).

The relationships between these Material Master Types and other key Material Master Data objects that are used in the manufacturing process (BOMs, Routings and PIRs) are briefly reviewed over next few pages.

Modeling a Finished Good Part in SAP.

Finished Good (FERT) Level Part:
Material Number = QS-8-K-BL-S-C ──────────────▶
Material Description = Quad Rocker Switch

The BOM for this Material, consists of three items:
The Cap; The Switches; The Circuit Board...

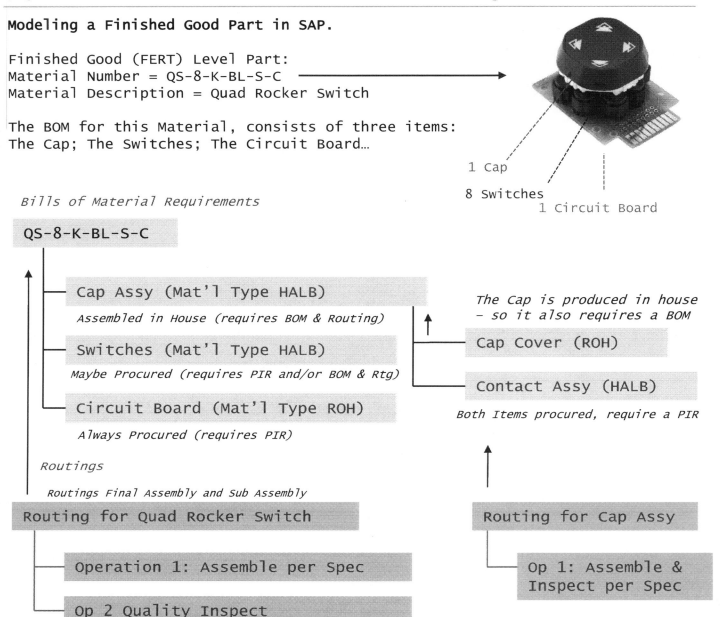

1 Cap

8 Switches

1 Circuit Board

Bills of Material Requirements

QS-8-K-BL-S-C

Cap Assy (Mat'l Type HALB)

Assembled in House (requires BOM & Routing)

Switches (Mat'l Type HALB)

Maybe Procured (requires PIR and/or BOM & Rtg)

Circuit Board (Mat'l Type ROH)

Always Procured (requires PIR)

The Cap is produced in house – so it also requires a BOM

Cap Cover (ROH)

Contact Assy (HALB)

Both Items procured, require a PIR

Routings

Routings Final Assembly and Sub Assembly

Routing for Quad Rocker Switch

Operation 1: Assemble per Spec

Op 2 Quality Inspect

Routing for Cap Assy

Op 1: Assemble &
Inspect per Spec

In this example above, (6) Material Masters are called for: the Final Assembly itself; its 3 components, and the 2 components in the Cap Sub Assembly.
- ✓ Production of the Final Assembly item and the Cap Sub Assembly in house requires (2) BOMs and (2) Routings. (Each Production Order requires a Material Master, BOM and Routing.)
- ✓ In this case, (4) PIRs (Purchasing Info Records) are also required for the items that are procured from vendors.

Material Master (MM). In SAP, the Material Master is the Data Object containing the information needed to Buy, Build or Sell the material. Three key Material Master Types are:
✓ FERTs (sellable Goods)
✓ HALBs (Sub-Assemblies)
✓ ROHs (Raw Materials)

Material Master records are defined at the Client Level and *views are extended to* Plant, Sales and Purchase Org Levels.

Bill of Material (BOM). Is the master data object that lists the component materials and the quantities of those materials required to build an FERT or an HALB material in the Plant.
✓ BOMs may contain any combination of Material Types with their own BOMs.
✓ BOMs are Plant specific.

Routing (Rtg). This master data object lists the operations and the manufacturing times necessary to build a FERT or HALB material in a Plant.
✓ Routings are Plant specific.

Purchasing Info Record (PIR). This is a master data record that establishes the purchase price for an FERT, HALB or ROH material when it is procured from a Vendor.
✓ PIRs are plant and purchasing organization specific.

Special Procurement Key (SPK). This is a material master field and is used when special procurement conditions exist for the material to include procurement from another plant.

Material Type	Produced (where)	Requires (what) Master Data
Finished Good (FERT)	In House (normal)	Material Master, BOM and Routing
Sub Assembly (HALB)	In House (normal)	Material Master, BOM and Routing
Finished Good (FERT)	Externally (exception)	Material Master, Purchasing info Record or Special Procurement Key
Sub Assembly (HALB)	Externally (exception)	Material Master, Purchasing info Record or Special Procurement Key
Raw Material	Externally (normal)	Material Master, Purchasing info Record or Special Procurement Key

MM Views. Material Master fields are presented in series of *Views*. The views required for any material are specified by the **material type**, are established in *configuration* and are specific to an **Org Structure** level.

Here are some examples:

✓ *All* Materials must have a **Basic Data View**. This view is maintained at the *client level* – meaning that *any* fields/values specified on the Basic Data View are applicable to *all* Plants, Sales and Purchase Orgs in the System.

✓ *Sellable* FERTs, HALBs and ROHs must have a **Sales Org View** – this view is specific to a Sales Org (multiple Sales Org Views can be maintained).

✓ ROH Materials must always have a **Purchasing** view and if planned, an **MRP** (Materials Requirements Planning) view.

✓ Material **MRP** Views *are Plant specific* – meaning that plants can plan materials differently using parameters/values applicable to their plant.

✓ FERTs and HALBs manufactured internally must have *work Scheduling Views*, also specific to the plant level.

✓ *Costing, Accounting and Storage Location views* are supported at the Plant level and in the case of Storage Location, down to Storage Location Level.

MM03 Display Material Master Transaction and the Example Views maintained for a material in SAP.

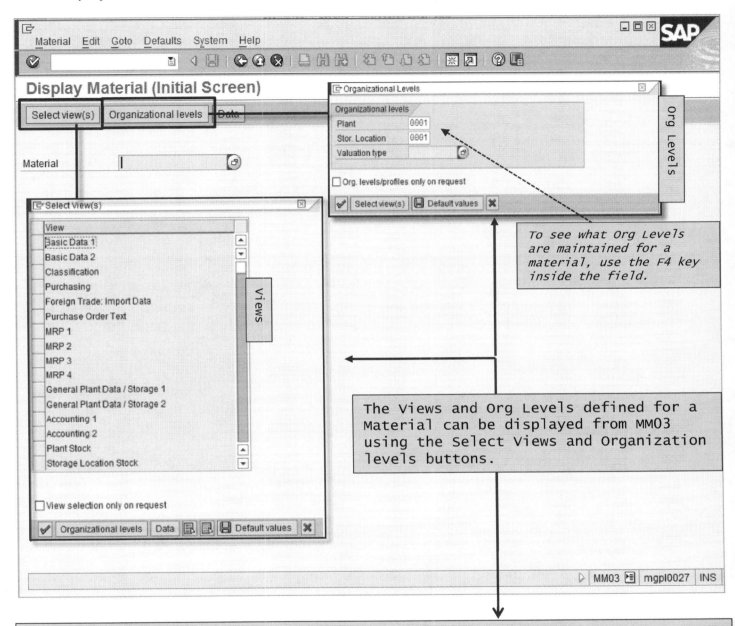

To see what Org Levels are maintained for a material, use the F4 key inside the field.

The Views and Org Levels defined for a Material can be displayed from MM03 using the Select Views and Organization levels buttons.

✓ Material Master Views required for a Material are determined by the Material Type as specified in the IMG (Implementation Management Guide).

✓ MM Views are Org Structure specific, *multiple* Plant and Sales Org Views for a material can be maintained. This allows Materials to be extended across multiple Plants, Sales and Purchasing Organizations for use globally.

The table below summarizes some of the most common Material Master Views in SAP. Remember, the details and field level requirements for each view are specified in configuration and vary from project to project.

View	Org Structure Level	Notes
Basic Data 1 & 2	Client	For use with all material types. Includes Material Number, Description, Catalog, Old Material Number, Design Drawing and Basic Unit of Measure Fields.
Classification	Client	Usually Optional. This view allows the assignment of the material into classification characteristics definable by the business.
Sales Org Data 1 & 2	Sales Org / Distribution Channel	For use with any material to be sold. This view is standard with all FERTs and HALBs. This view includes fields describing Distribution Channel and Taxation Status, and Delivery Plant information.
Sales General Plant Data	Plant	For use with any material to be sold. Key fields on this view include Availability Check and Profit Center.
Foreign Trade Export Data	Plant	For use with any material to be sold. Key fields include Country of Origin and Commodity Code .
Sales Text	Sales Org / Distribution Channel	Text entered on this View can be automatically entered on Sales Orders for the material.
Purchasing	Plant	Required for purchased materials. For ROH materials this is a standard view. Key fields include Purchasing Group (a buyers Code), Material Group and Purchasing Value key.
Foreign Trade Import	Plant	Required for purchased materials.
Purchase Order Text	Client	Text entered on this View can be automatically entered on Purchase Orders for the material.
MRP1 – MRP4	Plant	Materials Requirements Planning Views. The fields on these views are read when MRP is ran for the material. MRP Type (Standard, Reorder Point, etc), Lot Size, Safety Stock and MRP Controller (Planner) fields are examples of the fields found on these views.
Forecasting	Plant	If the MRP Type used with the Material requires forecasting, this view is maintained. Fields on this view would specify the forecasting method, period, history, etc.
Work Scheduling	Plant	This view is required for FERTS and HALBS manufactured in house. Fields on this view would include Production Scheduler and Production profile views.
Quality Management	Plant	View is required if Quality Management module will be used with material.
Plant Data Storage 1 & 2	Plant	These views contain fields specifying details for the storage and handling of the material in the plant - temperature conditions, storage life, etc.

Table continued

View	Org Structure Level	Notes
Warehouse Management 1 & 2	Storage Location	These views are required if the plant uses the SAP Warehouse Management (WM) module. For most small to medium size manufacturing companies, this functionality is not required; in these environments, inventory can be managed at the Storage Location level.
Plant Stock	Plant	These views show the material inventory in the Plant. Inventory data is divided into stock categories such as Unrestricted, Sales Order, Quality Inspection, Blocked, etc.
Storage Location Stock	Storage Location	Details Stock in a Storage Location.
Accounting 1 & 2	Plant	Describes Total Stock Value, Moving and Standard Price details for the material.
Costing 1 & 2	Plant	Provides Previous, Current and Future price details for the materials.

Remember: Not all views are required.

For example, and especially in smaller manufacturing enterprises, the Warehouse Management views may not be maintained because WM Module is not employed.

Some example SAP Material Master views are provided below. Remember that the list of fields and views are determined by configuration.

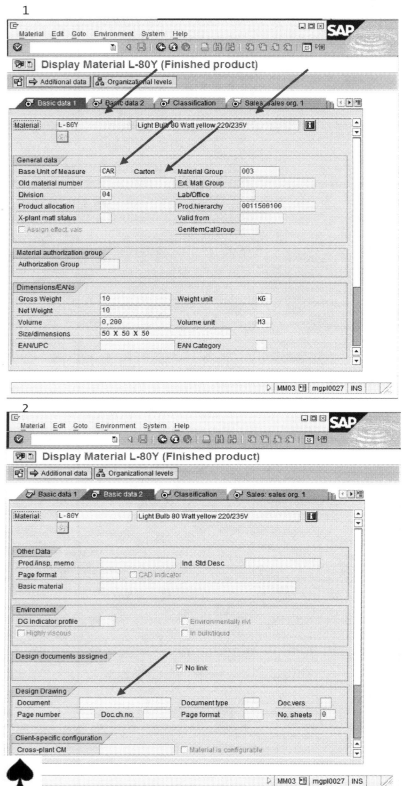

Basic data 1 view key fields:
(client specific)
- ✓ Material #
- ✓ Description
- ✓ Basic Unit of Measure
- ✓ Old Material Number

Basic data 2 key fields:
(client specific)
- ✓ Design Drawing Document

3 / 4

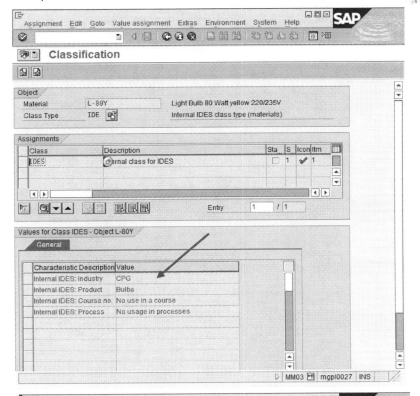

Classification view:
(client specific)
✓ Material classifications
   by Classes and
   Characteristic values
   defined by the business.

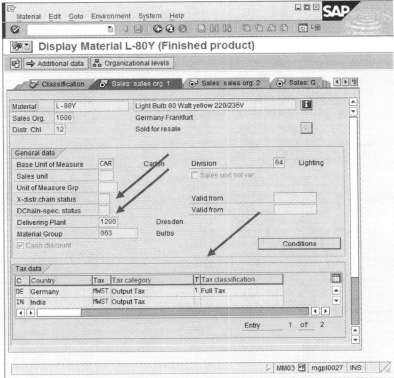

Sale org 1:
(Sales Org/Dist Ch
   specific)
✓ Distribution Chain
   Status
✓ Delivering Plant
✓ Taxation Status

5 / 6

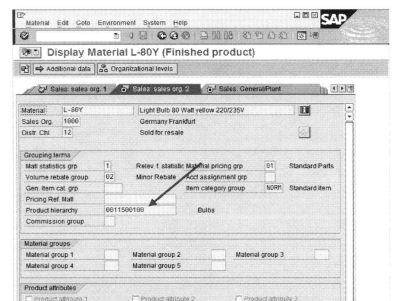

Sales Org 2:
(Sales Org / Dist Ch)
✓ Product Attributes

Sales General/Plant:
(Plant)
✓ Profit Center

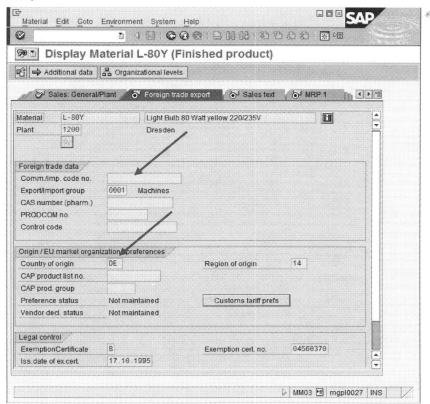

Foreign trade export:
(Plant)
✓ Commodity Code
✓ Country of Origin

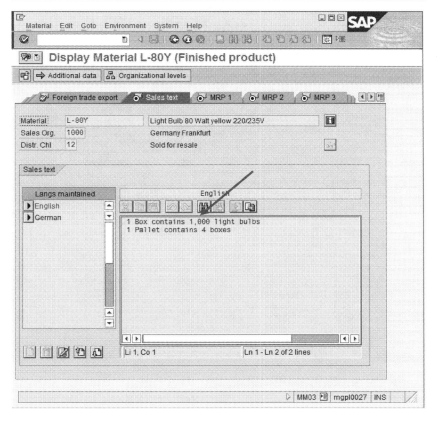

Sales text:
(Sales Org / Disti Channel)
✓ Text entered here
   appears on Sales
   Documents

9

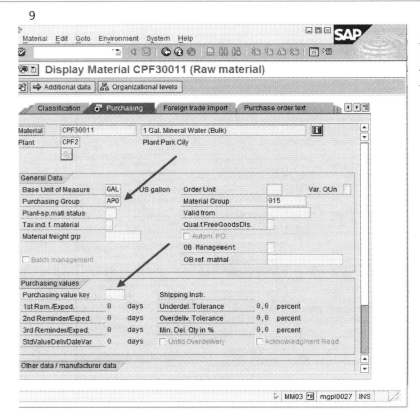

Purchasing:
(Plant)
✓ Purchasing Group
✓ Purchasing Value Key

10

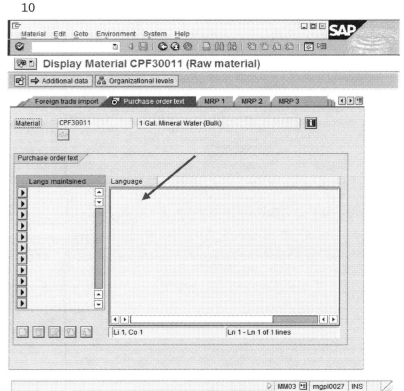

Purchase order text:
(Client)
✓ Text entered here appears
   on Purchase Orders

11 / 12

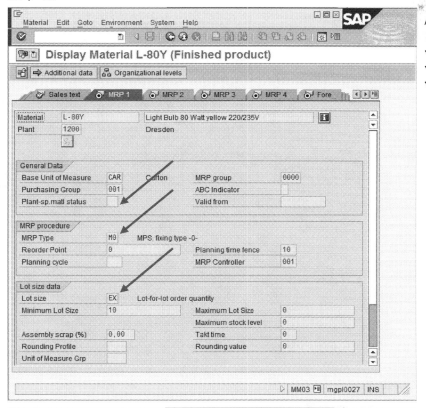

MRP 1:
(Plant)
✓ MRP Type
✓ Plant Material Status
✓ Lot Size Controller

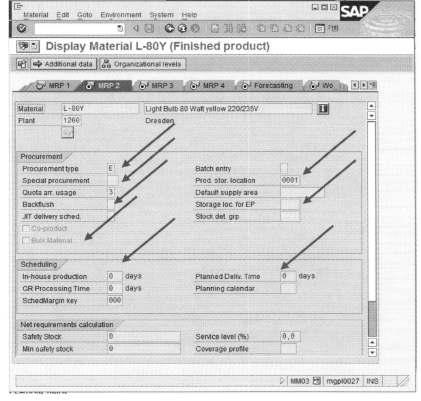

MRP 2:
(Plant)
✓ Procurement Type
✓ Special Procurement Key
✓ Backflush Indicator
✓ Bulk Indicator
✓ Storage Loc for Procurement
✓ Storage Loc for Production
✓ In House Prod Time
✓ Planned Delivery Time

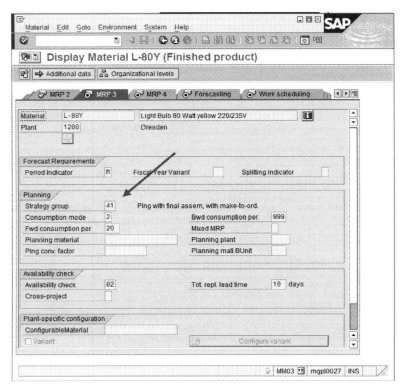

MRP 3:
(Plant)
✓ Strategy Group

MRP 4
(Plant)
✓ Selection method
✓ Individual Coll. Indicator

15 / 16

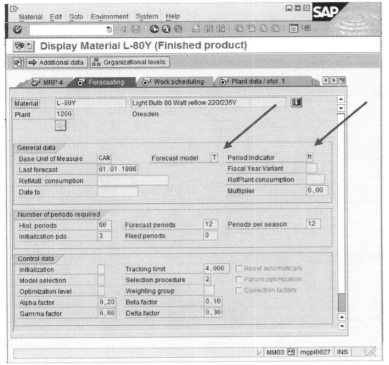

Forecasting:
(Plant)
✓ Forecast Model
✓ Forecast Period

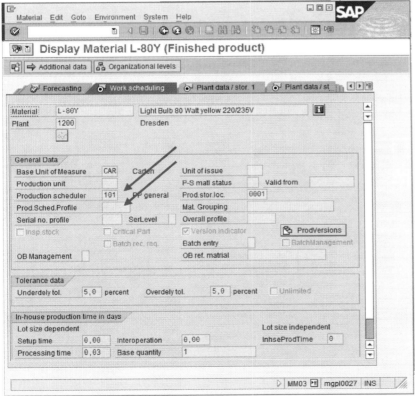

Work scheduling:
(Plant)
✓ Production Scheduler
✓ Prod. Sched. Profile

17 / 18

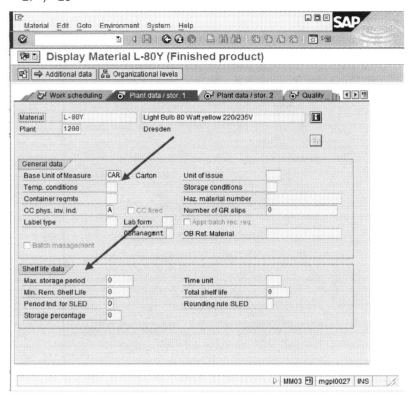

Plant data / storage 1:
(Plant)
✓ Temp. Conditions
✓ Shelf Life Data

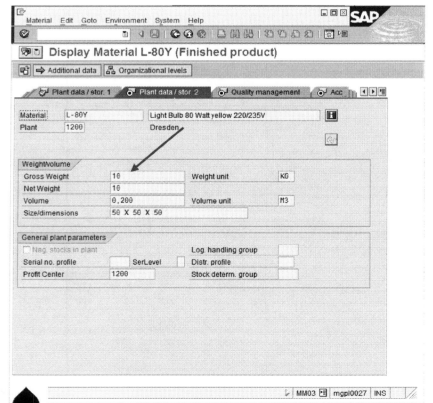

Plant data / storage 2:
(Plant)
✓ Weight/Volume/Dimensions

SAP ECC in Manufacturing: *An Operator's Guide*

19 / 20

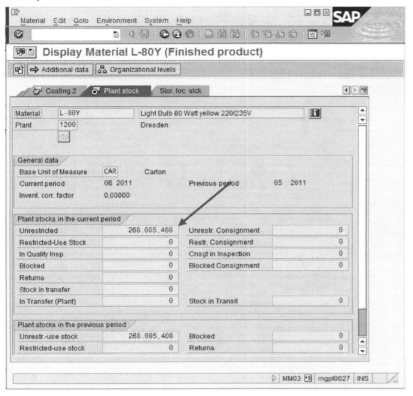

Plant stock:
(Plant)
✓ Material Stock by Stock
  Category

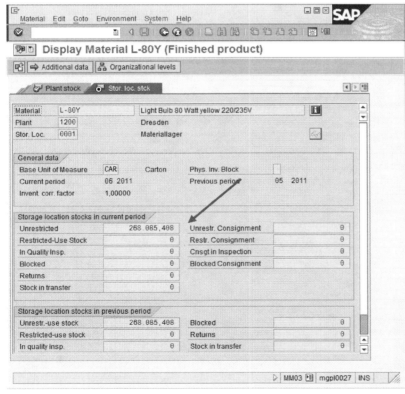

Storage loc. Stock;
(Storage location)
✓ Material Stock by Stock
  Category

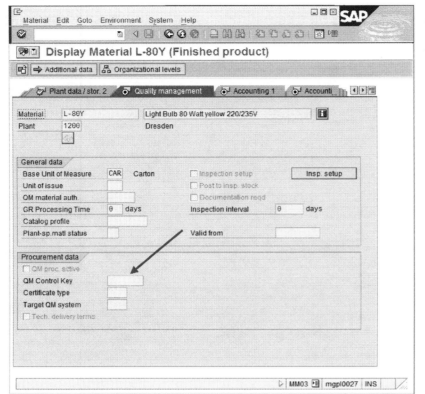

Quality management:
(Plant)
✓ QM Control Key

Accounting 1:
(Plant)
✓ Price Unit
✓ Standard Price
✓ Total Stock
✓ Total Stock Value

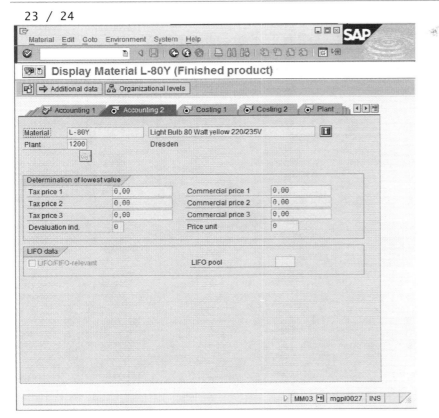

Accounting 2:
(Plant)

Costing 1:
(Plant)

25

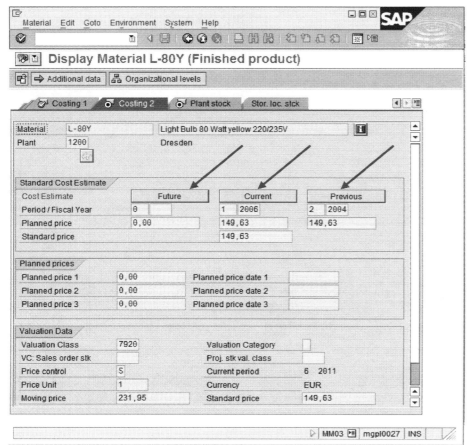

Costing 2:
(Plant)
✓ Future, Current,
  Previous Price.
✓ Price reflected from the
  Assembly to include
  material (components /
  BOM), Manufacturing
  (Routings) & Purchasing
  (PIR) costs.
✓ Not the Sales price.

With over 500 field level values that can be maintained, it is easy to get overwhelmed by the complexity of the material master. Provided below is a table that discusses 30 fields that are of critical use in many SAP project implementations. The fields are listed by their MM View order.

Material Master Key Fields Summary

Field	View	FERT	HALB	ROH	Description
Material Number	Basic Data View 1	Y	Y	Y	This is the part number that SAP will use to store the material record. Often times, Part numbers must be changed in the switch to SAP because the legacy part number is already used or does not meet SAP conventions.
Material Description	Basic Data View 1	Y	Y	Y	Part/Material Number Description. Sometimes, but not always, accompanies the SAP Material Number in list displays etc.
Catalog Number	Basic Data View 1	Y	Y	Y	Usually the 'Part Number', at least to the customer, used when ordering the material.
Basic Unit of Measure	Basic Data View 1	Y	Y	Y	Once defined, cannot be changed, so, get it right - make sure it is the **Base** measure. If you order in Feet but occasionally use centimeters – the base unit of measure needs to be centimeters. Alternate UOMs can be described from the Base UOM up.
Distribution Chain Status		Y	Y		This field is used to restrict the material for certain sales activities by Dchain Status. The distribution chain is made up of the Sales Org and the Distribution Channel.
Delivering Plant		Y	Y		If the delivering plant is not set in the customer material info record or the customer, it is determined from Material Master.
Availability Check		Y	Y	Y	The Availability Check enables the system to check availability of stock on a particular date against a sales order or other requirements. If it is not set in the material master, it will not be included when availability check is run.
Plant Material Status		Y	Y	Y	This Material Status restricts the usability of the material for certain activities by plant.

♠

MM Fields continued

Field	View	F E R T	H A L B	R O H	Description
Purchasing Group			Y	Y	It is also known as the Buyer code. An example would be the name of the person assigned to the buyer code who is responsible for buying the raw material.
MRP Controller		Y	Y		Thousands of materials are used to make materials and these material can be organized by an MRP controller code which can be a product line or the production planner (person) responsible for it.
Lot Size		Y	Y	Y	Defines what quantity of the material needs to be produced or procured.
Procurement Type		Y	Y	Y	This field determines whether the material is produced in house or procured. Raw materials can be external, while Finished goods are produced in house.
Special Procurement Key		Y	Y		This Key refers to the procurement type. A material could be externally procured (F) for example through a consignment order or a stock transport order from another plant.
Backflush Indicator			Y	Y	When a material is withdrawn for a production order, it is usually marked as goods issued upon confirmation. This is generally used where manual goods issues (MIGO_GI) are avoided.
Bulk Material Indicator				Y	Bulk materials are usually not part of materials planning. An example of a bulk material could be paint. This indicator is found in the MRP2 view.
Production Storage Location		Y	Y	Y	The material storage location is where the material is issued from a backflush. It can also be defined as the goods receipt location.
External Procurement Storage Location				Y	Storage location for externally procured materials copied to the purchase requisition.

MM Fields continued

Field	View		F E R T	H A L B	R O H	Description
MRP Type			Y	Y		This key determines whether a material is planned or not. It also determines which MRP procedure is used in planning that material.
MRP Group			Y	Y		MRP group is used to group materials for MRP control parameters that differ from the plant parameters.
In House Production Time			Y	Y		Time required to build a material in-house in work.
Profit Center			Y	Y	Y	Profit centers are assigned in the Sales: General/Plant view of the material master.
Current Std Price			Y	Y	Y	Standard price is the cost to obtain the material. It is different from the moving average price and is explained in detail in the costing chapter.
Sched Margin Key			Y	Y		This key defines the opening period, production floats and release periods.
Purchase Value Key					Y	Key that defines when a vendor needs to be reminded about an order. Also sets the under and over delivery tolerances.
Sales Order Text			Y	Y		Text related to the Sales process can be maintained here and this text can be copied into a sales order.
Purchase Order Text					Y	Text related to the Purchasing process can be maintained here and this text can be copied into a Purchase requisition or a purchase order.

Remember SAP field level help - for more info on any field - press the F1 key in the field.

MM03 is used to display a material master record.

Example: *Find the Delivering Plant on the MM Sales Org View for a material.*

Info Required.
- ✓ Material Master Number or find via Field Search function
- ✓ MM View(s)
- ✓ Org Structure

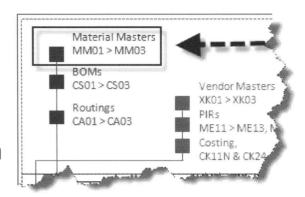

Transaction Flow.

1

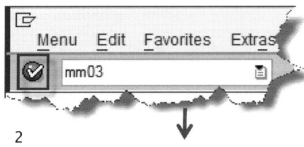

Enter MM03 and press the Green Check button

2

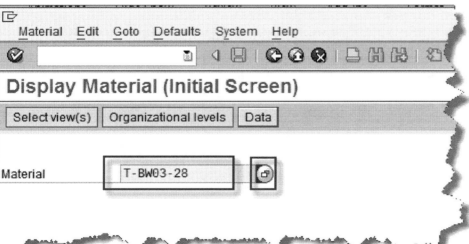

Enter Material Number or Find with MM Search Field

3

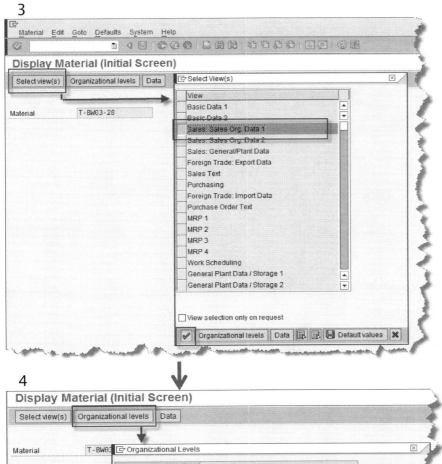

Click on Select view(s) button, Select Sales: Sales Org Data 1 view...

And then click on Green Check button...

4

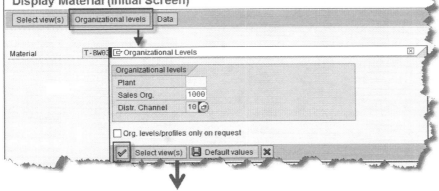

Click on Organization levels button, enter Sales Org and Distribution Channel...

And then click on Green Check button...

5

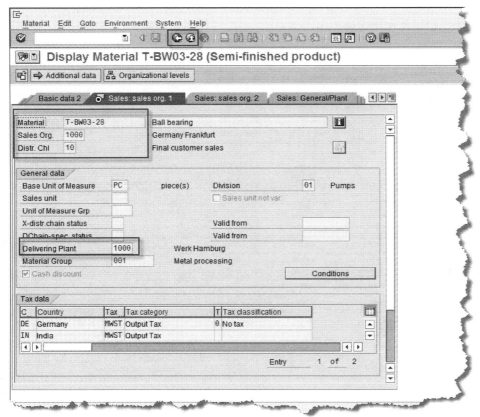

Sales: Sales Org. 1 view of the Material Master is displayed...

✓ Plant 1000 is the Delivering Plant for this Material and Sales Org combination.

Use the Green back or Yellow exit buttons to exit the view...

MM02 is used to change a material master record.

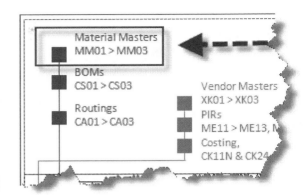

Example: *Change a material MRP type from Standard SAP Planning (MRP type 'PD') to Reorder Point ('VB') and specify a Reorder Point Level of 100.*

Info Required.
- ✓ Material Master Number or find via Field Search function
- ✓ MM View(s) / Org Structure

Transaction Flow.

1

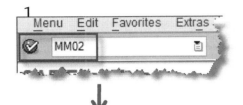

Enter transaction code MM02 and press the Green Check button

2

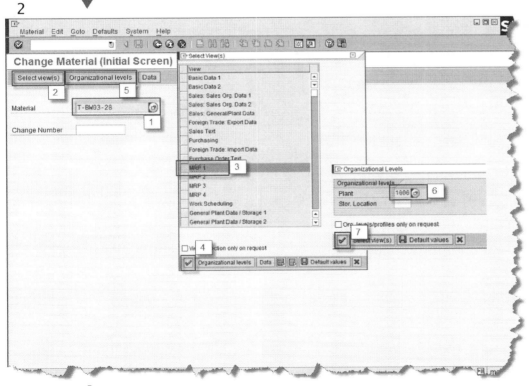

Enter Material Number or Find with MM Search Field...

Select View, MRP1 and Org Level, Plant...

3

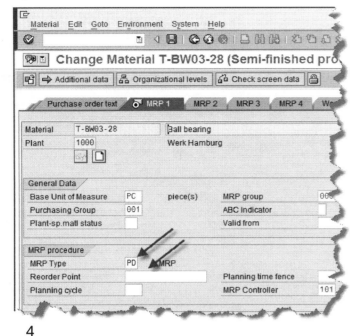

Change MRP Type from PD to VB...
Add 100 to Reorder Point field...
Click the Enter key to check...

4

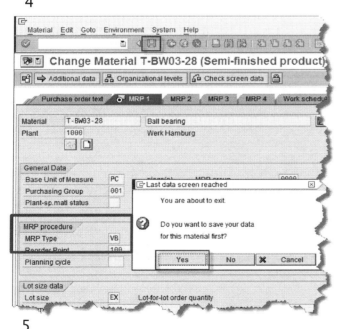

Because only one view was selected, SAP
asks if you want to save the data –
click on the Yes button...

o   note: Save button not active because
    of dialog...

5

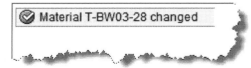

Confirmation Message that Save was
carried out.

MM01. MM01 is used to create a new material master or to extend an existing material master to a new Plant and/or Sales Org.

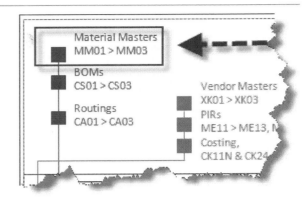

Example: *Create the Basic Data & MRP Views for a new Material similar to another material and set X-Plant Material Status field to blocked until the remaining views are created.*

Info Required.
- ✓ *New Material Master Number*
- ✓ *MM View(s) required*
- ✓ *Org Structure(s) required*
- ✓ *(highly recommended) Reference MM Number and Org Structure for the copy function.*

Transaction Flow.

1

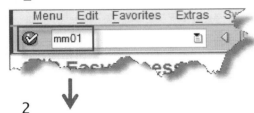

Enter transaction code MM01 and press the Green Check button...

2

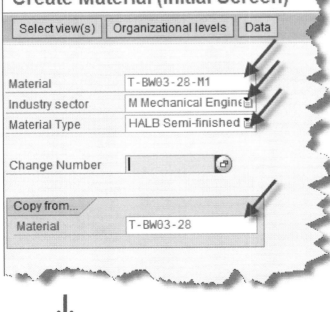

Enter:
1) (new) Material Number
2) Industry Sector
3) Material Type
4) Copy from Material number

Press the enter key

3

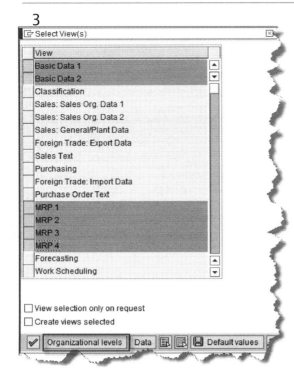

Click on Views to be created and then on Organization levels button.

4

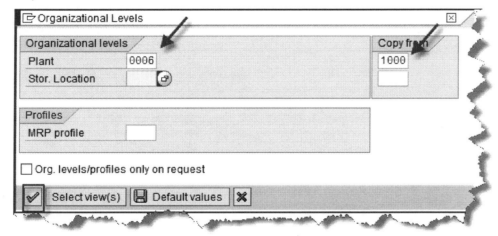

Enter Copy from and New Org Level values – e.g. the existing and new Plant numbers…

Click on the Green Check button…

5

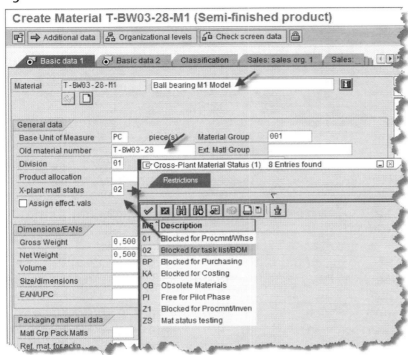

Change any fields that should
be changed...

Here:
✓ Change the Material
  Description
✓ Enter the old material
  number
✓ Set X-plant matl status

Press the enter key...
the next MM View will be
displayed – Set the field
values on that view as
required.

6

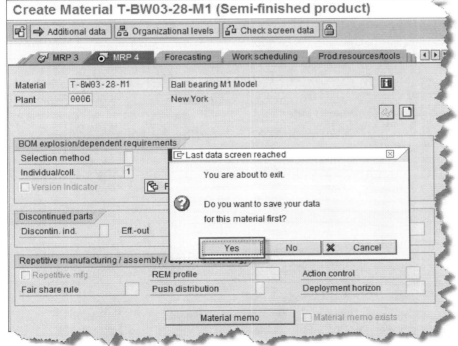

Pressing the enter key on the
last view, will cause SAP to
display a confirmation
message, asking if a Save
should take place...

Click Yes.

7

Confirmation Message that the Material
has been created.

BOM Transactions.

Create	Change	Display	List	Special
CS01	CS02	CS03	CEWB	CS13 CS15

Key Concepts:

✓ A Bill of Material defines the component materials and quantities required to produce an Assembly.

✓ BOMs are necessary for the Material Requirements Planning (MRP) run; and are copied into a production order when it is created.

✓ Structurally, a BOM consists of **header** and **component items**.
> ✓ The BOM Header consists of the data that refers to the entire BOM. It includes data like the material number, revision number and plant.
> ✓ BOM Items: Specify each of the components used in making the Assembly. BOM Item fields include item component, component description, quantity, unit of measure and an **Item category** (e.g. Stock or Text Item).

✓ BOMs have a **Status** (Created, Approved, etc...) and an **Effectivity Date**:
> ✓ The Effectivity Date establishes the validity period for the BOM; and allows for multiple BOMs to be maintained for a single material.
> ✓ The BOM Status code defines whether a BOM can be used in a production order and included in the MRP run. Inactive BOMs cannot be used in demand planning.

✓ **BOMs have a Type** and the usage field of the bill of material defines in what kind of process that BOM is used in – example BOM Types include:
> ✓ Production
> ✓ Engineering/design
> ✓ Universal (most common)
> ✓ Plant maintenance
> ✓ Sales and distribution
> ✓ Costing

✓ Transaction-wise, **CS01** is used to create a BOM; **CS02** is used for BOM changes and **CS03** is used to display a single BOM.
> ✓ Transaction code **CEWB** provides access to Engineering Workbench and Mass Maintenance capabilities.
> ✓ **CS13** provides a summarized BOM Display.
> ✓ **CS15** provides a BOM component item 'where used' list.

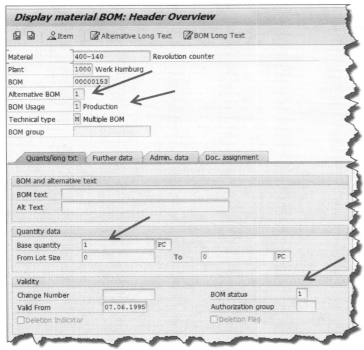

BOM Header Display - Key Fields
- ✓ Alternative BOM
- ✓ BOM Usage
- ✓ Base Quantity
- ✓ BOM Status

BOM Component Item Display –
Item Category Selections

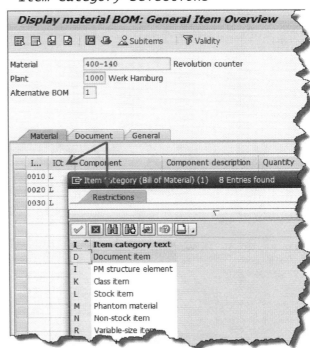

Sales BOM Example –
Sales BOMs are used in sales orders to ship parts to a customer that they assemble to complete the finished product.

Both the finished product and the components are displayed as line items in the Sales Order.

Overview. CS03 is the transaction to display a BOM. In the example below, we show how to perform a simple search for Materials in a Plant with BOMs and then how to display the BOM object.

Info Required.
✓ Material Number.
✓ Plant.
✓ Effectivity Date.

Transaction Flow.

1

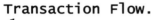

2

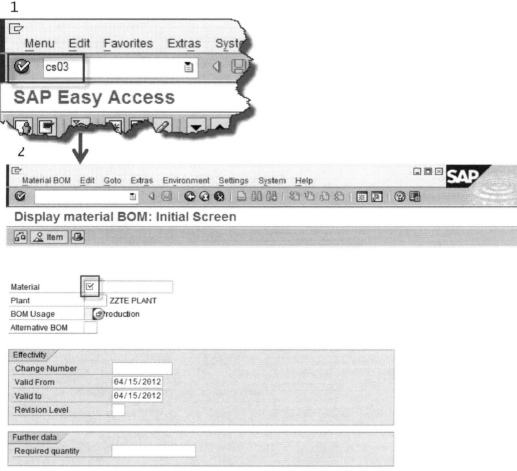

CS03 Initial BOM Display

Material is a required field – press F4 key Field selection dialog

♠

3

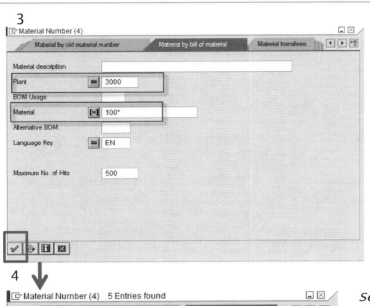

CS03 Material Master Field – Search Dialog – Search by Bill of Material Tab displayed.

Search for BOMs in Plant for Material Numbers starting with 100... (and display first 500 results).

4

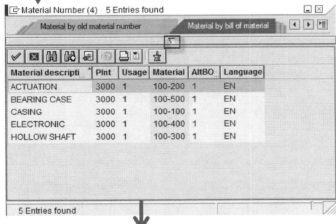

Search Results – Double click on a line to select that line or click on the down triangle icon to re-display the search dialog.

5

CS03 Initial Display with a Material – Plant BOM as selected from the Search Dialog.

CS03 Display BOM – Component Display Fields and Controls Overview.

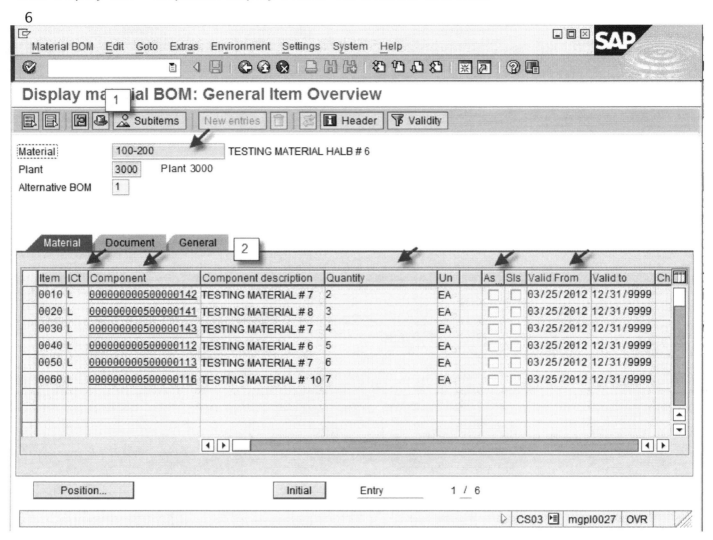

BOM Fields & Controls:
1. BOM Header (Next Overview)
2. BOM Components
   - ✓ Line Item Number
   - ✓ BOM Component Type – L Stock; T Text item
   - ✓ Component Material Number and Description
   - ✓ Required Quantity
   - ✓ Unit of Measure
   - ✓ Assembly indicator (indicates this BOM has a BOM)
   - ✓ Validity Period

CS03 Display BOM – Header Display Fields and Controls Overview.

7

Material BOM	Edit	Goto	Extras	Environment	Settings	System	Help

Display material BOM: Header Overview

[Item] [Summ BOM] [Alternative Long Text] [BOM Long Text]

Material	000000000000002268	TESTING MATERIAL HALB # 6
Plant	ZZTE	ZZTE PLANT
BOM	00003047	
Alternative BOM	1	
BOM Usage	1	Production
Technical type		
BOM group		

Quants/long txt	Further data	Admin. data	Doc. assignment

Quantity data

Base quantity   1   EA

Validity

Change Number		BOM status	1
Valid From	03/25/2012	Authorization group	
☐ Deletion Indicator		☐ Deletion Flag	

▷ CS03 ▣ mgpl0027 OVR

BOM Header Controls & Fields:
- ✓ Component Item Display control.
- ✓ BOM Long Text control.
- ✓ Alternative BOM Number – indicates multiple versions of BOM are maintained.
- ✓ BOM Usage – usually 1 Production; 3 Universal, etc…
- ✓ Base Quantity
- ✓ Valid From Date
- ✓ Status = 1 Active, 2 Inactive, etc…

Production Routing Transactions.

Create	Change	Display	Special
CA01	CA02	CA03	CR03 – Display Work Center (used in a Routing)

Key Concepts:
A routing describes the operations needed to produce an Assembly in house. It lists the steps in manufacturing sequence to include the work centers involved, and the associated machine and labor times.

✓ Routings are a required item in the costing of any material produced in house. Based on the Routing – and its work centers and times – production costs for the in house manufacture of an assembly can be established.

✓ Along with BOM, the routing for a material is copied into the production order when it is created.

✓ Routings have a Usage code that describes its intended use – example usage codes include:
   1 Production
   2 Engineering/design
   3 Universal
   4 Plant maintenance

✓ Routings have Validity Dates that define the effective period of the routing.

✓ Routings have a Status code that indicates its lifecycle status; Example Routing status codes include:
   1 Created
   2 Released for order
   3 Released for costing
   4 Released (general)

✓ A material can have multiple routings.

continued

Routing Key Concepts (cont'd)

✓ Structurally, Routings have a **Header** and one or more **Operation** Steps.

✓ Each Operation is assigned to a **Work Center**. In SAP, work centers can be created to track production costs for any of the following:
   - ✓ Machines
   - ✓ People
   - ✓ Production lines
   - ✓ Maintenance groups

✓ For costing purposes, each Work Center is assigned to a Cost Center.

✓ The production costs associated with each operational step in a Routing can be established by tracking **Labor, Machine and Set up Times** of the Work Centers involved.

✓ Each Operation Step in a Routing is assigned a Confirmation Control Key. These keys are used to define what happens when the Operations Step is complete. Confirmation Control Keys can be created to:
   - ✓ Confirm the Operation itself;
   - ✓ Confirm the Operation and all previous Operations;
   - ✓ Confirm All Operations and move the final Assembly into Inventory in a designated Storage Location.

✓ Transaction wise, CA03 is used to display a Routing; CA02 is used to change a Routing; and CA01 is used to Create a Routing.

Selected Routing Screenshots.

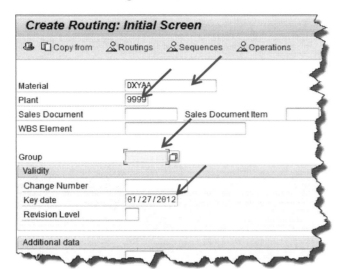

Create Routing Screen Key Fields
- ✓ *Material to be produced*
- ✓ *Plant*
- ✓ *Routing Group - initially blank - created by the system when the Routing is saved*
- ✓ *Key Date*

Change Routing Operations Overview Key Fields
- ✓ *Operations Step Number*
- ✓ *Work Center*
- ✓ *Confirmation Control Key*
- ✓ *Operations Text Description of the Task to be performed*

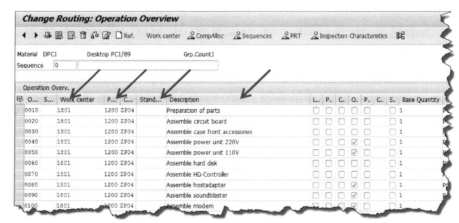

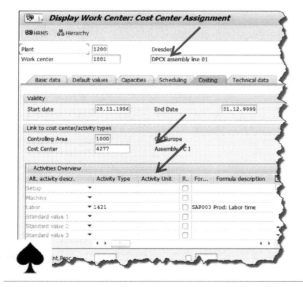

Work Center - Cost Center Key Fields
- ✓ *Work Center*
- ✓ *Cost Center*
- ✓ *Activities -*
  - ✓ *Setup Time*
  - ✓ *Machine Time*
  - ✓ *Labor Time*

- ✓ *Cost Center Rates x Activity Times establish Cost of the Operation.*

Overview. CA03 is the transaction to display a Production Routing. In the example below, we show how to search for Materials in a Plant with a Routing and then how to display them.

Info Required.
- ✓ Material Number.
- ✓ Plant.
- ✓ Key Date.

Transaction Flow.

1

2

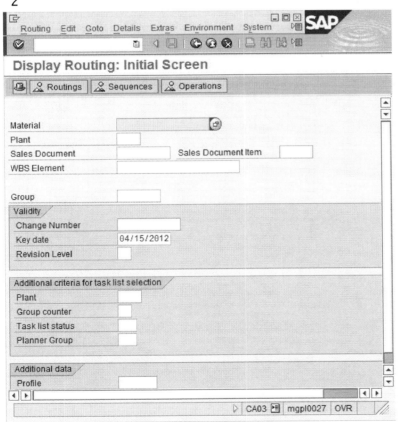

Display Routing Initial Screen.

Click on Field Selection Icon next to the Material Field or click on Function Key 'F4' to begin a Routing Search

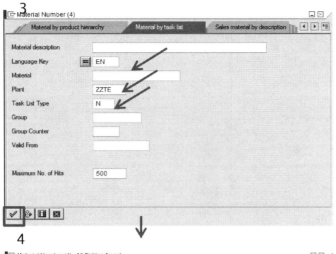

Display Routing Material Search Dialog. Enter a Plant and Routing Type (usually N) and press the Enter Key to begin a search...

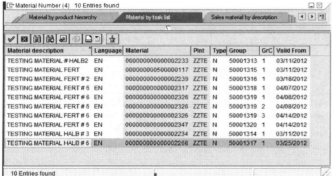

Double clicking on a Routing selects the Routing and enters its values into the CA03 display field.

Display Routing: Initial Screen

Routings | Sequences | Operations

Material   000000000000002268
Plant   ZZTE
Sales Document   Sales Document Item
WBS Element

Group
Validity
Change Number
Key date   04/15/2012
Revision Level

Additional criteria for task list selection
Plant
Group counter
Task list status
Planner Group

Additional data
Profile

CA03   mgpl0027   OVR

Press the Enter Key to continue to the Routing Display Operation Overview screen.

CSA3 Display Routing – Operations Fields and Controls Overview.

6

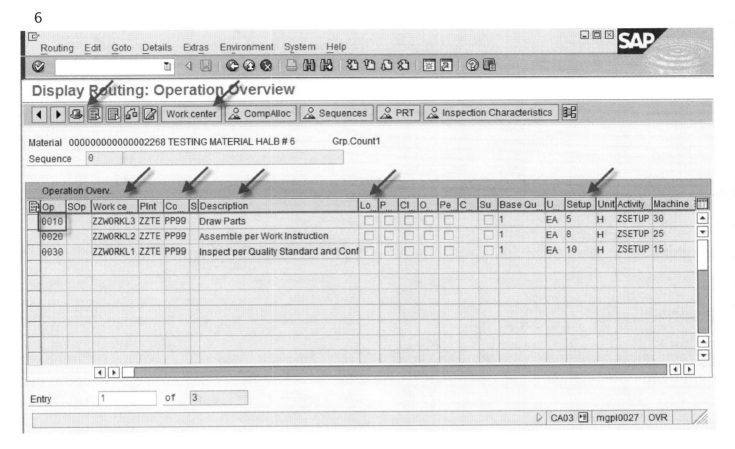

Routing Operations Controls & Fields:
- ✓ Display Routing Header.
- ✓ Display Work Center.
- ✓ Routing Operations Overview
    - ✓ Work center
    - ✓ Plant
    - ✓ Routing Confirmation Control Key
    - ✓ Operations Text
    - ✓ Long Text Indicator
    - ✓ Operations Setup, Machine and Labor Time values

Double clicking on an Operations Number displays the Operations Detail Screen.

CSA3 Display Routing - Operations Detail Screen Fields and Controls Overview.

7

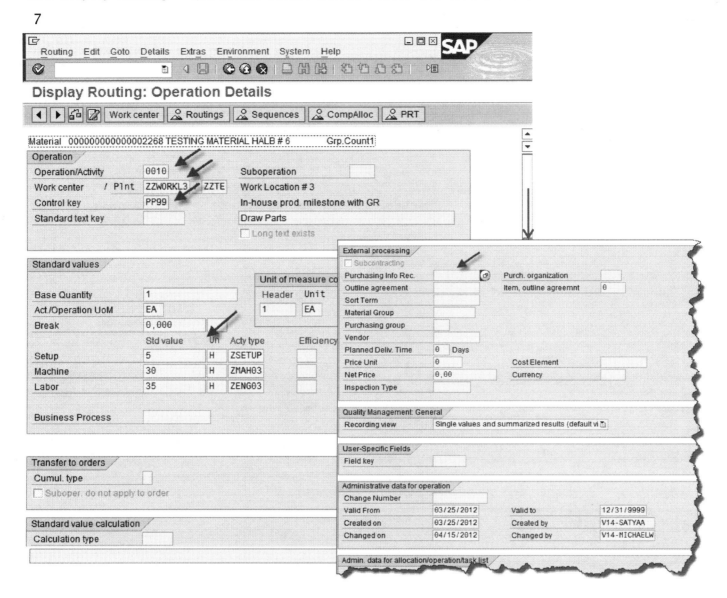

Routing Operations Detail Controls & Fields:
- ✓ Operations Number.
- ✓ Work Center / Plant / Confirmation Control Key
- ✓ Setup, Machine & Labor Values
- ✓ Furth down the screen — Purchasing Info Record Field — used in External Processing Scenarios.

Vendor Master Transaction Series:

Create	Change	Display	Special
XK01	XK02	XK03	XK05 – Block Vendor

Key Concepts:

Vendor (and Customer) Masters are defined around a **Business Partner** concept that uses **Account Group** and **Partner** functionality.

✓ **Vendor account groups** define which fields are required during a vendor creation process.
  - ✓ Each account group also determines a partner type and the information required to create the record.
  - ✓ Standard Vendor Account Groups include Vendors, Goods Supplier, Alternative Payee and Forwarding Agent type records.

✓ **Vendor Partner Functions** establish the relationship between Vendor records.
  - ✓ For example, a large supplier may have multiple sales office locations organized either regionally and/or functionally by product line. To model this in SAP, multiple "OA" (Ordering Address) Vendor Partner Records would be created for these offices and then linked to a single "VN" (Vendor) Record.
  - ✓ Examples partner functions standard in SAP include:
    - ✓ OA Ordering address
    - ✓ VN Vendor
    - ✓ CR Carrier
    - ✓ GS Goods Supplier

✓ In most SAP implementations, the Accounts Payable department is responsible for creating and maintaining Vendors Masters.

Vendor Account Groups

0001	02	☐	Vendors
0002	XX	☐	Goods supplier
0003	XX	☐	Alternative payee
0004	XX	☐	Invoice presented by
0005	XX	☐	Forwarding agent

XK03 Display Vendor screen

SAP Vendor Master is divided into three areas:

✓ *General Data: Defined at Client level, Address information is maintained here.*

✓ *Company Code Data: This data is company code specific. Financial information like Reconciliation Account Numbers are maintained at this level.*

✓ *Purchasing Organization Data: This data is purchasing org specific and includes information like the Purchasing Group, Payment and INCO terms, etc.*

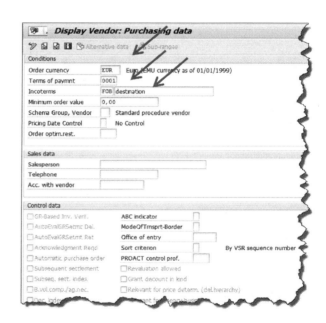

Vendor General Data Key Fields

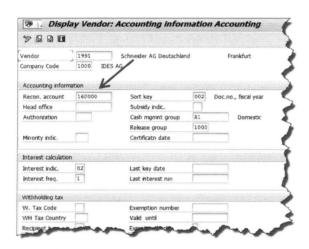

Vendor Company Code Key Fields

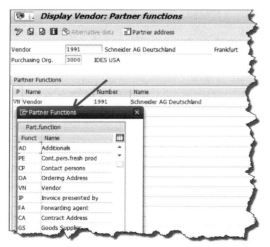

Vendor Purchasing Org Key Fields

Vendor Purchasing Org Partner Functions

PIR Transactions.

Create	Change	Display	List
ME11	ME11	ME13	ME1M

Key Concepts:
A Purchasing Information Record (PIR) contains the purchase price for a material from a supplier (vendor). PIRs can be manually created by the Planner/Buyer or created automatically from the information entered on a Purchase Order. Information maintained in a PIR is copied into the purchase order when it is created.

✓ PIRs can be maintained at the following organizational levels:
  ✓ Purchasing Organization
  ✓ Plant

✓ Each PIR has a **Type** depending on the procurement scenario it is used in:
  ✓ Standard
  ✓ Subcontracting
  ✓ Pipeline
  ✓ Consignment

✓ Key PIR field includes:
  ✓ Vendor
  ✓ Material
  ✓ Purchasing Organization
  ✓ Ordering Unit of Measure (UoM)
  ✓ Pricing
  ✓ Applicable Tax Code
  ✓ Planned Delivery Time
  ✓ Availability period during which the vendor can supply the material

Overview. ME1M can be used to display and/or change a list of PIRs as selected by various criteria.

Info Required.
Usually some combination of
✓ Material Number
✓ Plant
✓ Vendor
✓ Purchasing Group
✓ Purchasing Organization.

Transaction Flow.

1

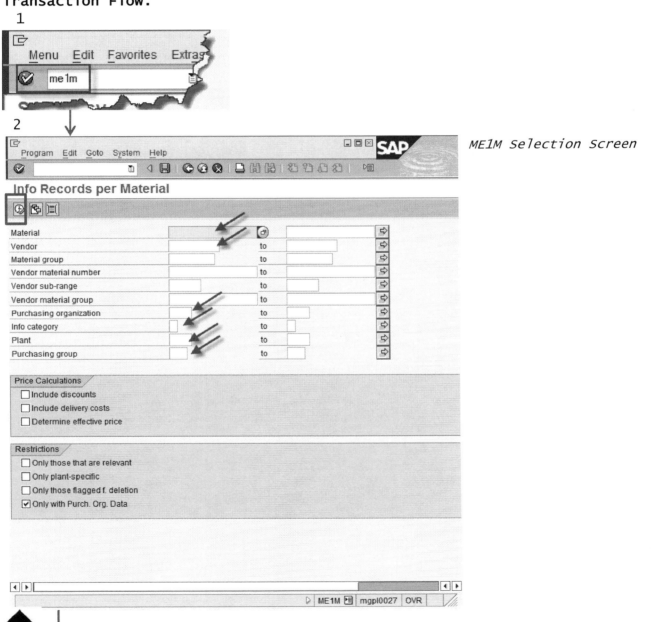

2

ME1M Selection Screen

Transaction report ME1M.

3

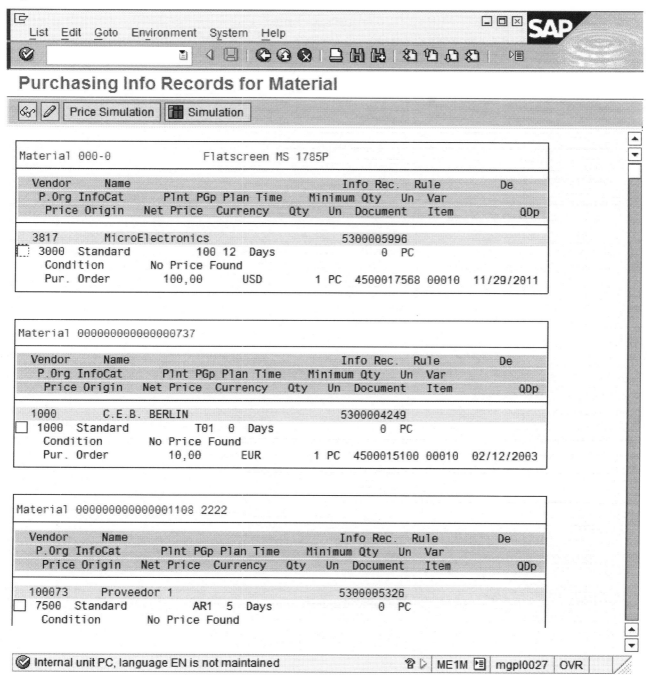

↓   *Double clicking on a PIR Line with a checkbox will display the PIR...*

ME13 Purchasing Info Record – Purchasing Org View Display.

4

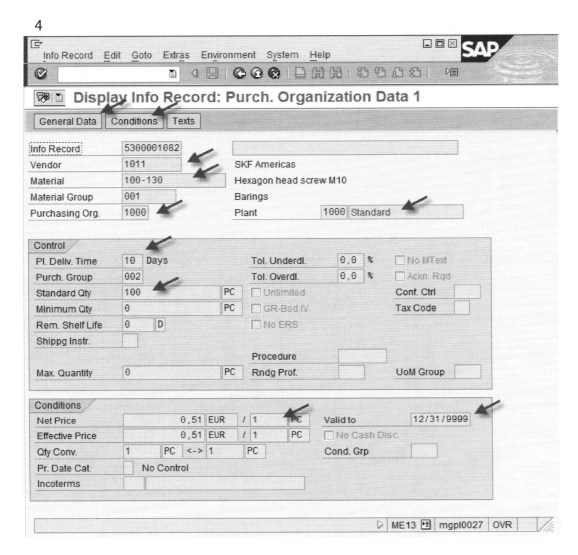

PIR Controls & Fields:
- ✓ General (Vendor Detail) Display.
- ✓ Pricing Conditions Display.
- ✓ Plant-Purchasing Org – Vendor – Material fields.
- ✓ Planned Delivery time and Purchasing Group ('Buyer') fields.
- ✓ Standard Quantity per Buy.
- ✓ Net Price
- ✓ Valid to Date.

Costing Transactions.

Create	Change	Display	Special
CK11N CK24	(Same)	MM03	CK40N

Key Points.
Costing is the process through which an expense (cost) to make a material is analyzed and updated in the material master. Costing puts a value on the inventory maintained in the system. Costs can be calculated based on quantity (also known as **Cost Estimate With Quantity Structure**), and for materials where the cost constantly varies, it can be calculated without taking quantity into consideration (**Cost Estimate Without Quantity Structure**).

There are two main costing values:

Standard Price. This is a relatively static price that is maintained for the material and will not change automatically when a goods receipt is done for that material.

Moving Average Price. This is a dynamic costing value applied to inventory using the cost price of a material per each goods receipt. When a goods receipt is done, the material price is automatically updated in the material master.

Creating a Material Cost Estimate. The material cost estimate is created using transaction **CK11N**. To create a cost estimate for an Assembly Material the Routing, Bill of Material and PIRs for all the components of the assembly are required.

Marking and Releasing a Cost. Once the material has been costed, it can be released to the material master. This can be done with transaction **CK24** to update the standard price for that material.

✓ Once a material cost is released, it can be displayed on MM03.

✓ Only released costs can be applied to inventory and used in Sales, Purchasing and Production Order related functions.

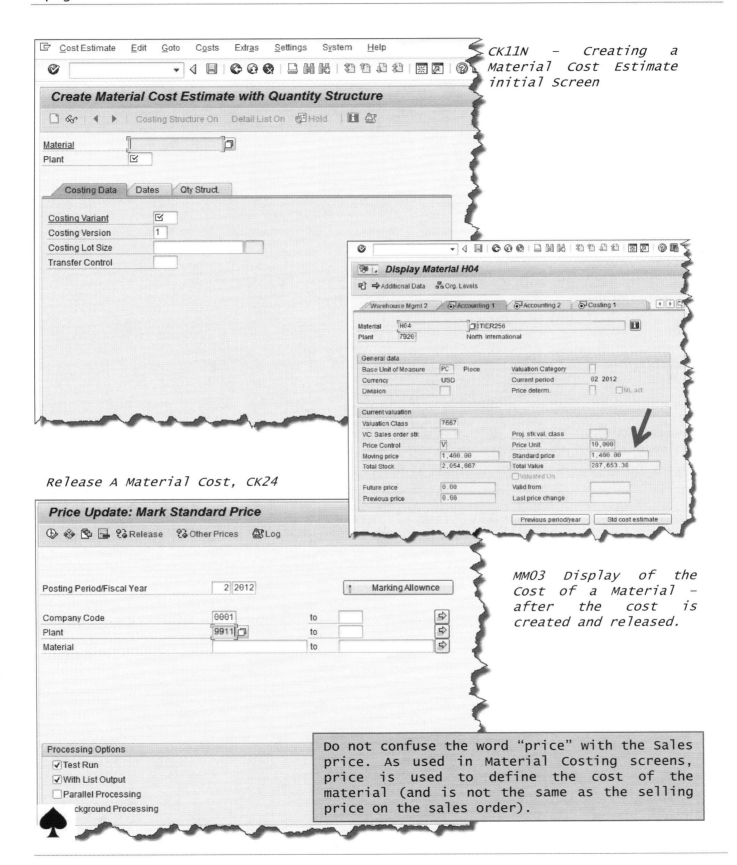

CK11N – Creating a Material Cost Estimate initial Screen

Release A Material Cost, CK24

MM03 Display of the Cost of a Material – after the cost is created and released.

Do not confuse the word "price" with the Sales price. As used in Material Costing screens, price is used to define the cost of the material (and is not the same as the selling price on the sales order).

Customer Master Transactions.

Create	Change	Display
XD01	XD02	XD03

Key Concepts:

Customers are business partners in SAP and to sell a product, the first step is to define those customers. This process is usually handled by the accounts receivable department of a company.

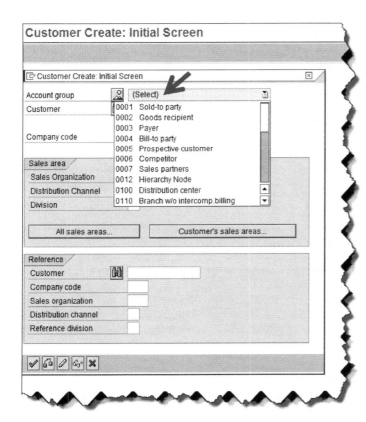

Partner Functions. A Customer's related business partners can be linked to each other using partner functions. Examples include:
- SP-Sold to Party
- SH-Ship to Party
- BP-Bill to Party
- PY-Payer

Each Partner can have separate addresses. For example: a Macys 'Sold To' party can be located in NJ but the product can be shipped to a NY store (e.g. 'Ship To' Partner address).

Account Groups are used to define what field level information is required for each partner. For example: addresses can vary for each partner and therefore different address fields can be chosen for different account groups. Account groups are then linked to each partner function type in configuration.

The customer Master is divided into three areas:

✓ General Data: Contains the address and is client level information.
✓ Company Code Data: Contains the recon. account, payment terms and other financial information.
✓ Sales Area Data: Contains information like shipping conditions, delivering plant, sales office and incoterms.

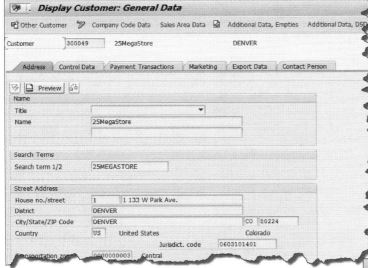

Once the customer is created, the company code data can be extended to another company using the create transaction XD01.

The Partner Functions can be found in the sales area.

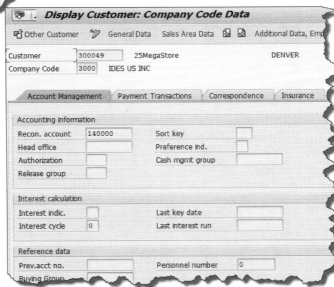

Transactions.

Create	Change	Display
VK11	VK12	VK13

Key Points.

Pricing in SAP is determined using a condition technique.
- ✓ When selling (or buying), the system will calculate the net price by taking into account the list price and all the associated discounts and surcharges.

- ✓ Pricing can be maintained manually or determined by the system.

Condition Types. Different pricing; such as discounts, list prices and surcharges, are modeled in the system as a Condition Type.
- ✓ Condition Types are differentiated by using a 4 character alphanumeric code.
- ✓ Condition types are arranged in a sequence and are added and subtracted to the get their respective totals.

Access Sequence. The access sequence defines the search strategy to retrieve a price. An access contains different accesses or keys.

Access. This is a combination of fields for which a price is defined. An example would be, Sales Organization/Distribution channel/Material.

Condition Record. The condition record is where the Pricing Business Analyst maintains the price per unit and enters other information like scales, etc.

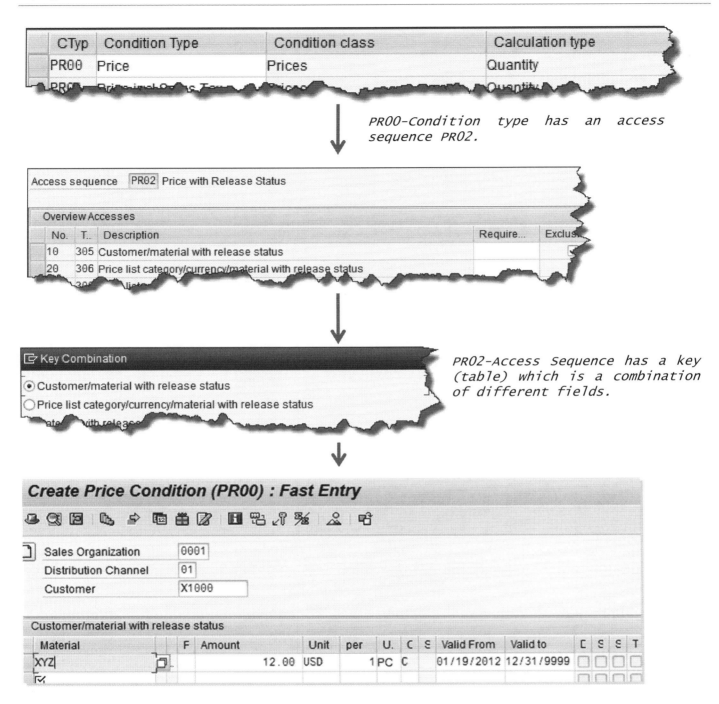

CTyp	Condition Type	Condition class	Calculation type
PR00	Price	Prices	Quantity
PR00	Price incl.Sales Tax	Prices	Quantity

PR00-Condition type has an access sequence PR02.

Access sequence PR02 Price with Release Status

Overview Accesses

No.	T..	Description	Require...	Exclus..
10	305	Customer/material with release status		
20	306	Price list category/currency/material with release status		

PR02-Access Sequence has a key (table) which is a combination of different fields.

Key Combination

◉ Customer/material with release status
○ Price list category/currency/material with release status

Create Price Condition (PR00) : Fast Entry

Sales Organization	0001
Distribution Channel	01
Customer	X1000

Customer/material with release status

Material	F	Amount	Unit	per	U.	C	S	Valid From	Valid to	C	S	S	T
XYZ		12.00	USD	1	PC	C		01/19/2012	12/31/9999				

Based on the above combination (table), a price is entered. In this case (in transaction VK11), based on the Sales Organization/Distribution Channel/Customer and Material fields.

Map Area 2A
Customer Service Sales Order Entry

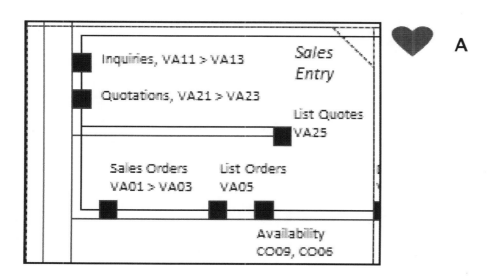

A

In this section, we describe the primary transactions used to capture customer inquiries, create quotations and enter sales orders.

Also covered in this section are key reports used in the management of Sales Documents, to include the Availability check and Incompleteness Procedure transactions that determine order promise dates.

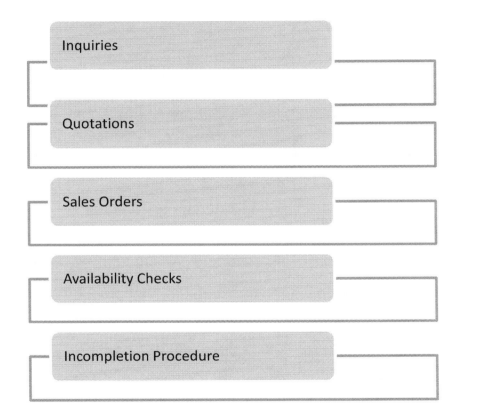

Sales Entry Section Topics

- Inquiries
- Quotations
- Sales Orders
- Availability Checks
- Incompletion Procedure

♥ A

Transactions.

Create	Change	Display
VA11	VA12	VA13

Key Points.

The sales and distribution flow begins with an inquiry.

✓ An inquiry is used when a customer requests preliminary information about a product. These requests are logged as documents in SAP to be used as performance metrics or converted into quotations.

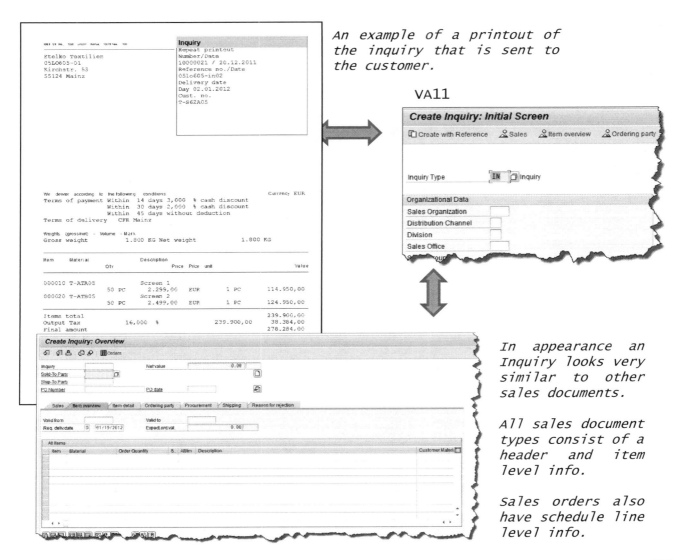

An example of a printout of the inquiry that is sent to the customer.

In appearance an Inquiry looks very similar to other sales documents.

All sales document types consist of a header and item level info.

Sales orders also have schedule line level info.

Transactions.

Create	Change	Display	List
VA21	VA22	VA23	VA25

Key Points.
Quotations are generally used as a bid/proposal provided to the customer to estimate the cost of a product or service. Quotations can be created with reference to an inquiry, which means the systems copies information from an existing inquiry without having a user key it in.

Document Types. The two most common types of quotations used are:
- ✓ Project Quotations
- ✓ Standard Quotations

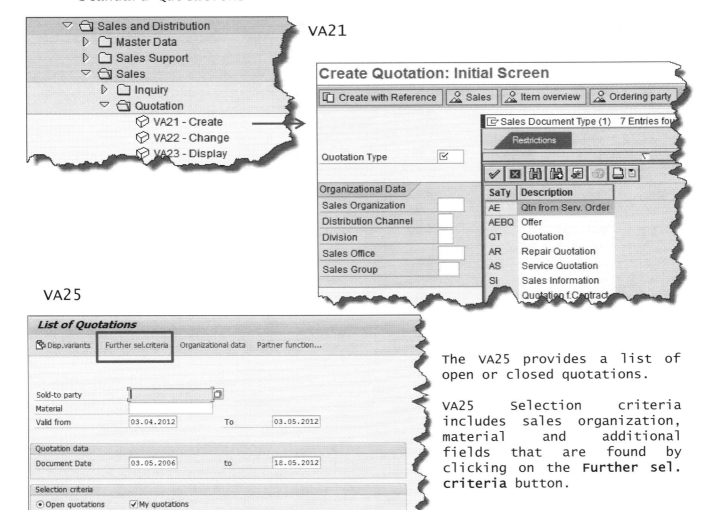

VA21

The VA25 provides a list of open or closed quotations.

VA25 Selection criteria includes sales organization, material and additional fields that are found by clicking on the **Further sel. criteria** button.

Transactions.

Create	Change	Display	List
VA01	VA02	VA03	VA05

Key Concepts.
A sales order is a legally binding document containing information such as quantities and delivery dates on which the customer will receive the product. Sales Orders can be created with reference to a quotation.

Sales Order Types are defined per company requirements. Example Sales Order Types standard in SAP include:

✓ **OR- Standard Order:** Used for a standard sale.

✓ **RE- Return:** A returns order is processed when a customer returns a product, for example, if the product is defective.

✓ **SO- Rush order:** In this type of order, the delivery will be created as soon as the sales order is created, although the customer is billed later.

Follow On Documents.   Delivery and Billing documents can be created from sales orders.

Printing.   The Sales order acknowledgement can be printed on paper, sent via EDI or faxed from SAP to the customer.

Key Sales Tables.   Include:
✓   VBAK- Header Information
✓   VBAP- Item Information
✓   VBFA- Document Flow
✓   VBEP- Schedule Line Item

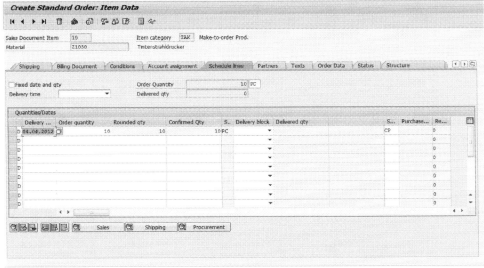

Enter the sales order type. The organizational data is determined by the customer and can be preset to a sales area by setting the parameter ids. The Sold to Party determines the ship to party and other partner types on the order. The Purchase order number is provided by the customer and is usually mandatory, especially for standard orders

Materials and the quantity needed to be shipped to the customer are entered at the line item level. The plant and shipping point are determined at the line item level and can vary for each material.

The schedule line will display important information like the confirmed quantity on the order which can be shipped to a customer.

🔄 Display Pricing

📇 Run Availability Check

🗂 Document Flow

👤 Display Sold to Party

📄 Display Document Header

💾 Once all the required fields in the order are complete, click on the save button to save the order.

☑ Standard Order 12643 has been saved

 A

SAP ECC in Manufacturing: *An Operator's Guide*

Delivering Plant. The Delivering plant can be entered manually and can be determined automatically from the sources in the sales order in the following sequence:
- ✓ Customer Material Info Record
- ✓ Customer Master
- ✓ Material Master

SD Route Determination. Route determination defines the mode of transport and influences the time to schedule it. The elements that influence it are the country, transportation zone, shipping conditions and transportation group. The route can be determined in the sales order and is copied to the delivery.

Credit Limit Check. Credit Limit check is Sales module functionality, although the credit is set in the finance module. The credit check determines if the customer is eligible for a shipment; otherwise, it blocks the sales order from being delivered.

Pricing. Pricing determination is required for calculating prices in a sales order. The pricing in a sales order is determined by:
- ✓ Sales Organization
- ✓ Distribution Channel
- ✓ Division
- ✓ Sales Document Type (example, an OR – Standard Sales Order)
- ✓ Customer pricing Procedure (assigned in the customer master sales area data)

Availability Check. The availability check is triggered at the sales order line level to search for materials in inventory. The availability check is discussed in detail later in the chapter.

Transactions.

Special
V_V2

Availability Check.   When an item is entered in a sales order, an availability check is performed (either automatically or manually) to confirm if goods are available on the customer's requested delivery date.

Availability checks are also performed at the delivery level.

The scope of availability check defines which elements are taken into account. For example, different stock types; including inward and outward stock flows like production orders, purchase orders and deliveries, may be considered.

Once the system runs an availability check, the confirmed quantity and dates can be seen at the schedule line level of the order.

Batch jobs can be setup to run availability checks across all orders at different times of the day – this eliminates the need for sales personnel to run the transaction manually.

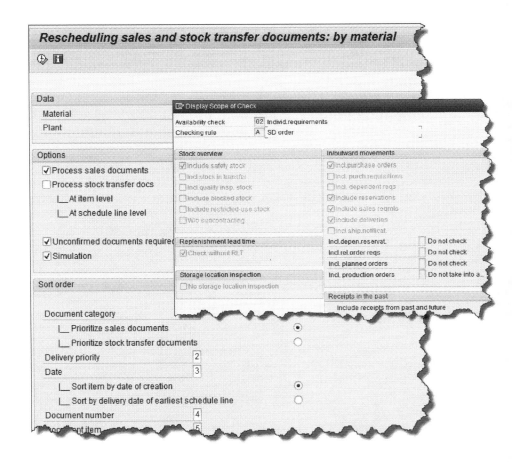

Transactions.

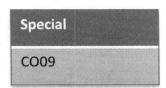

Special
CO09

CO09 provides an overview of a materials availability at the plant level.

✓ Receipts are shown as a positive quantity in the Rec./reqd qty column, while the issues are shown as negatives.

✓ Goods issues can be related to sales orders or deliveries; Goods receipts can be from a stock transport order.

The **Checking Rule** defines what elements (for example, sales orders or unrestricted stock) are taken into account.

The **Availability Check** field identifies the MRP elements used when running an availability.

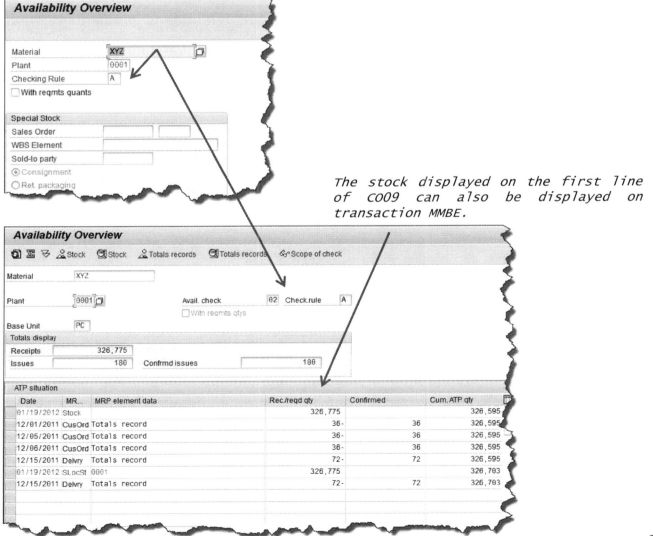

The stock displayed on the first line of CO09 can also be displayed on transaction MMBE.

Transactions.

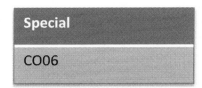

Special

CO06

This transaction is very similar to CO09 and is used in **back order processing** – The process of reassigning stock from one sales order to another based on customer order priorities and required dates.

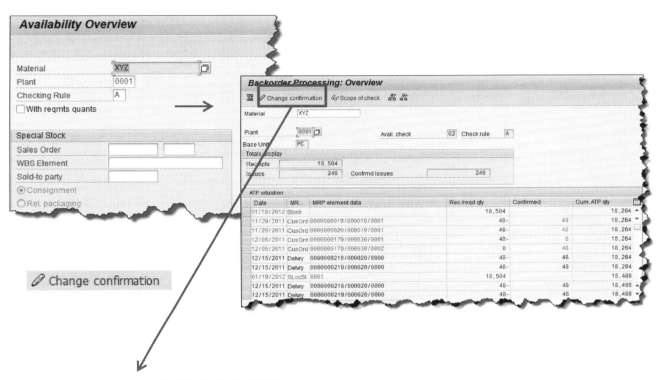

Change confirmation

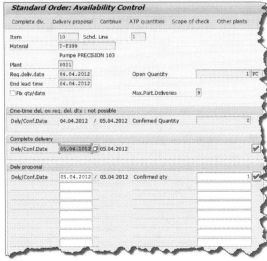

Using CO06, sales order stock can be unassigned from one order and reassigned to another order.

♥ A

Concept. An incompleteness procedure can be carried out for every sales order or delivery document to ensure that all the required data is entered correctly. The Incompletion Procedure is normally carried out when the Sales Order or Delivery is being saved.

✓ Incomplete Sales Documents cannot be processed further if the required data is missing.

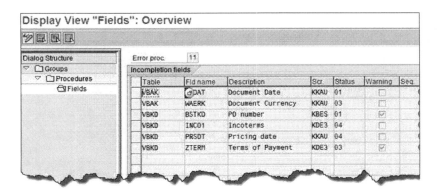

The incompletion procedure is managed as a configuration item in SPRO.

Users interact with the Incompletion Procedure via a Menu Item. In transactions VA21 or VA01 the procedure is under the Edit menu...

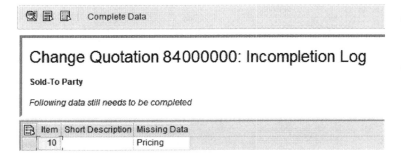

Example Incompletion Procedure for a Quotation.

In this example, Pricing data is missing from the Quote.

Transactions.

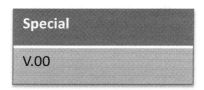

V.00 is used to find the list of incomplete sales documents. Any such document that has a missing value in a mandatory field, will show in this report.

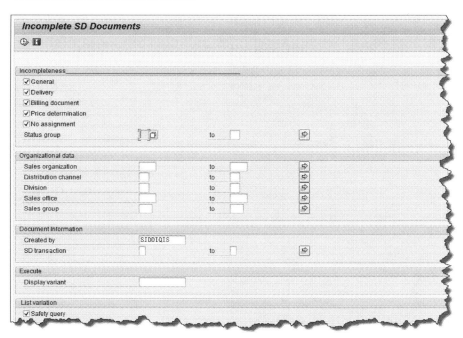

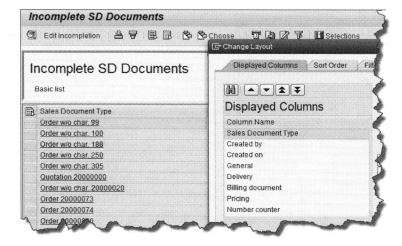

Use report V.00 to drill down into individual sales documents to make corrections...

♥ A

Map Area 2B
Deliveries and Billing

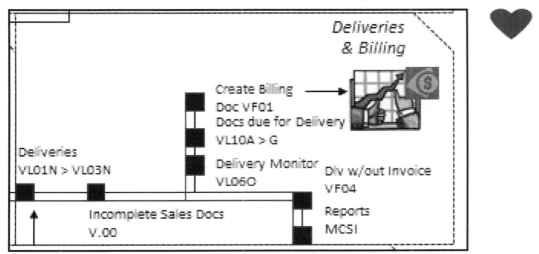

B

Transactions.

Create	Change	Display
VL01N	VL02N	VL03N

Outbound delivery documents in SAP can be created from the sales order document or a stock transfer order. The **Post Goods Issue (PGI)** of a Delivery Document indicates that 'Goods have left the building...' and are on the way to the Customer.

Delivery document functionality supports three main shipping processes:
- ✓ Picking
- ✓ Packing
- ✓ Post Goods Issue

SAP standard delivery document types include:
- ✓ LF – A Standard Delivery...
- ✓ LO – Delivery without reference...

In SAP, Inbound deliveries can also be created to receive stock, for example, on a Purchase order or a return sales order (RMA).

Once a delivery has a post goods issued, it can be billed.

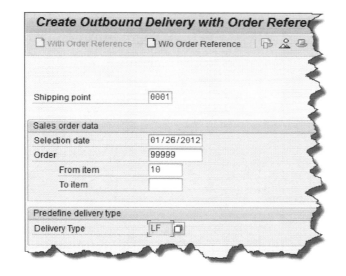

Example delivery being created with reference to a sales order for a particular line item.

Main elements of the SAP Delivery Process:

Pick   Pack   Ship / PGI

♥ B

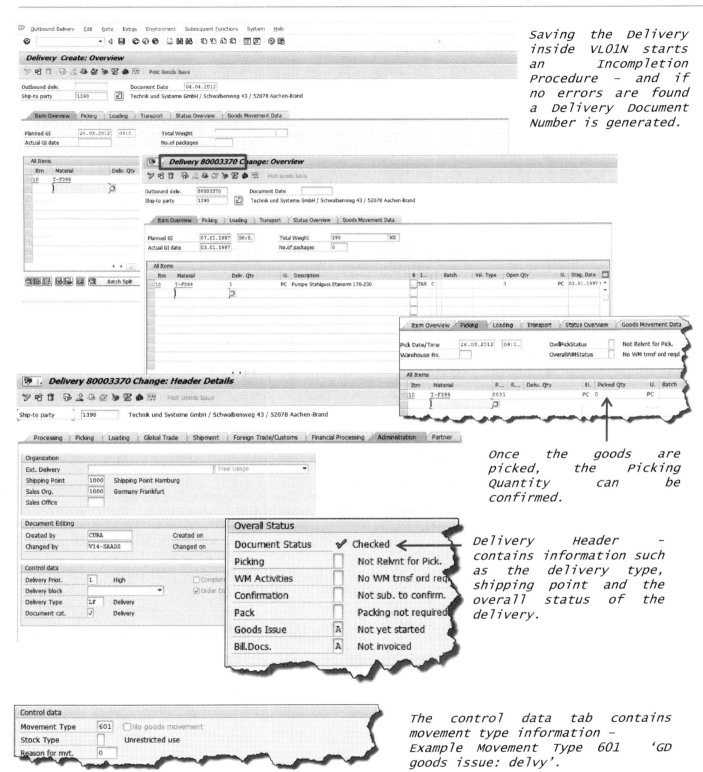

Saving the Delivery inside VL01N starts an Incompletion Procedure - and if no errors are found a Delivery Document Number is generated.

Once the goods are picked, the Picking Quantity can be confirmed.

Delivery Header - contains information such as the delivery type, shipping point and the overall status of the delivery.

The control data tab contains movement type information - Example Movement Type 601 'GD goods issue: delvy'.

Transactions.

Special	Notes
VL10	User Specified
VL10A	for Sales Orders
VL10B	for Purchase Orders
VL10I	for Schedule Lines

This transaction series can be used to collectively process multiple Sales and Stock Transfer Orders for delivery.

Where VL01N will only allow you to create one delivery at a time, VL10 series allows creation of deliveries in mass and in groups.

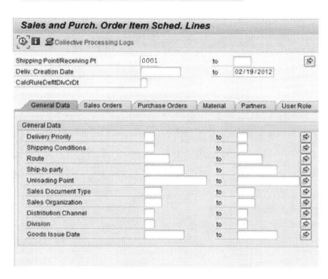

Once the shipping point is entered and the delivery creation date selected, the transaction will display a list of sales orders and purchase orders that can be delivered.

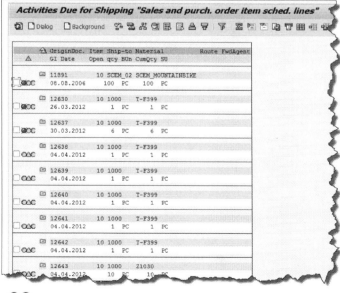

Traffic lights indicate which deliveries can be processed.

Batch jobs can be scheduled to create deliveries in the background using this transaction.

 B

Transactions.

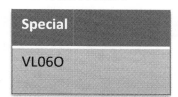

Special
VL06O

The Outbound Delivery Monitor can be used to select deliveries at various stages of completion and by other values, such as Shipping Point, Sales Area or Create Date.

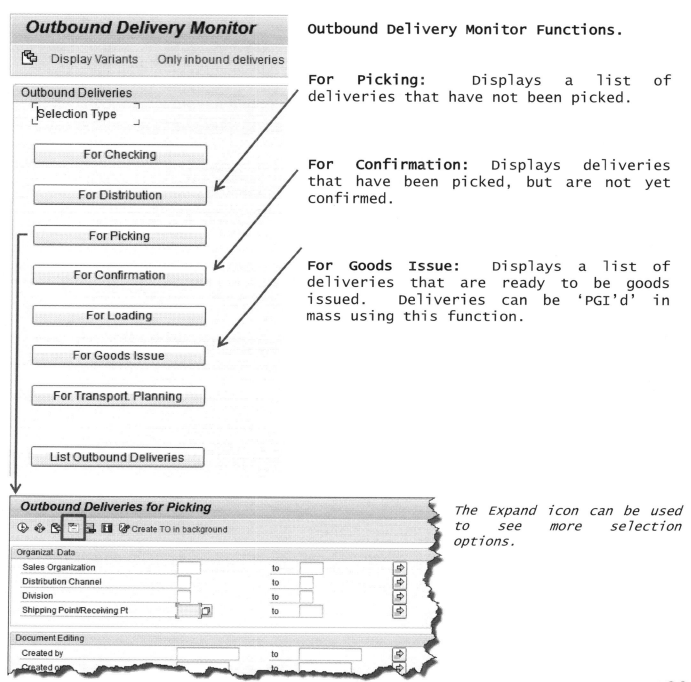

Outbound Delivery Monitor Functions.

For Picking: Displays a list of deliveries that have not been picked.

For Confirmation: Displays deliveries that have been picked, but are not yet confirmed.

For Goods Issue: Displays a list of deliveries that are ready to be goods issued. Deliveries can be 'PGI'd' in mass using this function.

The Expand icon can be used to see more selection options.

B

Transactions.

Create	Change	Display
VT01N	VT02N	VT03N

Shipments are used within SAP to group and track deliveries from the shipping plant to the final customer destination.

Key Points.

For the shipment functionality to work, a transportation planning point needs to be defined in configuration.

Shipments can be used to post goods issue the deliveries contained in the shipment.

Shipment functionality incudes:
- ✓ Creating shipments
- ✓ Managing Shipment costs/settlements
- ✓ Freight handling
- ✓ Tracking information
- ✓ Printing the Shipment manifest or Bill of Lading

Shipments also contain other information like route, forwarding agent and container id etc.

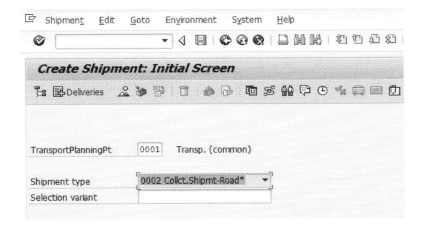

The VT01N transaction requires the transportation planning point be configured.

 Click on the deliveries button to add deliveries to the shipment. A shipment is like a truck containing multiple packages to multiple destinations.

 B

SAP ECC in Manufacturing: *An Operator's Guide*

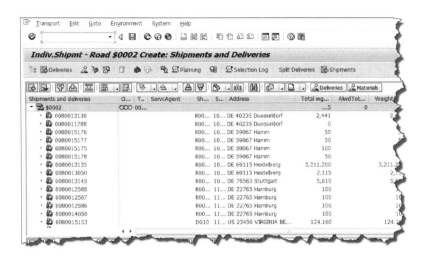

This screen shows all the deliveries contained within that shipment and in the create mode, you can add and delete them. Information such as the weight and the ship to address of the deliveries can be viewed from this screen.

Once the shipment has been saved, the different stages of the shipments are entered. For example, if the loading of the truck has ended, the Loading End button will log the time and date. Each of these buttons can trigger actions, like printing the Bill of Lading documents, once the shipment is complete.

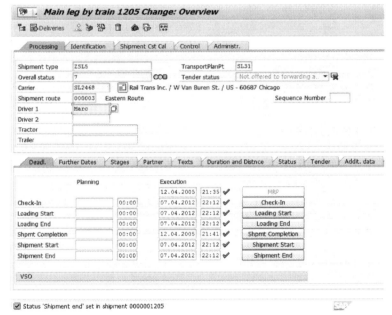

Loading End

The tracking information is entered in the identification tab. The tracking information includes the tracking number, container id, etc.

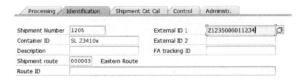

B

Transactions.

Create	Change	Display	List
VF01	VF02	VF03	VF04

Billing in SAP is carried in the final step of the sales and distribution process and includes printing the customer invoice.

Key Points.

The billing document type controls the final steps in the sales process. Standard billing document types in SAP Include:

✓ **F2:** The standard billing type used for creating an invoice to the customer. An output will be generated to print the invoice.
✓ **F8:** Used to generate a pro-forma invoice for customs. This billing type has no impact on the General Ledger accounts.
✓ **G2:** Used to create a credit memo to issue customer credit on returns.

In VF01, enter the delivery or sales order number and press save to create the billing document.

The posting status in the header of the billing document provides more information on the billing, terms of payment, errors and financial postings.

Click on the coin to check the pricing in the sales document.

Click on the accounting button to view the accounting documents if the billing document has been released to accounting.

♥ B

Invoice List. An invoice list is also a type of billing method. The invoice list is used for grouping billing documents into one document and sending it to a payee.

Billing Plan. Billing Plans allow items to be billed according to a schedule. There are two basic types of billing plans – **Periodic** and **Milestone**.

✓ Periodic billing works by charging the total amount due on particular billing dates. Examples of Periodic Billing would include Weekly or Monthly Rentals where the total amount of the item is charged at the end of the period.

✓ Milestone Billing works by charging for portions of a total project at specified milestone dates/stages.

Rebate Agreements. A rebate agreement is a discount provided to the customer after the product has been purchased at the list price.

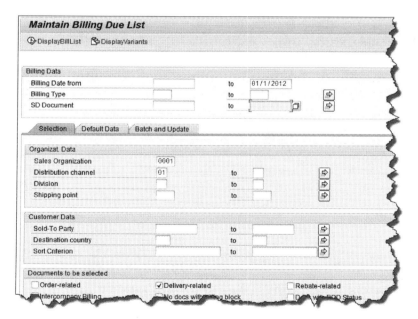

Transaction VF04 can be used to generate multiple billing documents at a time.

Billing documents can be combined into one invoice or printed separately for each sales order.

Billing documents can be generated from an order or a delivery.

Transactions.

List	Notes
VA05	List Sales Orders
VA25	List Quotations
MCSI	Sales Order Information System

SAP sales reporting options include standard sales reports series, Sales Information System Reports, custom reports created in SQ01 and SQVI and BW reporting tools.

VA25. This report is very similar to the VA05 report, except it is used to gather information on quotations. It gives you information on open quotations, user created quotations, material number, customer and validity dates.

VA05. One of the most used SAP standard reports in the sales and distribution module is VA05. VA05 can track sales orders and provide various information, including order values, delivery dates and detailed line information, among other options.

MCSI. This report is part of the Sales Information System (SIS) and can be used once the SIS info structures are activated. MCSI supports analysis for sales orders by multiple criteria, including Sales Organization, Customer, Order Types, Values and Date Ranges.

♥ B

Map Area 3
MRP, Production and Inventory

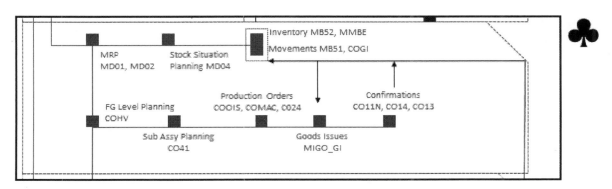

This section provides an overview of transactions in the MRP, Production and Inventory area of the map and include:

✓ MD01 and MD02 – the transactions for Running MRP at the Plant and Material Level;

✓ MD04 – for viewing MRP results;

✓ MMBE, MB51, MB52 and COGI – transactions for viewing Inventory and associated Goods Movements;

✓ COHV, CO41, COOIS, COMAC and CO24 – transactions for reviewing Planned Orders and managing the release of Production Orders to the shop floor.

✓ MIGO_GI, CO11N, CO13 and CO14 – transactions used to issue materials to Productions Orders to make and review (and if necessary reverse) Production Order Confirmations.

These transactions are normally performed by Production Planners and Operations/Shop Floor and (in the case of Goods Issues) by Warehouse personnel.

The section begins with two concept overviews:
✓ *Material Requirements Planning*
✓ *Production Order* and *Production Planning*

The section then moves on to cover the mechanics of the transactions listed on the map.

16 Key Transactions in MRP, Inventory and Production Planning.

Transaction	Area	Notes
CO11N	Production	Production Order Confirmation.
CO13	Production	Production Order Confirmation – Reversal.
CO14	Production	Production Order Confirmation – Display.
CO24	Production	Missing Parts Information System (Report).
CO41	Production	Planned Order to Production Order Conversion. (Single Material Field Input).
COGI	Production (Inventory Errors)	List Production Order / Cost of Goods Issue Errors.
COHV	Production	Planned Order and Production Order Mass Processing (Multiple Material Selection Inputs).
COMAC	Production	Production Order Collective Availability Check / Production Order Missing Parts Update.
COOIS	Production	Production Order List Report / List Orders by Shortage, Created, Released and other criteria.
MB51	Inventory	List Material Goods Movements.
MB52	Inventory	Inventory Report (Multiple Material Inputs).
MD01	MRP	MRP Planning – Plant Level.
MD02	MRP	MRP Planning – Material / Multi-Level.
MD04	MRP and Inventory	Current Stock Situation and MRP Requirements Display; Individual and Collective Material Display options.
MIGO_GI	Production (Goods Issues)	Issue Materials to Production Orders.
MMBE	Inventory	Material Inventory Report.

In SAP, Materials Requirements Planning (MRP) is driven by the configuration of multiple settings defined at the Plant and Material level. We introduce the basics of Material Requirements Planning (MRP) for those new to SAP with this statement:

When MRP runs, SAP creates a new *Supply Element* for any *Demand* not covered in the *Planned Stock Situation*.

These three conceptual terms: MRP Supply Elements, MRP Demands and Planned Stock Situation – are briefly discussed below.

Supply Elements: There are two basic types…
- ✓ **Planned Order:** An internal requirement for action by the Production Planner; The Production Planner converts Planned Orders to Production Orders and schedules them for release to the shop floor.

- ✓ **Purchase Requisition:** An external requirement for action by the Buyer; The Buyer converts Purchase Requisitions into Purchase Orders and releases them to Vendors that supply the materials.

The type of supply element that MRP creates – either the Planned Order or Purchase Requisition - *is driven the Procurement Type Field Setting* on the Material Master.

Demands: Demands can be traced to a Customer Requirement such as a Sales Order (and in certain cases, a Quotation) or a forecasted element.

- ✓ A demand in MRP is created for the Final Assembly itself and for *all* component materials, as specified in the Bill of Material (BOM) - i.e. **Component Demands**.

Planned Stock Situation: This is a view of the stock situation for a material over time. It starts with Current Inventory level and is adjusted to include supply increases (from the receipts into inventory of supply elements) and stock withdrawals (external shipments to customers or internal goods issues to production orders).

As supplies come in and demands go out, the Planned Stock Situation for a material *changes over time*.

Concept Diagram for understanding SAP ECC MRP processing.
✓ MRP can be run at Plant or Material Level.
✓ The main goal is to create procurement or production proposals to cover demands.
✓ MRP does not allocate stocks – MRP is not Available to Promise (ATP) processing.

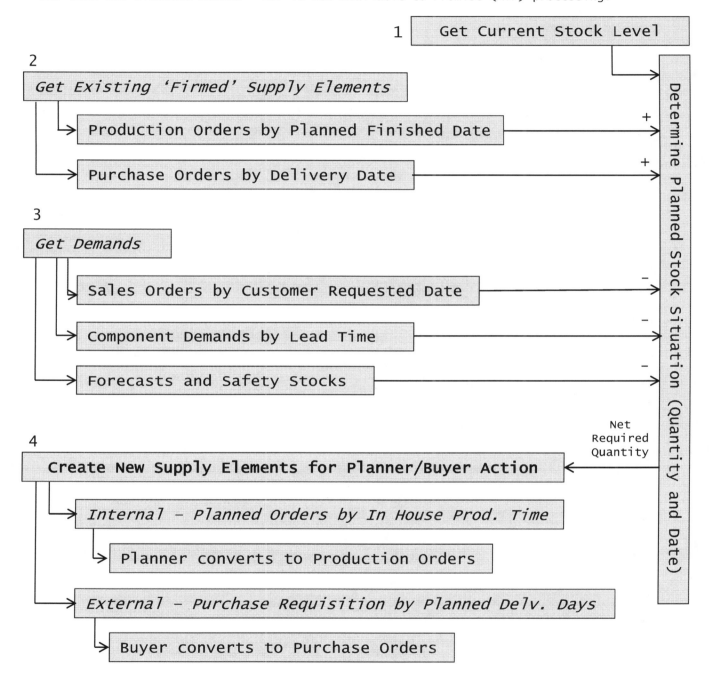

Remember this is a high level concept description of what happens in a SAP ECC MRP run. MRP is driven by MM, PP, and SD configuration elements and settings on Material Master.

Production Orders specify the work to be completed by the shop floor. A Production Order identifies:
- ✓ The assembly to be manufactured along with the component materials required - as listed in the Bill of Material (BOM);
- ✓ The operational steps in the manufacturing process - as specified in routing;
- ✓ The work centers involved in the manufacturing process and expected time and cost (components and labor).

Most production orders are converted from Planned Orders created during the MRP run - As the Production Planner reviews Planned Orders, he/she has the option to adjust order quantities and planned finish and start dates, thereby consolidating requirements into a single Production Order.

Production Order Status: Production Orders contain *status codes* that can be queried and tracked in the Production Order Information System ('COOIS'). Some of most common codes and are described here:
- ✓ When Production order is first converted from a planned order it has the status **CRTD** (created);
- ✓ Created orders with component part shortages have the additional status of **MSPT** (Missing Parts), while orders will all component parts fully available are marked with the status **MACM**;
- ✓ Orders released to the shop floor have the status **REL** (Released); in most SAP installations, Released Production Orders are automatically printed - and so would have another status of **PRT** (Printed).
- ✓ Orders fully confirmed and delivered into inventory have the status of **CNF** (Confirmed) and **DLV** (Delivered)
- ✓ Orders may be marked as technically complete (**TECO**) to restrict further processing or, if released, may have a Deleted (**DEL**) status.

Goods Issues: Materials can be issued to Production Orders, removing them from inventory at the start of the production process. When this is done (usually with MIGO_GI transaction), the Production Order status of **GMPS** is assigned. As an alternative, component materials can be removed or *backflushed* from inventory when the order is confirmed. The Backflush setting is specified in the Material Master and the BOM.

Confirmations: Confirming the Production Order can be done at the Routing Operations step or the Order/Header level. A confirmation is a controlling action indicating that one or all of the steps in the routing have been completed. Confirmations can be for *full* or *partial* quantities - and include *scrap* and final *yield* quantities.

CO03 Display Production Order - Fields and Controls Overview.

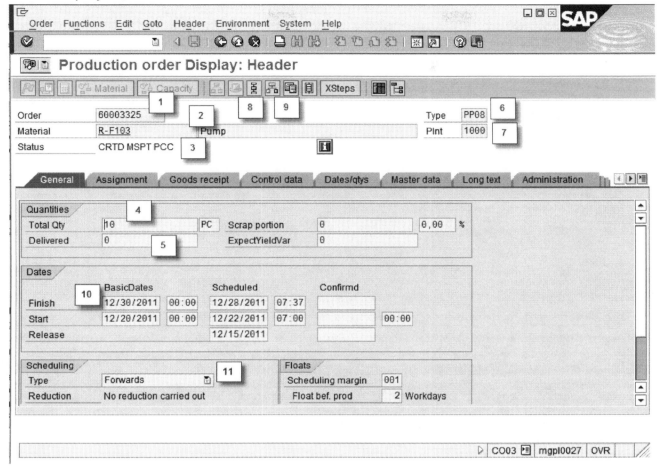

Production Order Overview Fields & Controls:
1. Production Order Number.
2. Material Number and Description - Material to be produced.
3. Production Order Status Codes - shown CRTD (created) and MSPT (Missing Parts).
4. Order Quantity.
5. Delivered (Actually Produced) Quantity.
6. Production Order Type.
7. Production Plant.
8. Routing Control - Displays Production Order Routing.
9. BOM Control - Display Production Bill of Materials.
10. Planned Finish and Start Dates.
11. Production Order Scheduling Type - Forward Scheduling selected (setting Start Date will automatically set Finish Date).

Concept. There are certain tasks that production planners must do on a daily basis to manage the work going to the shop floor. **MD04 is a key transaction in this regard** – *but in many cases* – especially in small to medium size manufacturing companies, where one planner is responsible for hundreds or even thousands of materials – MD04 by itself may not be not enough. So we introduce the idea of collective production order planning – based on a review of Sales Order Demands.

When we train new Production Planners we summarize the suggested approach to their key tasks as follows:
1. *Plan Top Down but Build Bottom Up –*
2. *Plan FERTs, then HALBs, then ROHs –*
3. *Check for and Work Production Order Shortages –*
4. *Release Production Orders when all materials are available.*

Example Production Planner Daily Tasks.

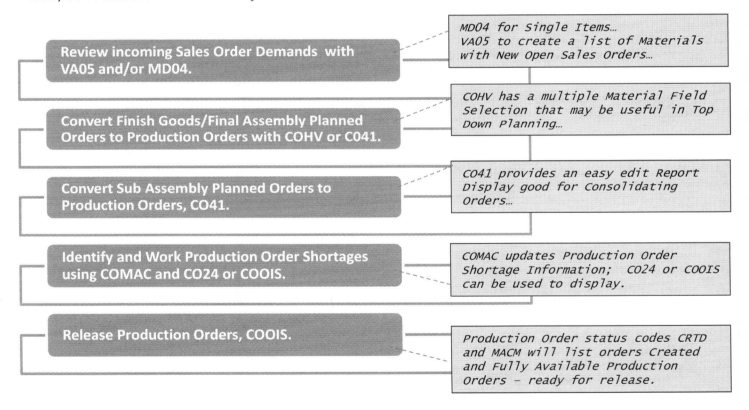

Review incoming Sales Order Demands with VA05 and/or MD04.

MD04 for Single Items…
VA05 to create a list of Materials with New Open Sales Orders…

Convert Finish Goods/Final Assembly Planned Orders to Production Orders with COHV or C041.

COHV has a multiple Material Field Selection that may be useful in Top Down Planning…

Convert Sub Assembly Planned Orders to Production Orders, CO41.

C041 provides an easy edit Report Display good for Consolidating Orders…

Identify and Work Production Order Shortages using COMAC and CO24 or COOIS.

COMAC updates Production Order Shortage Information; CO24 or COOIS can be used to display.

Release Production Orders, COOIS.

Production Order status codes CRTD and MACM will list orders Created and Fully Available Production Orders – ready for release.

Overview. In the ECC Learning Map, we identified COHV as a primary transaction to accomplish planned order to production order conversion for final assemblies - immediately after the MRP run for the site is completed. We identified COHV for this task ahead of other planned order processing transactions like CO41, because COHV includes the capability to allow for multiple material selections/inputs.

So, it is possible to use COHV with a list of materials from an open sales order report (e.g. created with VA05) - and thereby begin the production planning process in a top - down manner, focusing attention on the planned orders tied directly to Final Assemblies being sold by the company.

Top Down Planning Concept -
Below we summarize a technique for using COHV to accomplish Final Assembly Planned Order Conversion based on a Material Selection from VA05 Open Sales Order Report.

1. MRP for the site runs Planned orders are created based on new sales demands.

2. Planner runs VA05 Sales Report to view new/open sales orders. Planner copies list of VA05 materials to Windows clipboard/and or excel file.

3. Planner runs COHV using VA05 materials list… Planner reviews, consolidates and converts planned orders to production orders - for the Final Assemblies as ordered by Customers.

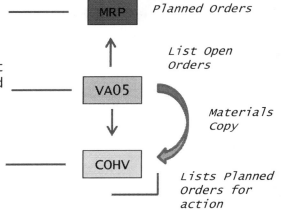

Result: Final Assembly Production Orders are reviewed and created against incoming Customer Orders.

VA05 to COHV Material Selection Copy: An example of driving Planned Order conversions from Sales Order requirements in a top down manner.

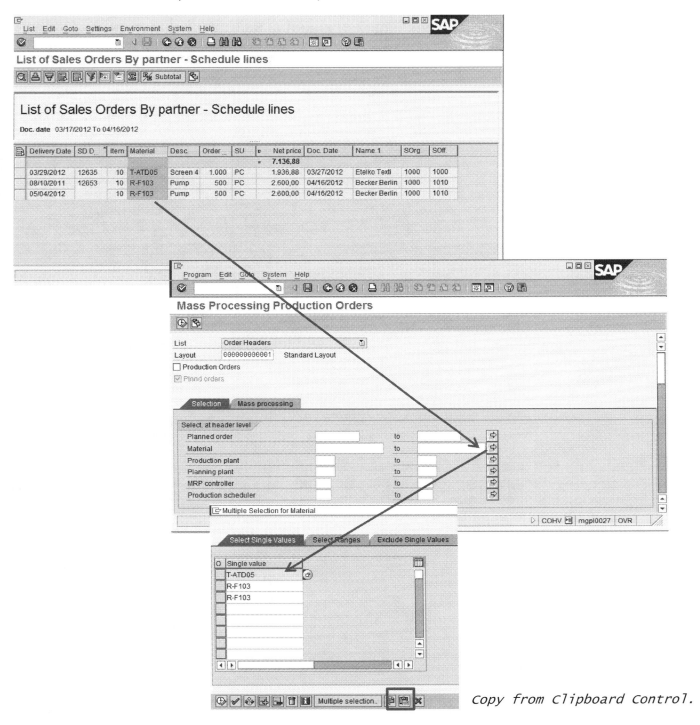

Copy from Clipboard Control.

COHV Overview. Allows Mass Processing of Production and Planned Orders.

Info Required.

✓ Usually some combination of Plant, Material, MRP Controller or Production Scheduler Purchasing Group or MRP Controller or Production Scheduler selection fields.

✓ In the Learning ECC Finished Goods Planning scenario – the Plant and list of Materials from VA05.

✓ Also required, the selection of mass process function to be performed – in this case the conversion of Planned Orders to Production Orders.

Transaction Flow.

1

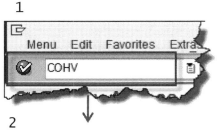

2

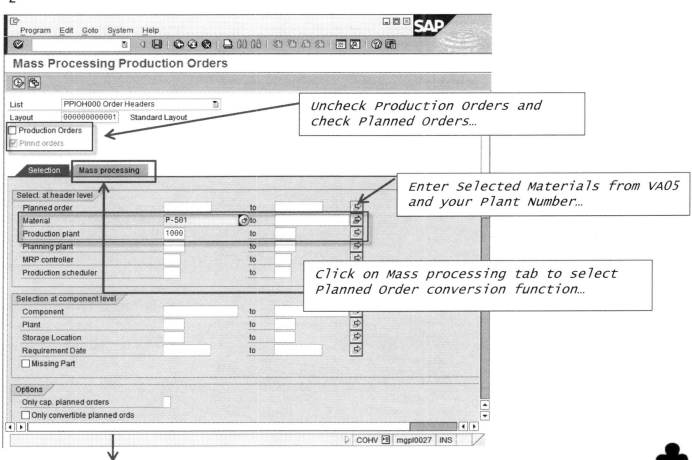

COHV Mass processing tab.

3

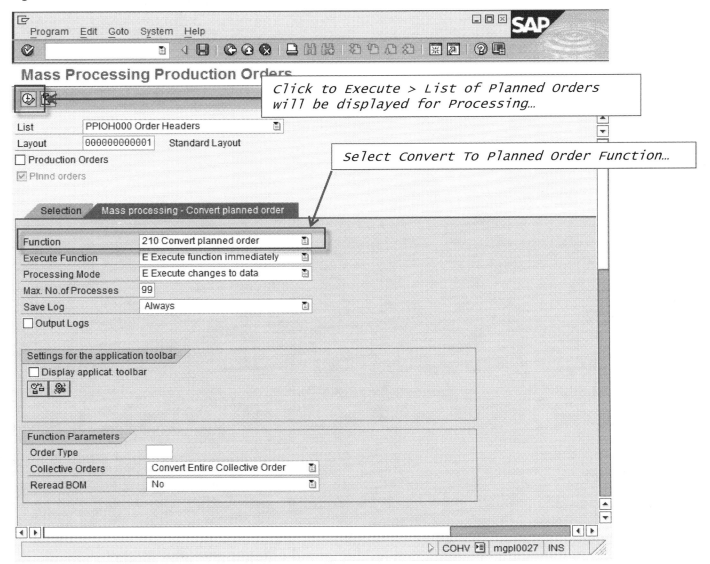

COHV Report Display.

4

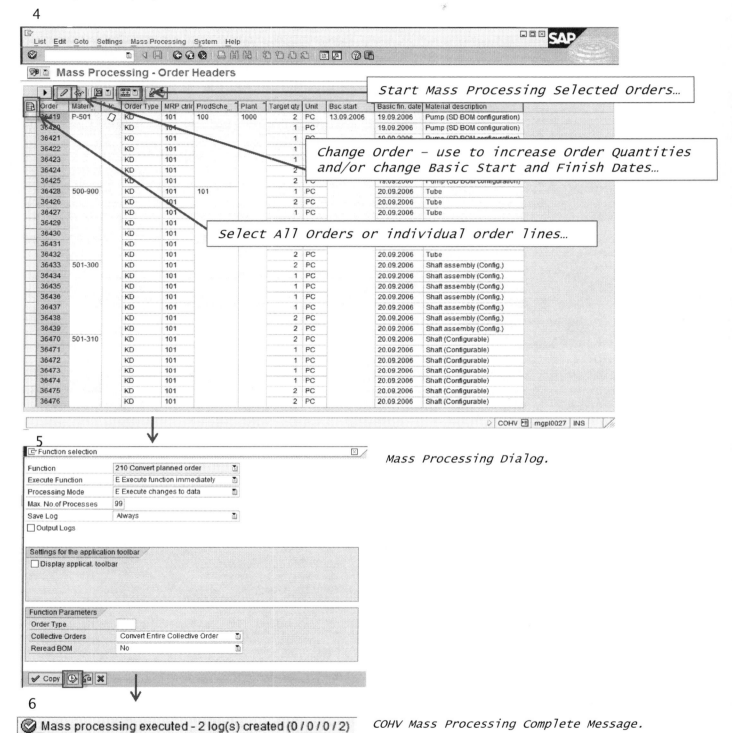

Mass Processing Dialog.

6

COHV Mass Processing Complete Message.

CO41. Allows conversion of Planned Orders to Production Orders.

Info Required.
- ✓ Usually some combination of Plant, MRP Controller or Production Scheduler selection fields.
- ✓ In the Learning ECC Map, CO41 is used for conversion of Sub Assembly (component level) planned orders.
- ✓ CO41 does not include a multiple material field selection capability, whereas COHV, does provide this option.
- ✓ CO41 can be used in place of COHV for conversion of Finished Good / final assembly planned orders – **if another field such MRP Controller or Production Scheduler can be used to distinguish between Final and Sub Assembly Materials.**

Transaction Flow.

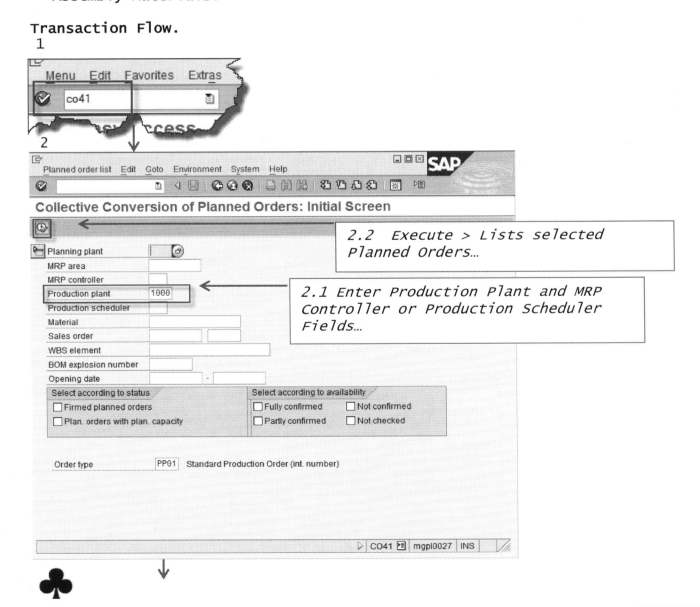

1

Menu   Edit   Favorites   Extras

co41

2

Planned order list   Edit   Goto   Environment   System   Help

Collective Conversion of Planned Orders: Initial Screen

2.2 Execute > Lists selected Planned Orders…

Planning plant
MRP area
MRP controller
Production plant   1000
Production scheduler
Material
Sales order
WBS element
BOM explosion number
Opening date

2.1 Enter Production Plant and MRP Controller or Production Scheduler Fields…

Select according to status
☐ Firmed planned orders
☐ Plan. orders with plan. capacity

Select according to availability
☐ Fully confirmed   ☐ Not confirmed
☐ Partly confirmed   ☐ Not checked

Order type   PP01   Standard Production Order (int. number)

▷ CO41 ▣ mgpl0027 INS

C041 Display.

3

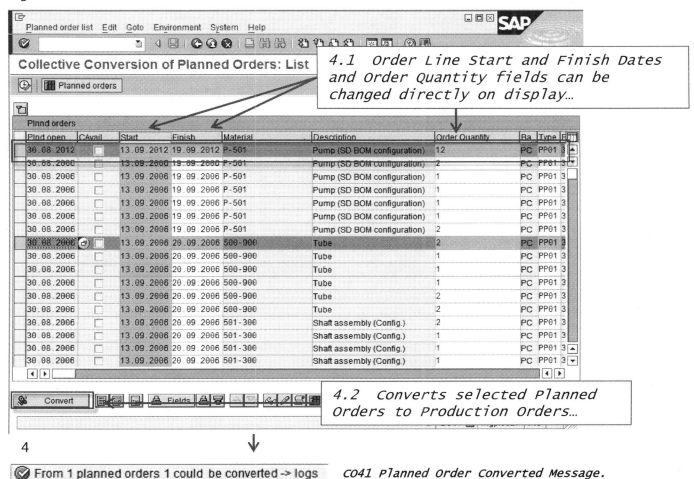

> 4.1 *Order Line Start and Finish Dates and Order Quantity fields can be changed directly on display...*

> 4.2 *Converts selected Planned Orders to Production Orders...*

4

⊘ From 1 planned orders 1 could be converted -> logs   *C041 Planned Order Converted Message.*

COOIS is Interactive report for viewing and editing Production (and Planned) Orders by various criteria.

Info Required.
- ✓ Usually Plant and some combination of Production Order Status Codes.
- ✓ In the Learning ECC Map, COOIS is used to identify Production Orders in two categories:
    - ✓ Orders that are Created and Fully Available (status codes CRTD and MACM) - these orders can be released to the shop floor for work.
    - ✓ Orders that are Created and Missing Parts (status codes CRTD and MSPT) – these orders are held by the Production Planner for further shortage review and action.

Transaction Flow.

1

2

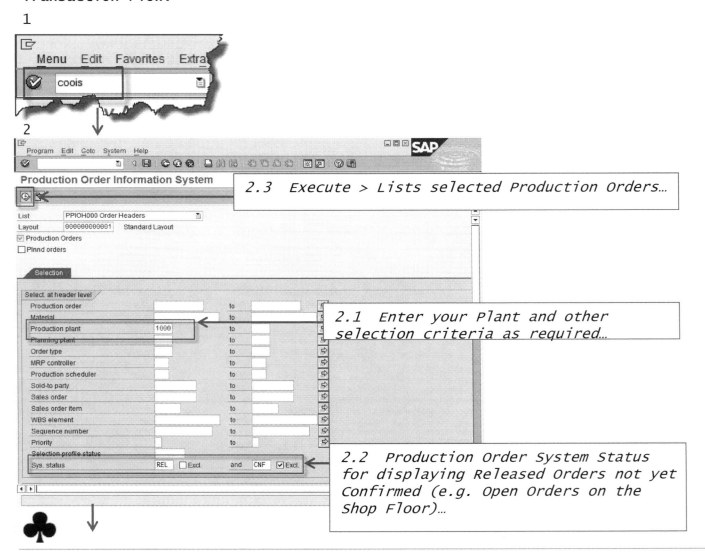

2.3 Execute > Lists selected Production Orders…

2.1 Enter your Plant and other selection criteria as required…

2.2 Production Order System Status for displaying Released Orders not yet Confirmed (e.g. Open Orders on the Shop Floor)…

SAP ECC in Manufacturing: *An Operator's Guide*

COOIS Display.
3

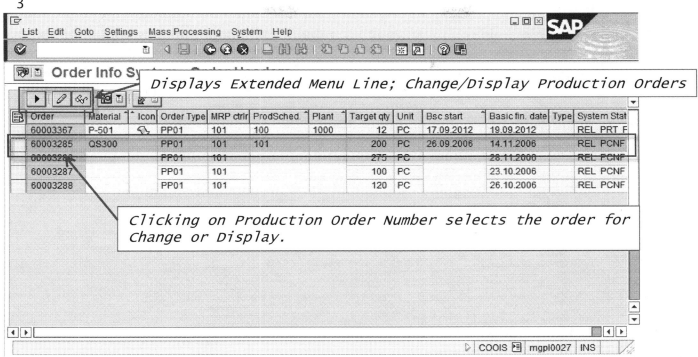

Displays Extended Menu Line; Change/Display Production Orders

Order	Material	Icon	Order Type	MRP ctrlr	ProdSched.	Plant	Target qty	Unit	Bsc start	Basic fin. date	Type	System Stat
60003367	P-501		PP01	101	100	1000	12	PC	17.09.2012	19.09.2012		REL PRT F
60003285	QS300		PP01	101	101		200	PC	26.09.2006	14.11.2006		REL PCNF
00003288			PP01	101			275	PC		28.11.2006		REL PCNF
60003287			PP01	101			100	PC		23.10.2006		REL PCNF
60003288			PP01	101			120	PC		26.10.2006		REL PCNF

Clicking on Production Order Number selects the order for Change or Display.

COOIS mgpl0027 INS

Additional Production Order Status Selections:

Created and Missing Parts

Sys. status	CRTD	☐ Excl.	and	MSPT	☐ Excl.

Created and All Parts Available

Sys. status	CRTD	☐ Excl.	and	MACM	☐ Excl.

Partially Confirmed and Not Closed

Sys. status	PCNF	☐ Excl.	and	TECO	☑ Excl.

Delivered and not Closed

Sys. status	DLV	☐ Excl.	and	TECO	☑ Excl.

COMAC. This transaction is used to update Missing Parts data contained in a Production Orders. Once updated, missing parts info can be displayed with CO24 or COOIS.

Info Required.
✓ Criteria normally includes Plant and a Scope of Selection for the Material Availability Check – usually Available To Promise (ATP) Check for All Materials.

Transaction Flow.

1

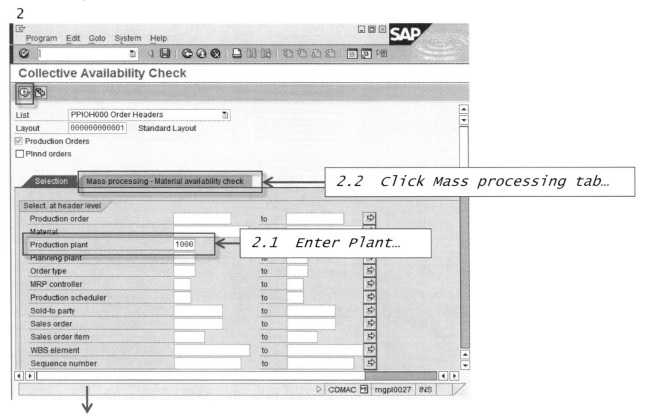

2

3   *COMAC Mass processing selection.*

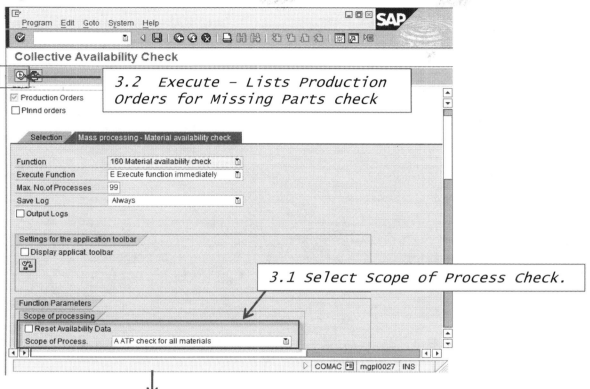

3.2 Execute - Lists Production Orders for Missing Parts check

3.1 Select Scope of Process Check.

4   *COMAC Display.*

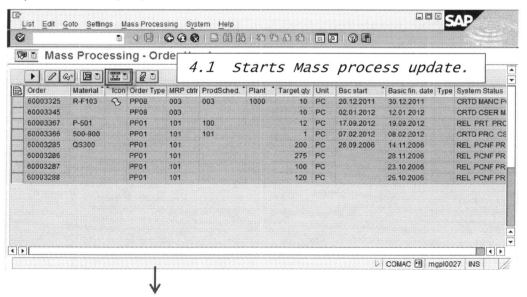

4.1 Starts Mass process update.

✅ Mass processing executed - 0 log(s) created (0 / 0 / 0 / 0)   *COMAC Mass processing complete message.*

CO24. CO24 generates a Missing Parts Report for a selected group of production orders. It is usually run after COMAC, the Collective Availability Check transaction. COMAC updates shortage information by checking for goods receipts against required component materials for a production order. CO24 provides a reporting tool against the latest availability information. COOIS can be used to generate a similar shortage report.

Info Required.
✓ Plant Number.

Transaction Flow.

1

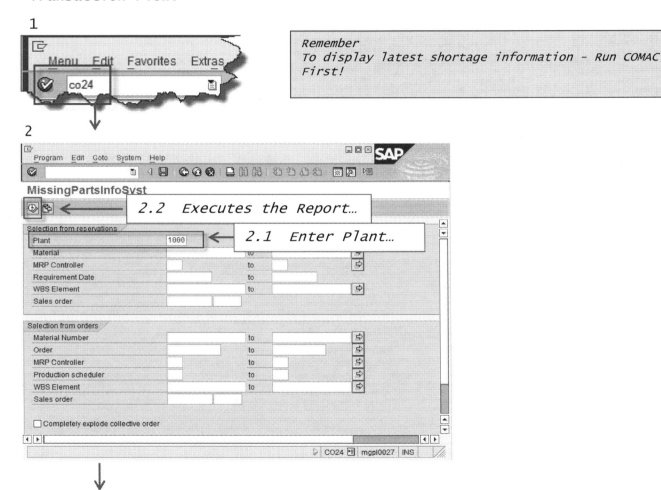

Remember
To display latest shortage information – Run COMAC First!

2.2 Executes the Report...

2.1 Enter Plant...

CO24 Report.

3

Missing Parts Info System

Material	ReqmtDate	Order	Reqmts qty	Committed qty.	Unit	Plnt	StLc	MRPC	Reserv	It	Sales Order
R-B103	04.01.2012	60003345	10	0	PC	1000	0001	003	67056	1	
R-B303	22.12.2011	60003325	10	0	PC		0001	003	67047	3	
	04.01.2012	60003345	10	0	PC		0001	003	67056	3	
R-B403			10	0	PC		0001	003	67056	4	

> *Shortage Materials listed by Requirements Date and Production Order.*

CO24 mgpl0027 INS

MIGO_GI. This transaction is used to issue materials to Production Orders. The goods issue is normally the first step of the production order routing.
✓ Goods issues are not required for production order components marked with the Bulk Item or Backflush Indicator - both of these fields are specified on the MRP View 2 of the Material Master.
✓ Posting a Goods Issue normally executes a Movement Type 261 - Goods Issue to a Production Order inventory movement; reducing the component material inventory by the quantity issued to the production order.

Info Required.
✓ Production Order Number.
✓ Component Material Quantities issued to the Production Order.

Transaction Flow.

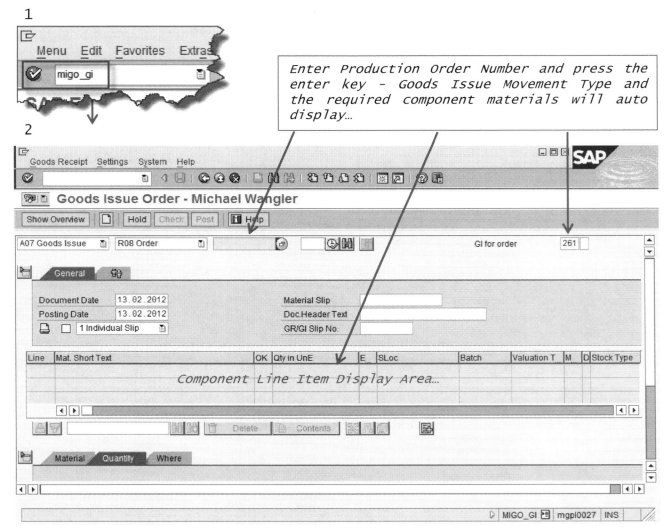

Enter Production Order Number and press the enter key - Goods Issue Movement Type and the required component materials will auto display...

MIGO_GI with Production Order Components Listed.

3

Goods Receipt Settings System Help

Goods Issue Order 60003394 - Michael Wangler

Show Overview | Hold Check Post | 1 | | 2 |

Goods Issue | Order | | GI for order | 261 |

General

Document Date	04/16/2012	Material Slip	
Posting Date	04/16/2012	Doc.Header Text	
Individual Slip		GR/GI Slip No.	

Line	Mat. Short Text	OK	Qty in UnE	E.	SLoc	Order	Bus	Co	Batch	
1	Casing	☐	100	PC	Materiallager	60003394	1000	1000		
2	Fly wheel	☐	100	PC	Materiallager	60003394	1000	1000		
3	Hollow shaft	☐	100	PC	Materiallager	60003394	1000	1000		

Delete | Contents

Material Quantity Where Reservation Account Assignment

| Qty in Unit of Entry | 100 | PC | 4 |
| Qty in SKU | 100 | PC | |

No. Containers

5

☐ Item OK   Line   1

▷ | MIGO_GI | mgpl0027 | OVR

MIGO_GI Overview:

1. Hold, Check and Post controls.

2. Material Movement Type.

3. Component Line Item Display.

4. Quantity to be issued.

5. Item OK, Previous and Next controls.

Overview. CO11N is used to confirm Production Orders. The Confirmation indicates that either an operational step in the production order, or the entire order itself, is complete. By 'complete' we mean that the final step in the Routing is finished. In this case, the assembly can be placed into inventory. This is normally accomplished by configuring the CO11N to execute a Movement Type 101 Goods Receipt when the confirmation occurs at the Production Order level.

Info Required.
✓ Production Order Number.
✓ *Optional:* An Operation Activity step from the Production Order Routing *IF* confirming at Operation level (normally not required).
✓ The confirmation type: Partial, Final or Automatic and Final
✓ The Yield / Quantity made.
✓ *Optional:* Scrap or Rework Quantities.

Transaction Flow.

1

2

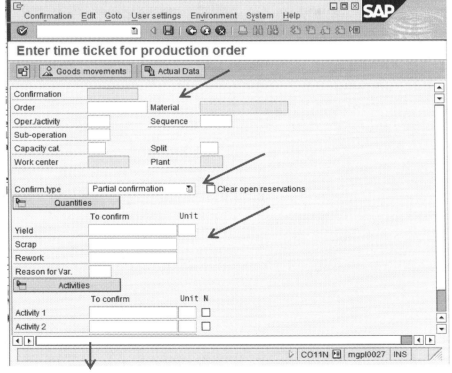

Enter:
✓ Order Number
✓ Confirmation Type
✓ Yield (Quantity Made)

And press the *Enter* Key – Information from the production order will be copied into the screen.

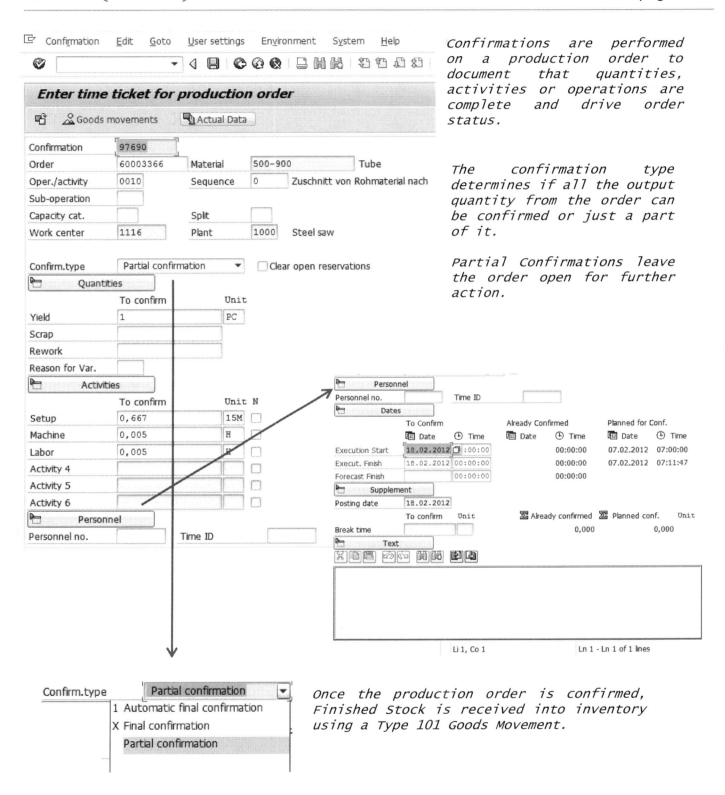

Confirmations are performed on a production order to document that quantities, activities or operations are complete and drive order status.

The confirmation type determines if all the output quantity from the order can be confirmed or just a part of it.

Partial Confirmations leave the order open for further action.

Once the production order is confirmed, Finished Stock is received into inventory using a Type 101 Goods Movement.

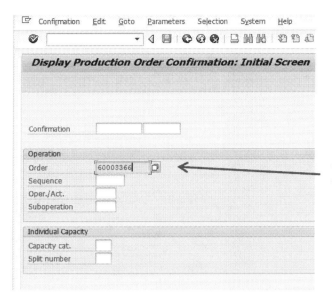

CO14 is used to display Production Order
confirmation data.

*Enter production order
number.*

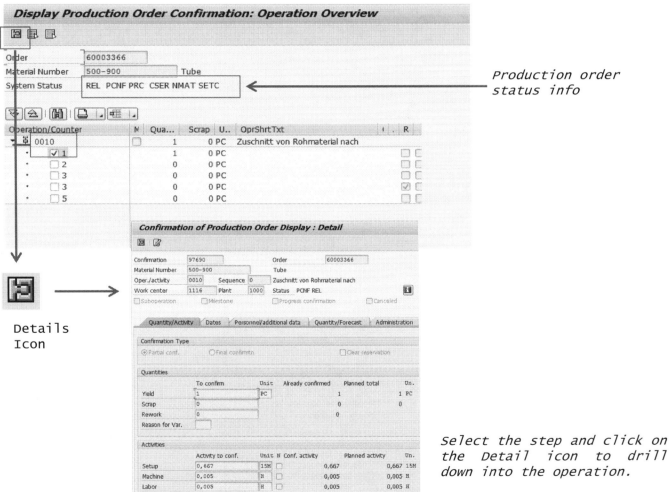

*Production order
status info*

**Details
Icon**

*Select the step and click on
the Detail icon to drill
down into the operation.*

Transaction CO13

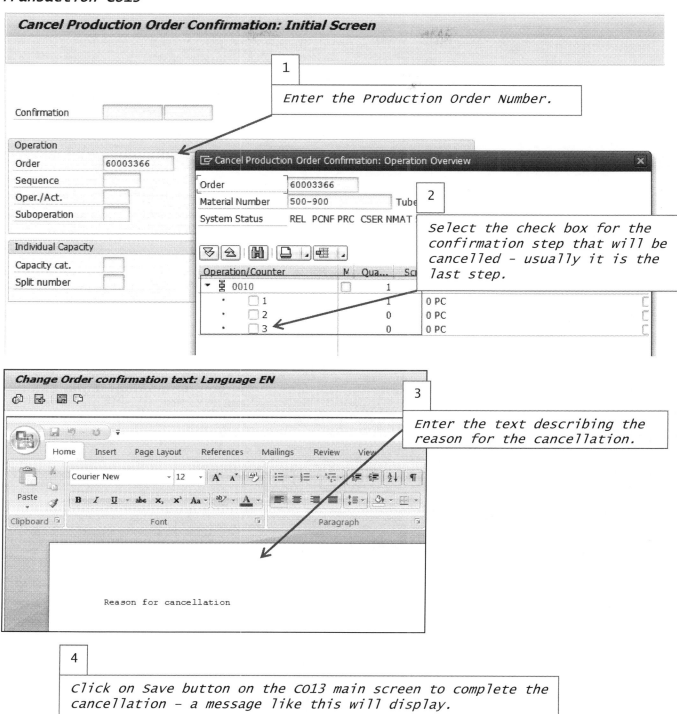

Cancel Production Order Confirmation: Initial Screen

Confirmation

Operation

Order   60003366
Sequence
Oper./Act.
Suboperation

Individual Capacity

Capacity cat.
Split number

1
Enter the Production Order Number.

Cancel Production Order Confirmation: Operation Overview

Order   60003366
Material Number   500-900   Tube
System Status   REL PCNF PRC CSER NMAT

2
Select the check box for the confirmation step that will be cancelled - usually it is the last step.

Operation/Counter   M Qua... Sc
▼ 0010   □   1
  ·   □ 1   1   0 PC
  ·   □ 2   0   0 PC
  ·   □ 3   0   0 PC

Change Order confirmation text: Language EN

3
Enter the text describing the reason for the cancellation.

Home Insert Page Layout References Mailings Review View

Courier New   12

Paste

Clipboard   Font   Paragraph

Reason for cancellation

4
Click on Save button on the CO13 main screen to complete the cancellation - a message like this will display.

☑ Confirmation of order 60003366 is cancelled

The COGI transaction is used to display and fix goods issue errors associated with Production Order confirmations. Typically, these errors can come about when the required quantity of a component material (set for backflush) is not available in the system. This can be caused when confirmations of sub-assemblies are lagging behind actual production – materials are available but not yet transacted/posted in the system.

Info Required.
✓ Usually Assembly Materials or Production Order Number(s).

Transaction Flow.

1

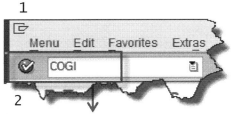

2

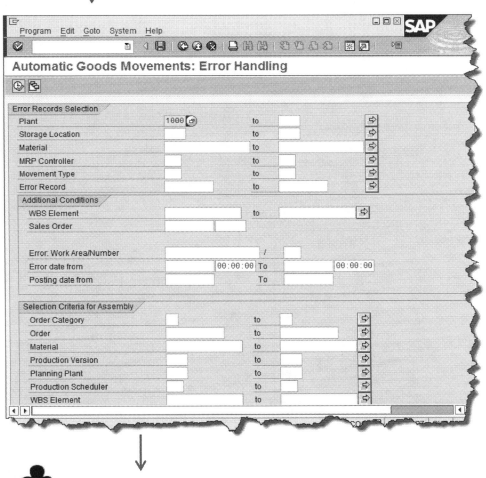

♣

SAP ECC in Manufacturing: *An Operator's Guide*

COGI (Cost of Goods Issue) Production Order Error Display.

3

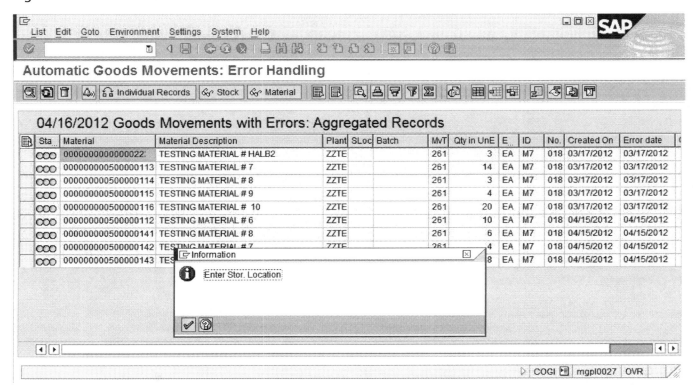

04/16/2012 Goods Movements with Errors: Aggregated Records

Sta	Material	Material Description	Plant	SLoc	Batch	MvT	Qty in UnE	E	ID	No.	Created On	Error date
OOO	0000000000000022	TESTING MATERIAL # HALB2	ZZTE			261	3	EA	M7	018	03/17/2012	03/17/2012
OOO	000000000500000113	TESTING MATERIAL # 7	ZZTE			261	14	EA	M7	018	03/17/2012	03/17/2012
OOO	000000000500000114	TESTING MATERIAL # 8	ZZTE			261	3	EA	M7	018	03/17/2012	03/17/2012
OOO	000000000500000115	TESTING MATERIAL # 9	ZZTE			261	4	EA	M7	018	03/17/2012	03/17/2012
OOO	000000000500000116	TESTING MATERIAL # 10	ZZTE			261	20	EA	M7	018	03/17/2012	03/17/2012
OOO	000000000500000112	TESTING MATERIAL # 6	ZZTE			261	10	EA	M7	018	04/15/2012	04/15/2012
OOO	000000000500000141	TESTING MATERIAL # 8	ZZTE			261	6	EA	M7	018	04/15/2012	04/15/2012
OOO	000000000500000142	TESTING MATERIAL # 7	ZZTE			261	4	EA	M7	018	04/15/2012	04/15/2012
OOO	000000000500000143	TES					8	EA	M7	018	04/15/2012	04/15/2012

Information — Enter Stor. Location

This Goods Movement generated a COGI error because the storage location was missing from the Production Order. The Goods Movement can be re-processed by entering the correct storage location for the material. When this is done, the COGI error will be eliminated.

MD01. This transaction is used to run MRP at the Plant Level. When it is executed, MRP is carried out for all materials assigned to the plant. Normally, planners are not given access to this transaction; instead the transaction is set up to run as a background job at specified time(s) through the day. (Background job scheduling is usually handled by the SAP Basis Team.) When part of a batch schedule, MRP may be run at multiple times during the day to provide Planners with up-to-date MRP results.

Info Required.
✓ Plant Number.
✓ MRP Processing Key Selection.

Transaction Flow.

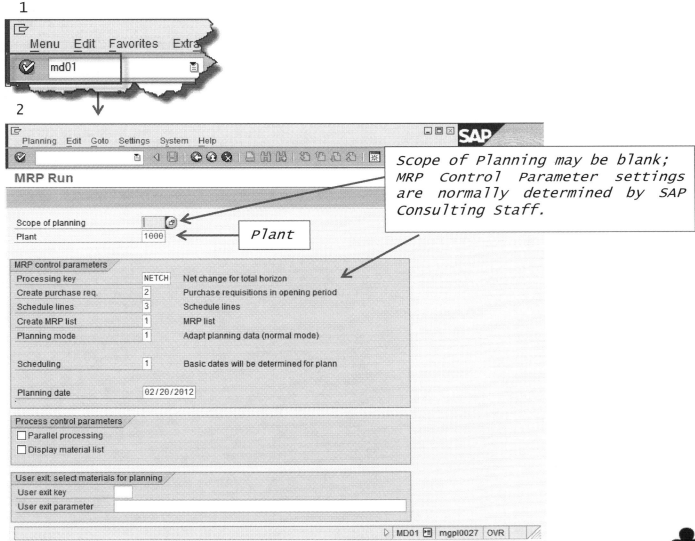

Scope of Planning may be blank; MRP Control Parameter settings are normally determined by SAP Consulting Staff.

Plant

MD01   Planning Run Dialog and Results Display.

3

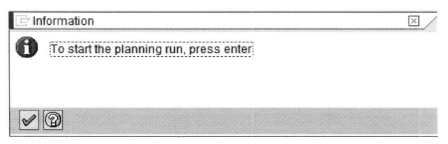

4

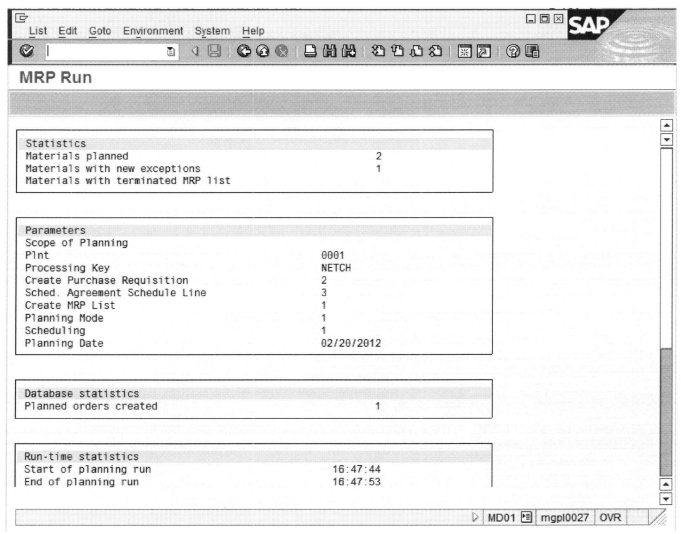

Overview. MD02 is the transaction used to run MRP for an Assembly and its Bill of Material components. Frequently, as Planners/Buyers process MRP planning elements, they will re-run MRP with this transaction to view the latest results.

Info Required.
✓ Material Number.
✓ MRP Processing Key Selection.

Transaction Flow.

1A

1B – Option

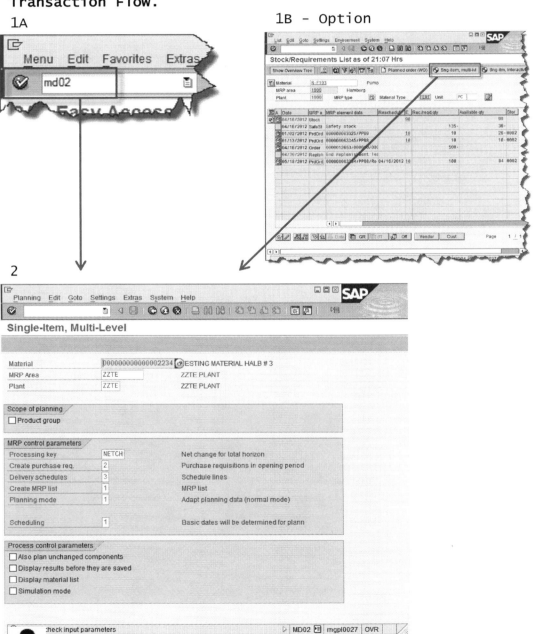

MD02 can be run from MD04 using a Navigation Profile that is found under the MD04 Settings Menu.

2

MD02 MRP Results Display.

3

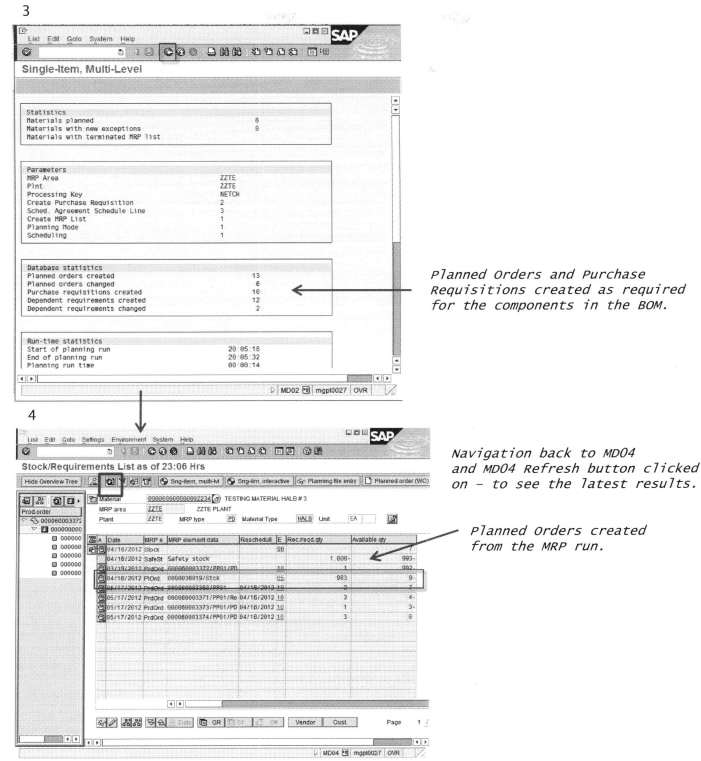

Planned Orders and Purchase
Requisitions created as required
for the components in the BOM.

4

Navigation back to MD04
and MD04 Refresh button clicked
on – to see the latest results.

Planned Orders created
from the MRP run.

Overview. MD04 is used to display current stock situation for a material. It is a key transaction in the Manufacturing Enterprise and is used by Planners, Buyers and a wide range of other personnel who need a quick look at the supplies and demands for a material over time.

Key Points.
- ✓ MD04 can be used in Single Material or Collective View modes.
- ✓ In the Collective View, Materials can be selected by various criteria – including MRP Controller, Procurement Type, Vendor, etc – and groups of materials can be viewed by user defined priorities ('Traffic Lights' functionality).
- ✓ MD04 also displays key MRP Parameters from the Material Master.
- ✓ MD04 is especially useful in understanding requirements for Material Assemblies – via its Overview Tree function – users can navigate through the Bill of Material structure of Assembly and pin point bottle necks and shortages.
- ✓ Each MRP element displayed on MD04 can be selected, viewed and/or edited – allowing Planners/Buyers to execute their most common transactions directly from this screen.

Transaction Flow.

1

2

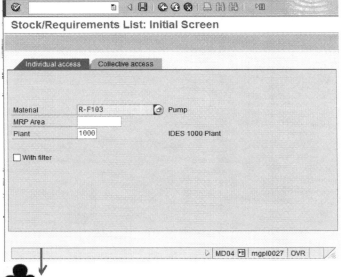

Info Required
(for individual access view):
- ✓ Material and Plant Numbers

3   *MD04 Results Display.*

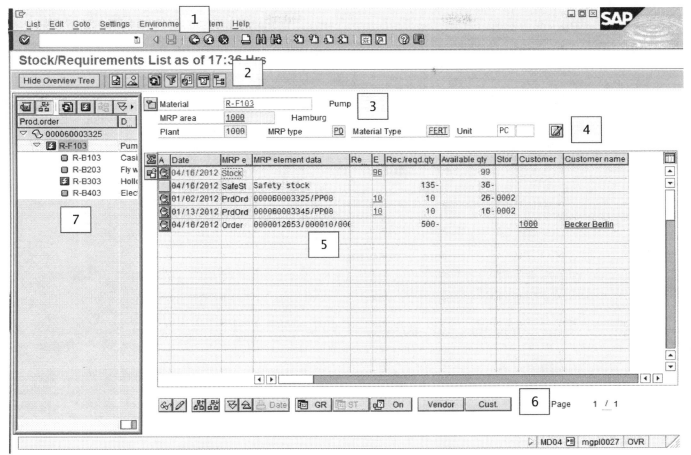

MD04 Overview:

1. **Menu line.** Go To menu allows navigation to other key Materials and Inventory Transactions; Settings menu allows set up of additional controls on the icon bar - including adding custom transactions, like MD02.
2. **Icon bar.** Displays/Hides Overview Tree, allows navigation between materials, provides filter controls and other services such as email.
3. **Material Parameters.** Key MRP Parameters from the Material Master can be displayed here.
4. **Text Comments control.** Planner text comments can be added with this control.
5. **Stock Situation panel.** Starting with current inventory in the Plant, MRP Supply and Demand elements are displayed.
    - ✓ Demand elements such as sales orders, are represented as negative numbers, reducing stock level;
    - ✓ Supply elements like Production Orders, are positive numbers, increasing stock;
    - ✓ Both Supply and Demand elements have Dates - indicating when they are required or available.
6. **Display controls.** Allows further display of MRP elements, MRP date display changes and display of Vendor and Customer data.
7. **Overview Tree panel.** Allows navigation to other materials in the Bill of Material. Green lights indicate that all of the required materials are available; Red Lights indicate that planner action is required.

SAP ECC in Manufacturing: *An Operator's Guide*

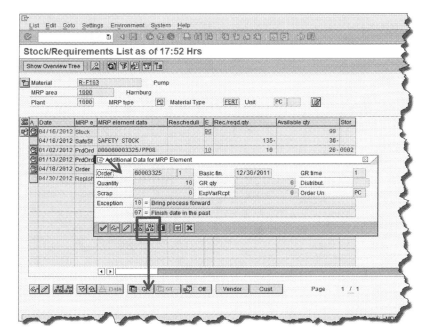

Double clicking on a MD04 MRP element — displays additional information and selected elements can be edited directly from MD04.

Navigation to CO02 from MD04

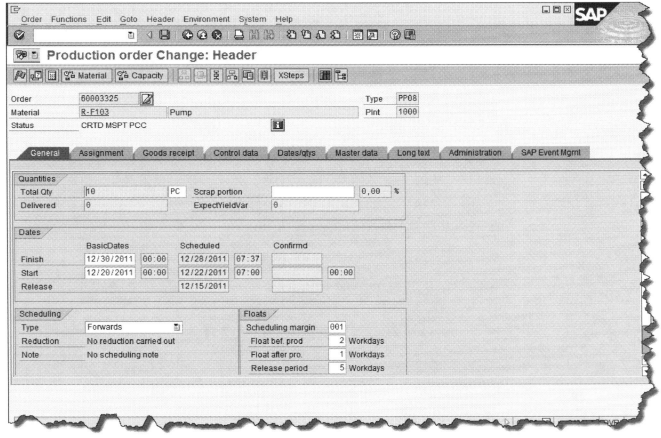

Selected MRP elements and their abbreviations.

MRP Element	Abbrv
Dependent reservation	OrdRes
Purchase requisition	PurRqs
Subcontractor requirements of material provided	SubReq
Order item schedule line	PchOrd
Gross requirements planning	----->
Process order	PR-ORD
Batch stock	BtchSt
Effective-out date	----->
Subcontracting purchasing	SubCon
Production order	PrdOrd
End of planning time fence	----->
Maintenance order	PMOrdr
In plant (only relevant for IS Automotive)	InPlnt
JIT call	JIT
Individual customer stock	Order
Consignment stock for customer (availability check)	C.Cons
Shipping notification	ShipNt
Storage location stock	StLcSt
SA schedule line	SchLne
JIT delivery schedule	JIT-DS
Stock with subcontractor	MatSub
Planned order	PlOrd.
Project stock	Projct
Planned independent requirement	IndReq
Forecast requirement	ForReq
Inspection lot for quality management	QM lot
Dependent requirement	DepReq
Safety requirement	SafReq
Safety stock	SafeSt

MRP Element	Abbrv
Simulation requirement	SimReq
Sim. dependent reqmts	SimReq
Release order for a stock transfer order	ConRel
Release order for a stock transfer requisition	PRqRel
Release order for a stock transfer order	ConRel
Release order for a stock transfer requisition	PRqRel
Request for quotation	Inqury
Quotation	Quote
Order	Order
SD scheduling agreement	SchAgr
SD scheduling agreement; external service agent	SA-ESA
Contract	Contr.
Delivery Free of Charge	Fr.del
Delivery	Deliv.
Goods issue	GIssue
Plant stock	Stock
Goods receipt	GRecpt
End replenishment period	Replsh

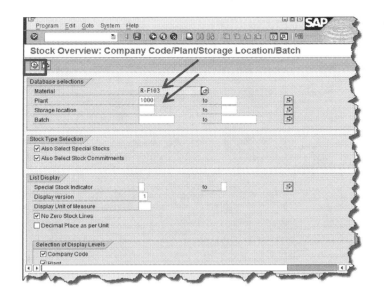

Transaction MMBE displays the inventory for a Material by Company Code, Plant and Storage Location (and if utilized, Batch) levels.

Within an Inventory Location - the stock may be assigned a category - such as Restricted Use or Quality Inspection.

Stock is moved between categories by a Goods Movement Transaction: e.g. Customer Returns can automatically move into a Blocked Stock Category; After Quality Inspection - they can be transferred to Unrestricted status.

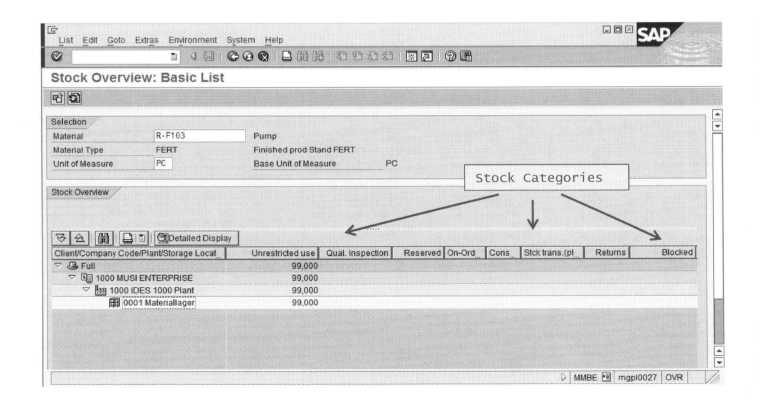

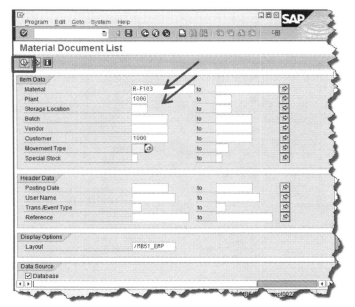

Transaction **MB51** displays the goods movements/postings for a material over time.

MB51 can be used to investigate possible stock transaction errors such as double postings, incorrect goods movements, etc.

MB51 Selection criteria is usually some combination of Plant, Material, Movement Type and/or Posting Date values.

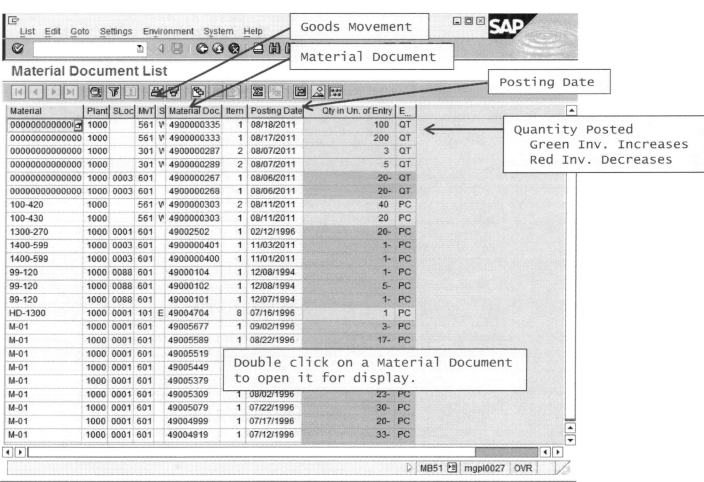

Double click on a Material Document to open it for display.

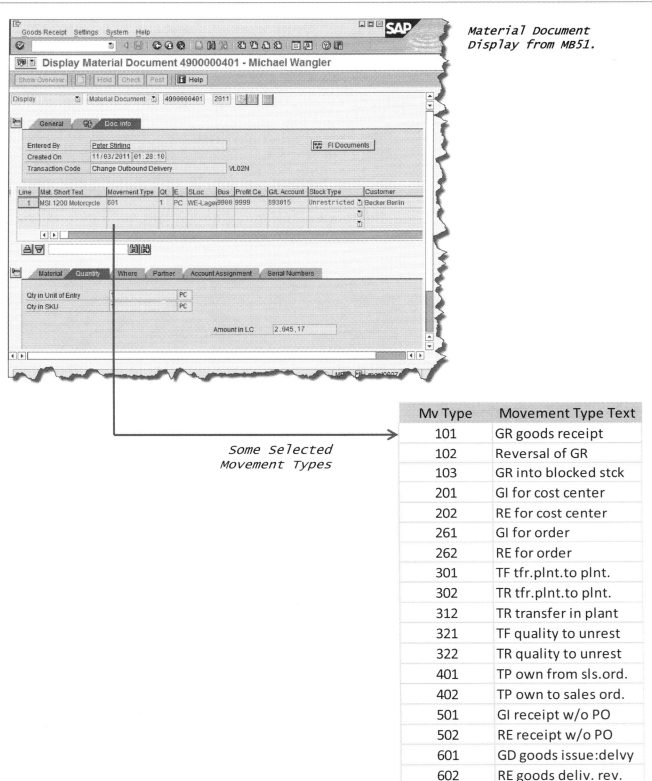

Material Document Display from MB51.

Some Selected Movement Types

Mv Type	Movement Type Text
101	GR goods receipt
102	Reversal of GR
103	GR into blocked stck
201	GI for cost center
202	RE for cost center
261	GI for order
262	RE for order
301	TF tfr.plnt.to plnt.
302	TR tfr.plnt.to plnt.
312	TR transfer in plant
321	TF quality to unrest
322	TR quality to unrest
401	TP own from sls.ord.
402	TP own to sales ord.
501	GI receipt w/o PO
502	RE receipt w/o PO
601	GD goods issue:delvy
602	RE goods deliv. rev.
651	GD ret.del. returns

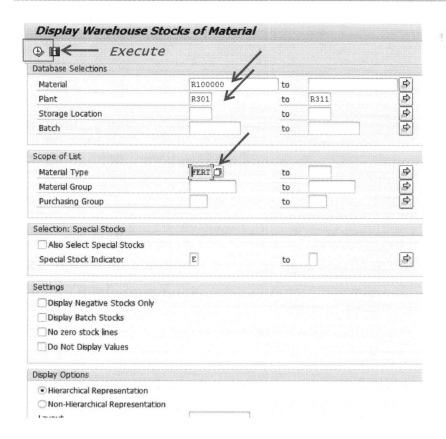

MB52 displays an Inventory Report for multiple materials.

✓ This report provides inventory data details similar to those in the MMBE transaction.

✓ The report also provides a total value of the inventory by material type.

✓ Typical report selections include Material Ranges, Plants and Material Types.

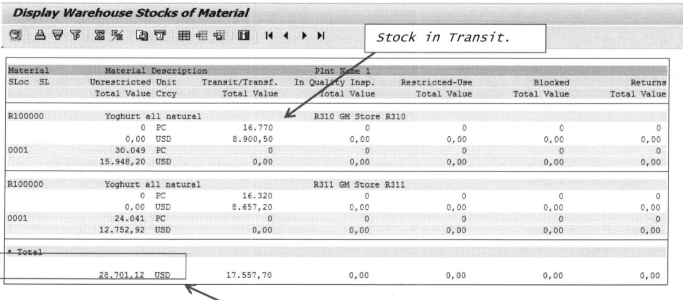

Stock in Transit.

Total value of Unrestricted stock.

Map Area 4
Purchasing and Receiving

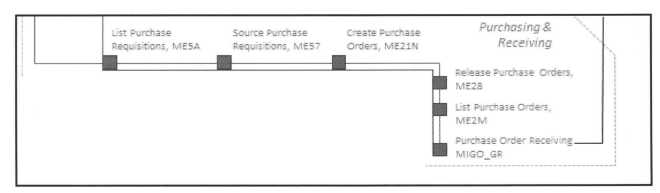

This section provides an overview of transactions in the Purchasing and Receiving area of the map to include:

✓ Purchase Requisition reporting and processing to include assigning a source of supply to a requisition;

✓ Purchase Order creation, release and reporting;

✓ Purchase Order material receiving.

These transactions are normally performed by Planners/Buyers and Warehouse personnel.

Purchasing Area Functions	Transaction
List Purchase Requisitions	ME5A
Source Purchase Requisitions	ME57
Create a Purchase Order	ME21N
Release Purchase Order	ME28
List Purchase Orders	ME2M
Purchase Order Goods Receiving	MIGO_GR

The section starts with a review of some basic concepts used in SAP Purchasing that are applicable to these transactions. Topics discussed include Direct vs. Indirect procurement, External vs. Internal purchasing and the general concepts for Subcontracting and Outside Processing in SAP.

Procurement Cycle. A generic purchasing cycle includes steps to Specify, Order, Receive, Consume, Pay and Evaluate the raw materials and semi-finished goods needed for production. In this section, our main focus is on steps in the 'Order stage' of the cycle.

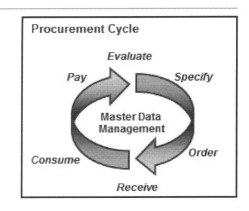

Procurement can also be described by its impact on Inventory: e.g. Direct vs. Indirect Purchasing.

Direct Procurement:

✓ Material Masters and Purchasing Info Records are maintained.

✓ Materials are ordered by Material Number and received into inventory.

✓ Materials are issued to production orders or the shop floor and consumed in the production process.

✓ Purchase Requisitions specifying Materials, Quantities and Planned Delivery Dates, created from the MRP process, drive the procurement cycle. Buyers convert Purchase Requisitions to Purchase Orders and release POs to Vendors.

> **Direct Procurement** for Materials consumed in the Production Process.

Indirect Procurement:

✓ Mainly used for goods and services and not directly used in the production process.

✓ Cost Centers are specified in the Purchase Order ('Cost Center Type K PO').

✓ Material Masters are not required. Purchasing Info Records may or may not be used.

> **Indirect Procurement** for General Goods and Services.

✓ Purchased Items are received by Goods Recipient and are not placed into inventory.

✓ Purchase Requisitions are manually entered and submitted to the Buyer for review and action. Approved Requisitions are converted to Purchase Orders and released to the Vendor.

Concept. SAP also distinguishes materials, goods and services purchased from external vendors from materials ordered from other plants in the company's business structure (internal Procurement).

The PO Type Field, NB Standard External Vendor / UB Stock Transport Order

In standard SAP, the PO Type field value **NB** is used to indicate external procurement (from outside Vendor), while the **UB** PO Type is used in an internal procurement (order from another Plant) order scenario.

Internal Procurement/Stock Transport Order (STO) Overview:

✓ For STO between two plants inside the same company code – no Invoice/Financial settlement document is required. This is because the company code represents a single business entity/chart of accounts.

✓ There is an additional STO case, in which the plants are assigned to different company codes – in this situation, an Intercompany invoice/settlement is required.

✓ In either case, the concept of **Stock In-Transit** is applicable. Stock in-transit is stock that has been issued by the supplying plant (via the Post Goods Issue on the Delivery Document), but not yet received in the ordering plant (via the posting of the Goods Receipt in the MIGO_GR transaction).

SAP External and Internal Procurement Options.

Materials Only versus Materials + Invoice Scenarios.

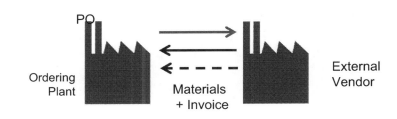

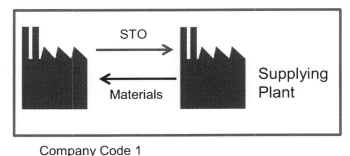

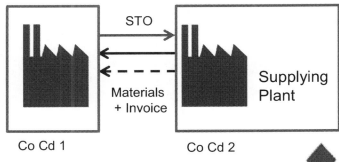

Overview. SAP supports two special procurement cases, in which a vendor is provided materials to finish, according to the specifications of the production process. These are the cases of **Subcontracting** and **Outside Processing**.

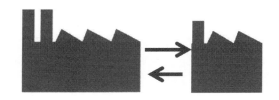

Subcontracting Concept:

✓ The materials used in the manufacture of the Subcontracted Assembly are procured for and sent to the Vendor. The Vendor assembles and delivers a new assembly.
  - ✓ At minimum, (2) Material Numbers, (at least) one component and the final assembly, are maintained in SAP.

✓ The External Procurement (F) and Special Procurement (30) keys are set on the Material Master for the subcontracted assembly.

✓ A Bill Of Material for the Assembly is maintained.

✓ A Subcontracting Type Purchasing Info Record is maintained.

✓ MRP generates a Subcontracting Purchase Requisition (identified by the Item category 'L').
  - ✓ The Requisition is converted into a Purchase Order and released to the Subcontracting Vendor by the Buyer.
  - ✓ No Production Order is created.

✓ Delivery documents are used to send Raw materials from the Plant to the Subcontractor (and also to ship the Assembly from the Vendor facility to the Plant).
  - ✓ Subcontracting Raw Materials appear as Inventory in SAP under the Subcontractor/Vendor Number in MD04.

✓ The receipt of the Purchase Order places the Subcontracted Assembly into inventory at the Plant and also *Backflushes* the Component Materials from Vendor Stock.
  - ✓ Two Movement Types (101 and 543) are transacted with the Goods Receipt.

Outside Processing (compared to Subcontracting):

✓ The Assembly is sent to the Vendor who performs a service such as Finishing, Painting or Stamping – the same Assembly/Material Number is returned to the Plant.
  ✓ Only (1) Material Number is maintained in SAP.

✓ The Internal Procurement Key (E) is maintained on the Material Master.

✓ A Standard Purchasing Info Record for the service performed – but this PIR includes only the service to perform – it contains no material number.

✓ A BOM and Routing for the Assembly is maintained in SAP:
  ✓ The Routing specifies an Outside Processing Step/Operation.
  ✓ The PIR for the Outside Service is referenced in the Procurement Details section of the Routing Operation.

✓ When a Production Order for the Assembly is created, the Assembly Routing (with the PIR) is read – and a Purchase Requisition for the Outside Process is created by SAP.
  ✓ (As with the Outside Process PIR) – the Purchase Requisition does not reference a Material Number.
  ✓ The Outside Process Purchase Requisition is converted to a Purchase Order by the Buyer.

✓ The Purchase Order and the Production Order accompany the Assembly when it is sent to the Vendor.
  ✓ No SAP Delivery Documents are generated in the process.

✓ No Backflush of Component Materials occurs because no Inventory exists at the Vendor location.
  ✓ When the Vendor has completed the Outside Process, the assembly is returned to the Plant – referencing the Purchase Order and Production Order.
  ✓ The Goods Receipt does not increase inventory at the Plant.
  ✓ The Goods Receipt is the signal to complete the Outside Process step in the Production Order Routing.

✓ The Production Order Confirmation completes the process.

Factor	Direct Procurement	Subcontracting	Outside Processing	Indirect Procurement
Material Number required	Yes	Yes	Yes	No
Service Items	NA	NA	Yes	Yes
Purchasing Info Record required	No	Yes	Yes	No
Bills of Materials required	NA	Yes	No	NA
Routing required	NA	No	Yes	NA
Purchase Requisition required	Yes	Yes*(1)	Yes	No*(2)
MRP generates the Purchase Requisition	Yes	Yes	Yes	No
Raw Materials/Components sent to Vendor	NA	Yes	No	NA
Service is performed at Vendor location	NA	No	Yes	NA
Service is performed in the Plant	NA	NA	No	Yes
Subcontracting Stock is visible at Vendor Location on MD04	NA	Yes	No	NA
Delivery Documents accompany Shipments to/from Vendor	NA	Yes	No	NA
Purchase Order Goods Receipt Increases Inventory	Yes	Yes	No	No
Purchase Order Goods Recipient is required	No	No	Yes	Yes
Backflush occurs with Goods Receipt	NA	Yes	No	NA
Production Order Operations Step completes Outside Process	NA	NA	Yes	NA

Notes:
1. Subcontracting Purchase Requisition.
2. If used - Cost Center Purchase Requisition.

ME5A Overview. This is the primary transaction to list, review and edit Purchase Requisitions. Requisitions are created directly by SAP during the Materials Requirements Planning (MRP) run and by other SAP Users requesting goods or services using the ME51N transaction. After reviewing Purchase Requisition quantities and requested delivery dates, the buyer assigns sources of supply, converts requisitions to orders and finally, releases purchase orders to vendors.

Info Required.
✓ Optional, usually some combination of Plant, Purchasing Group or MRP Controller fields.

Transaction Flow.

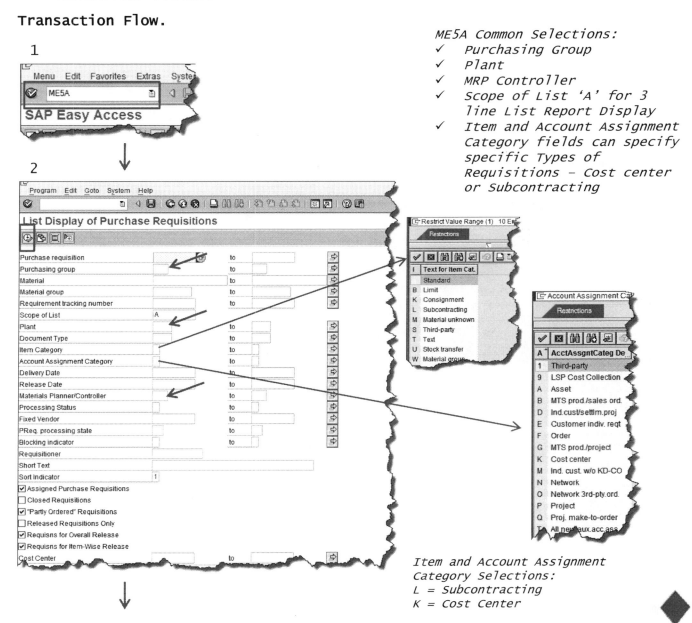

ME5A Common Selections:
✓ *Purchasing Group*
✓ *Plant*
✓ *MRP Controller*
✓ *Scope of List 'A' for 3 line List Report Display*
✓ *Item and Account Assignment Category fields can specify specific Types of Requisitions – Cost center or Subcontracting*

Item and Account Assignment Category Selections:
L = Subcontracting
K = Cost Center

ME5A Purchase Requisition List Report.

3

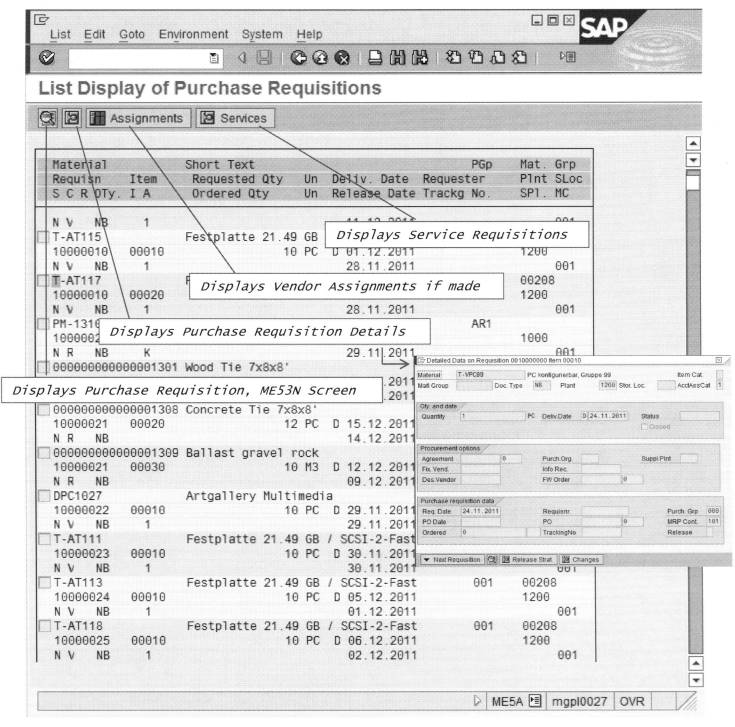

ME53N, Display Purchase Requisition – accessed from ME5A Purchase Requisition List Report.

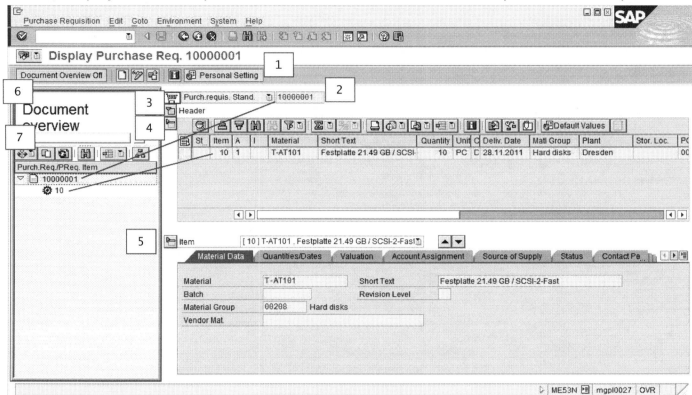

ME53N Purchase Requisition Overview:

1. Icon Bar. Provides controls to turn the Document Overview Panel On or Off, Create New Requisitions, Toggle between Change or Display modes, Display other Requisitions, General Info and Personal Settings.

2. Shopping Cart and Purchase Requisition Number. Requisitions Numbers from the Document Overview Panel can be dragged to the Shopping Cart for Screen Display.

3. Purchase Requisition Header (with Header minimized).

4. Purchase Requisition Line Items with Line Item "10" displayed.

5. Line Item Detail with Material Data Tab displayed.

6. Document Overview Control Panel. Provides icons to select/display requisitions and adopt Requisition directly into a Purchase Order.

7. Purchase Requisition Selection Variant control. Activates a selection screen that displays a list of Requisitions in the Document Overview Panel.

> Purchase Requisitions are internal documents used to indicate a procurement requirement/shortage quantity.

ME57, Purchase Requisition Assign Source Of Supply Overview.
✓ This transaction is used to assign Purchase Requisitions to Vendors.
✓ Once assigned, the requisition can be converted to a Purchase Order.
✓ Source of Supply can be specified from the Purchase Info Record.
✓ Source of Supply can also be set and sourcing automatically performed using Transaction ME01 – Create Source List.

Info Required.
✓ Optional, usually some combination of Purchasing Group, Plant and/or MRP Controller selections…

Transaction Flow.

1

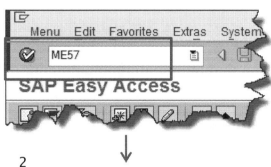

2

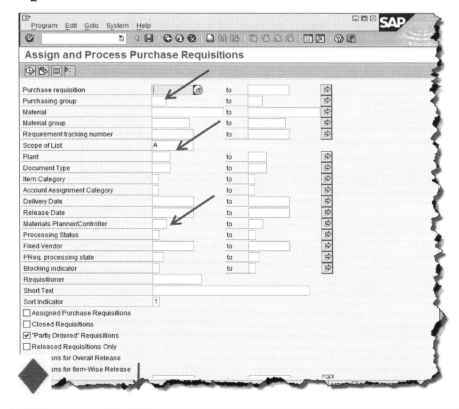

ME57 Selection Display with typical selection fields indicated:
✓ Purchasing Group
✓ Plant
✓ MRP Controller

ME57 Display.
3

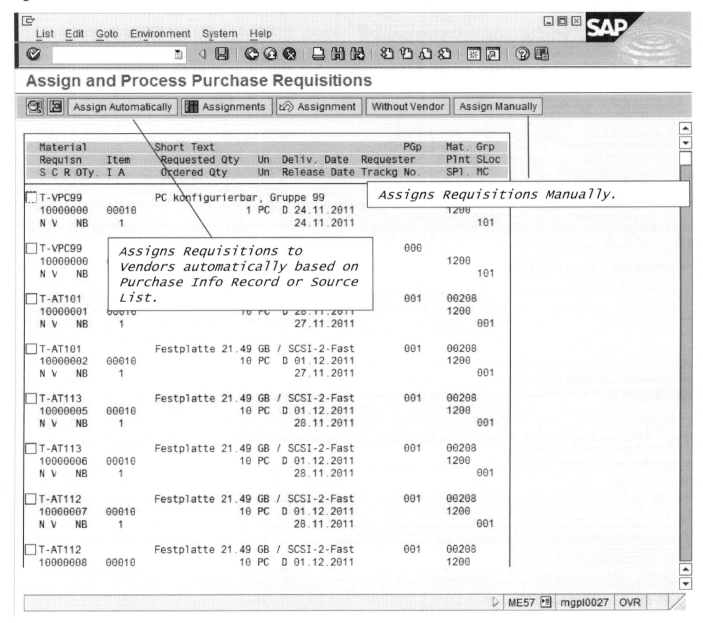

3 *ME57 Source Dialog.*

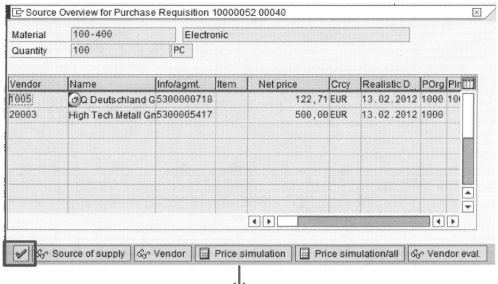

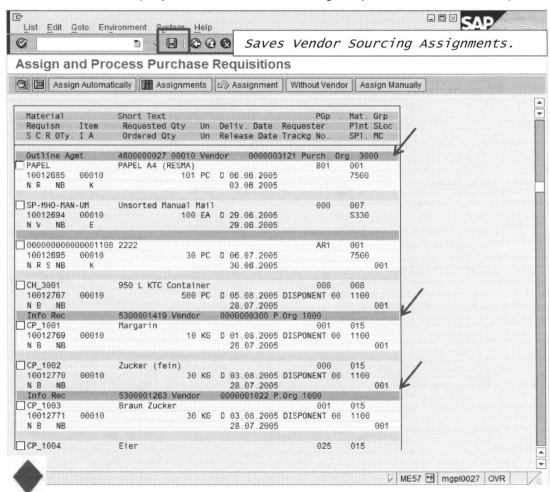

4 *ME57 Final Display - with Vendor Sourcing complete on selected Requisitions.*

Purchase Order (PO) Overview.

✓ This is a central document in SAP Purchasing.

✓ The Purchase Order is the formal request by the Purchasing Organization/Plant to a Vendor or another Supplying Plant to provide a quantity of goods or services at a specified location and date.

✓ In SAP, Purchase Orders are preceded by a Request For Quotations, Quotations, Purchasing Info Records and Purchase Requisition documents; and PO's can be replaced (for longer term supply arrangements) by Contracts and Scheduling Agreements.

✓ Purchase Orders can be used in Direct and Indirect, Subcontracting, Outside Processing, Consignment, Stock Transfer and External Service scenarios.

✓ Structurally, Purchase Orders consist of a Header and Line Items.

    ✓ PO header elements include the PO Type, PO Number and Vendor;

    ✓ PO line items specify individual materials or services, quantities and delivery dates.

✓ POs can be subject to a Release Strategy – which requires review and approval of each PO meeting certain criteria/value by a one or more designated Authorities.

✓ Pricing Condition Records are used in the PO header and line item level to determine the total overall and line item pricing.

✓ Output Conditions Records are used in PO's to determine how the PO Document itself is generated and transmitted to the Vendor. PO Output condition types include Hardcopy/Print, Fax, Email and EDI transmission.

✓ The PO Goods Receipt (MIGO_GR) indicates that the goods or services ordered have been delivered and it starts the Vendor Invoice Payment process.

Info Required.

✓ PO Type and Vendor for direct procurement, material number(s) and quantities (or from MRP, Purchase Requisition).

Transaction Flow.

1

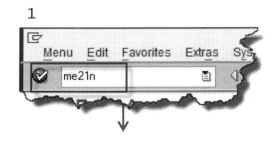

ME21N, Create PO Display.

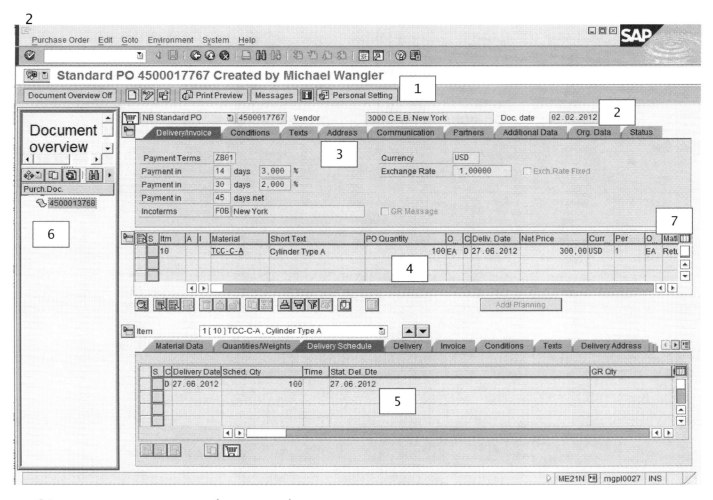

ME21N Create PO Transaction Overview:
1. **Icon Control Bar.** Includes controls to display or hide the Document Overview Panel; to create a New PO; to toggle between Display/Change Modes; to select a new PO for editing; Print Preview; PO Output Messages; Info and Personal Settings.
2. **PO Shopping Cart Control.** Requisitions in the Document Overview Panel can be dragged here to create a New PO; also includes PO Number Vendor and Document Date display fields.
3. **PO Header Tabs** (displayed Delivery/Invoice Tab).
4. **PO Line Item Display** includes columns and fields for PO Line Item, Material, Material Short Text, Quantity, Required Delivery Date and Net Price.
5. **PO Line Item Detail Display.**
6. **Document Overview Panel** – Selection Control allows PO and Purchased Requisitions to be displayed in this panel and then dragged to the Shopping Cart for action.
7. **Table Control** – controls the columns and column sequence in the PO Line Item Display.

Purchase Order Release Concept.
- ✓ The transaction ME28 is used By Purchase Order Approvers to display Purchase Orders for review/approval - if approved, Released orders can be transmitted to Vendors.
- ✓ The Release of a PO allows for PO Output and transmission of the document to a Vendor, in Hardcopy (Print), Fax, Email or EDI Form, to occur.
- ✓ Release Strategies are specified and implemented by the SAP consulting team as an IMG configuration task.
- ✓ A typical release strategy will include PO Value Ranges and multiple Approver levels:
  Example: POs valued below $1000 require could require no release strategy (and are thereby are under control of the Buyer); while PO's valued between $1001-$5000 require Purchasing Manager approval; PO's valued above that level would require a Company Director approval and so on.
- ✓ The Key Point is that PO Outputs for any PO are not to be created until PO release criteria for the PO is met.
- ✓ For many companies, a PO Release Strategy is implemented after SAP Go Live, meaning that manual procedures are used to review and control Purchase Orders until the Release Strategy is activated in SAP.

Info Required.
- ✓ Release Codes and Groups as defined in Configuration.
- ✓ Release Authorizations are set up in SAP User Administration System.
- ✓ Released Authorizations assigned to select SAP Users such as Buyers, Managers and Directors.

Transaction Flow.

1

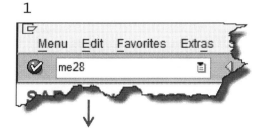

ME28, Release PO Selection Screen.

2

Release (Approve) Purchasing Documents

Program Edit Goto System Help

Release Code	1	←
Release Group	AA	←	to
☑ Set Release		
☐ Cancel Release		
☑ Release Prerequisite Fulfilled		
☐ List with Items		
Scope of List	BEST	
Puchasing Document Category	F	to
Purchasing Organization		to
Document Number		to
Document Type		to
Purchasing Group		to
Vendor		to
Supplying Plant		to
Document Date		to

> *Release Codes and Groups are defined in Configuration.*

▷ | ME28 | mgpl0027 | OVR

↓

ME28, Release PO Display Screen.

3

Release Purchasing Documents with Release Code G

🔓Release | Cancel Release | 🖼Release Strat. | Release + Save | 📑Print Preview

```
PO          Type Vendor     Name                         PGp Order Date
Release Strategy            Release Indicator     Release Option
  Item  Material            Short Text                    Mat. Group
  D I A Plnt SLoc             Order Qty    Un     Net Price Curr.   per Un

4500000030 ZNB  1107  COCA COLA                           OLC 11/30/2011
01/B1 FG-Sub FG             B Blocked             Release possible
  00010 G73                 COCA COLA                     03
        0001                        11  PC         0.50  USD     1 PC
    Still to be delivered           11  PC         5.50  USD  100.00 %
    Still to be invoiced            11  PC         5.50  USD  100.00 %
4500000063 ZNB  110757      INTERNATIONAL             MED 12/03/2011
01/B2 FG-Sub FG             B Blocked             Release possible
  00010 G1                                              03
        0001                    10,080  PC         2.00  USD     1 PC
    Still to be delivered       10,080  PC     20,160.00 USD  100.00 %
    Still to be invoiced        10,080  PC     20,160.00 USD  100.00 %
4500000067 INB  200212                                COD 12/05/2011
01/B1 FG                    B Blocked             Release possible
```

> *PO Release allows Purchase Order Output to be created.*

ME2M, List Purchase Orders Report Transaction Overview.
- ✓ Use this transaction to display and edit Purchase Orders created in SAP.
- ✓ Like ME5A, the ME2M report list is interactive - transactions ME22N or ME23N can be called from this report.

Info Required.
- ✓ Optional, usually some combination of Purchasing Group, Plant, Vendor, or other Material or Purchase Order selection.
- ✓ Scope of List, Account Assignment and Item Category fields are key selection criteria for creating different layouts and filtering PO's by Direct and Indirect, Subcontracting and Outside Processing categories.

Transaction Flow.

1

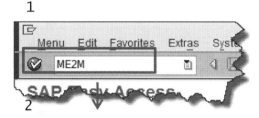

2

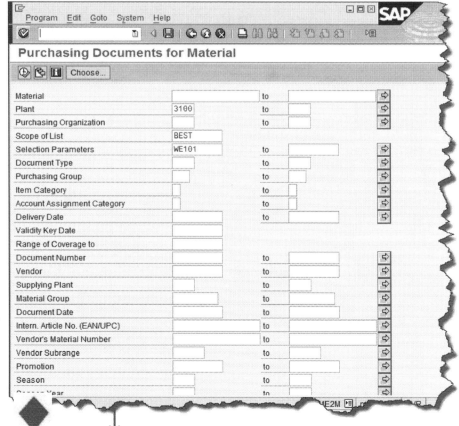

Data Entry:
- ✓ *Usually Plant, Purchasing Organization and Purchasing Group ('Buyer Code') entries.*

- ✓ *Scope of List Selection drives the look and format of list Display - i.e. single or multiple lines per order.*

- ✓ *Selection Parameter settings drive what PO's are displayed - e.g. All Orders or just POs with Open Goods Receipts.*

SAP ECC in Manufacturing: *An Operator's Guide*

ME2M Scope of List 'BEST' / Open Goods Receipt Example Report.

3

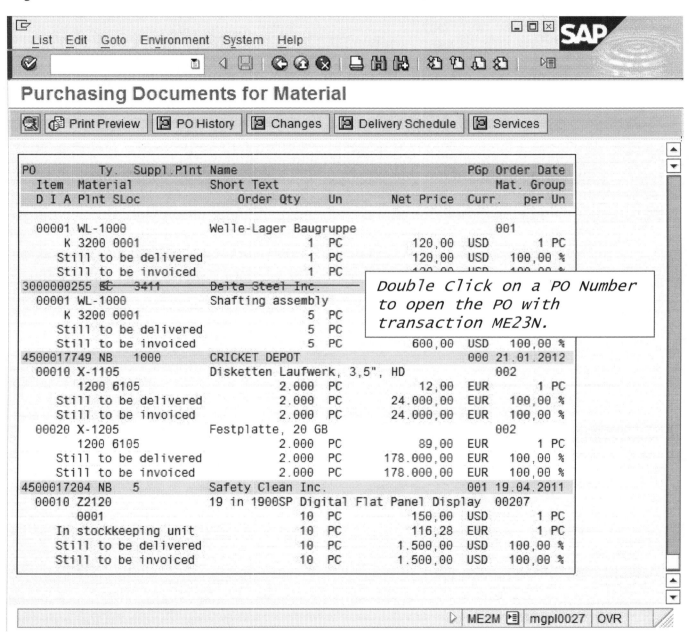

MIGO_GR, Goods Receiving Transaction Overview.
This transaction is used to receive Indirect and Direct Procurement Items into the Plant.

- ✓ Indirect Procurement Items are received to a Designated Goods Recipient as listed on the PO line item.
- ✓ Direct Procurement Items are received into the Storage Location listed on the PO line item.
- ✓ The PO Goods Receipt is a necessary step to allow for payment of the Vendor Invoice.
- ✓ The Inventory Management Goods Movement Type 101 is the standard goods movement type associated with the Goods Receiving process.
    - ✓ For a standard PO, 'Posting' the goods receipt moves the Stock from On Order (or In Transit) Stock categories to the Available/On Hand category in the Plant.
- ✓ If the flag, **Post to Inspection Stock**, is set on in the Material Master, the goods are received into the designated storage location in a Quality Hold stock category.

Info Required.
- ✓ Usually a Purchase Order Number, but other SAP documents such as a Delivery Document Number (for materials sent from one plant to another via Stock Transport Order) can also be used for goods receiving.

Transaction Flow.
1

2   *MIGO_GR Goods Receipt Transaction.*

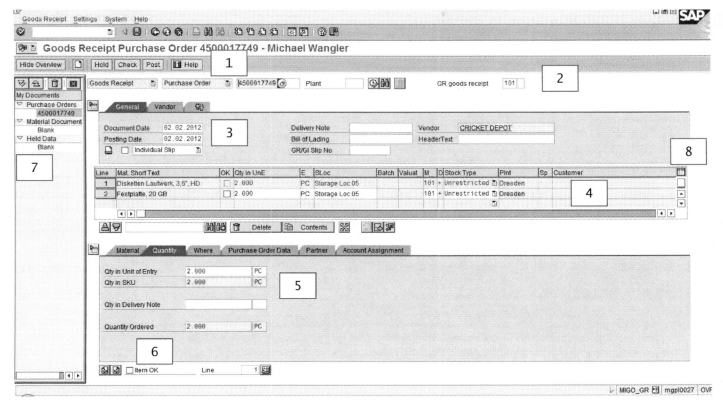

MIGO_GR Goods Receiving Transaction Overview:

1. Icon Bar. Provides controls to display/hide the Document Overview panel; and to Hold, Check or Post Items. 'Hold' status places the document on hold for action at a later time; 'Check' checks the existing document for errors and displays any warning or error messages encountered; 'Post' posts the document/completes the transaction executing the Goods Movement Type indicated.

2. Goods Receipt Control Group. Includes Goods Receipt selection, Purchase Order, and Goods Receipt Movement Type fields.

3. Document and Posting Date Fields.

4. PO Line Item Display with Material, Quantity, Movement and Stock Type and receiving Plant fields displayed.

5. PO Quantity Received.

6. Item Check Box, Next and Previous Item Controls.

7. Document Overview Panel.

8. Table Display Control – controls which columns are displayed in the PO Line Item Display.

SAP ECC in Manufacturing: *An Operator's Guide*

Map Area 5
Configuration and Systems Management

IMG/Configuration: SPRO
- Display Users: SU01D, SOBNO1
- Security: S_BCE_68001399
- Printing: SP01
- Background Jobs: SM37
- View & Maintain Tables & Queries: SE16N, SMB0, SQVI
- ABAP Editor, Transports & Errors: SE38N, SE10, SM12, ST22

Configuration & Systems Management

This section provides an overview (for Business Operators) of certain transactions used to manage an SAP environment.

The transactions referenced here are *not* be a part of the daily life of an SAP Operator – but knowledge of these transactions can be useful in Sandbox environments and training situations.

✓ Because of their system impact, *access to these transactions will be restricted* in a Production environment.

✓ Even in a Sandbox/Training environment, caution is needed in exercising these transactions – because of the chance of making unintended changes to the system.

Area	Function	Transaction
ABAP Editor, Transports & Errors	Display a Program	SE38N
	Display a Transport	SE10
	Display Table Locks	SM12
	ABAP Runtime Errors	ST22
Background Jobs	Background Job Selector	SM37
Configuration	Access to SAP Implementation Management Guide (IMG) Customization Tool of SAP.	SPRO
Display/Maintain Tables & Queries	Display a Table	SE16N
	Maintain a Z Table	SM30
	Build a Query	SQVI
Printing	Output Control/Print Management	SP01
Users & Security	Display a User	SU01D
	Find a User	SOBN01
	Review User Security Roles	S_BCE_68001399

ABAP Editor, Transports & Error Checking transactions.

Function	Transaction
Execute a Program	SE38N
Display a Transport	SE10
Display Table Locks	SM12
Display ABAP Runtime Errors	ST22

SE38N.   This transaction is used to execute a program by its program name. This may be required in cases where a Transaction code is not yet assigned to a program.

Info Required.
✓ A program name.

1

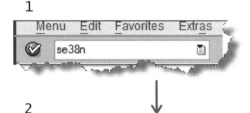

Enter transaction code SE38N in the command field and press the Green Check icon.

2

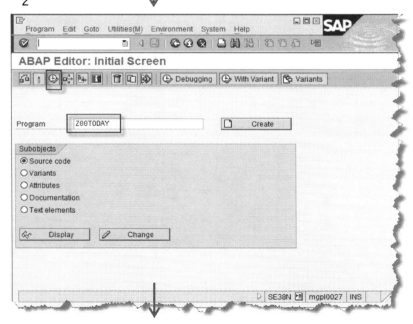

Enter the Program Name and click on the Execute icon to start the program.

SE10. This transaction is used to display the Transport Organizer. **Transports** are created by SAP Consultants and ABAP Programmers to move configuration and/or ABAP code between SAP Systems (e.g. from the Development client to Quality/Testing client through to Production).

Info Required.
✓ A transport number.

1

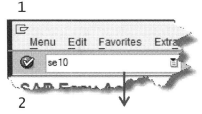

Enter transaction code SE10 in the command field and press the Green Check icon.

2

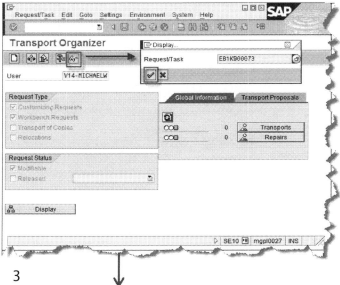

Click on the Glasses icon - enter the Transport Number...then click on the Green Check icon.

3

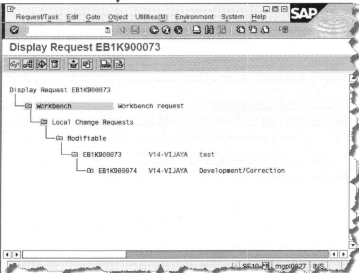

A summary info screen will appear with info on the Transport to include its status: Modifiable or Released.

SM12. This transaction is used to display Table Lock information. Table Locks may develop in a training or testing environment when users are accessing the same master data records at once. This is normally a rare error condition and if it is detected, it would be handled by the Project's Basis Team.

Info Required.
✓ A table or user name.

1

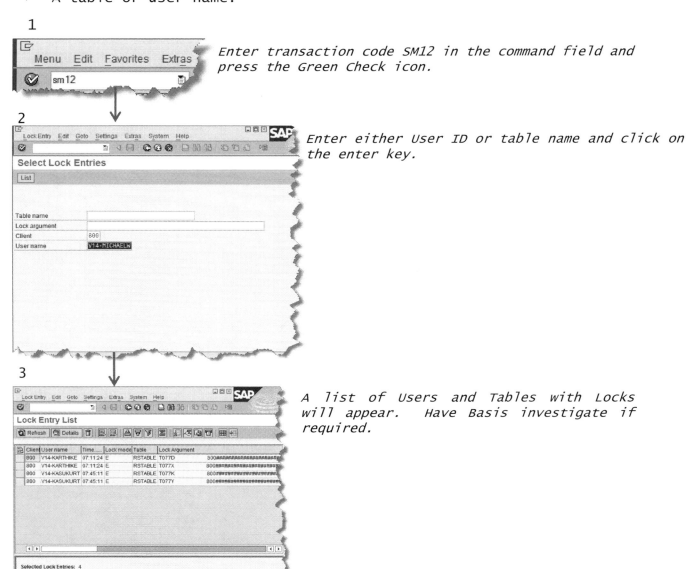

Enter transaction code SM12 in the command field and press the Green Check icon.

Enter either User ID or table name and click on the enter key.

A list of Users and Tables with Locks will appear. Have Basis investigate if required.

ST22. This transaction is used to display Table Lock information. Table Locks may develop in a training or testing environment when users are accessing the same master data records at once. This is normally a rare error condition and if it is detected, it would be handled by the Project's Basis Team.

Info Required.
✓ N/A.

1

Enter transaction code ST22 in the command field and press the Green Check icon.

2

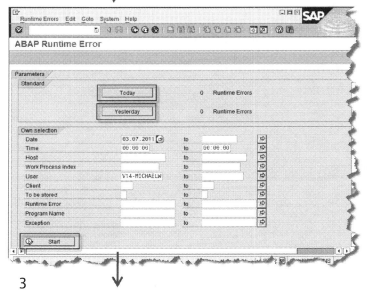

Click on the Today, Yesterday or Start buttons to start a date selection based search.

3

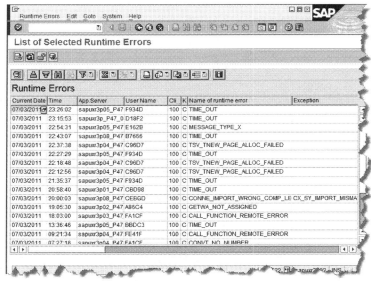

A list of Runtime errors for the selection criteria entered will be displayed. As necessary, have Basis Configuration or ABAP Programming Teams investigate and explain errors.

SM37. SAP divides its system work processing into two broad categories: online and background.

✓ *Online* processing includes all transactions directly executed by users;

✓ *Background* processing jobs – which are transactions/programs and variants scheduled to run at a certain date/time.

Function	Transaction
Display Background Jobs Display	SM37

Example: Display a list of Background Jobs.

Info Required.
✓ A Job Name.

1

Enter transaction code SM37 in the command field and press the Green Check icon.

2

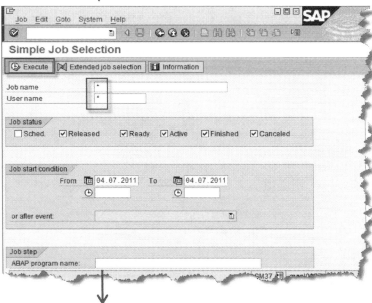

Enter the Job or User Name info or use the * key in both fields and click on the Execute button...

3

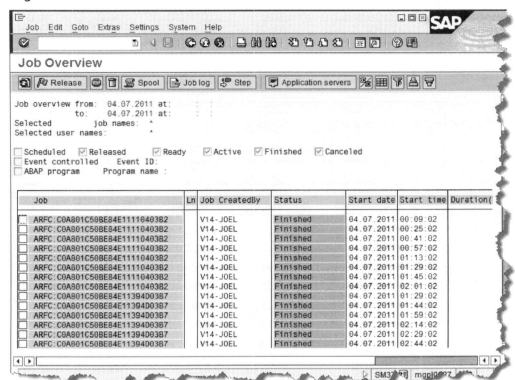

A list of Background Jobs, meeting the selection criteria will appear…

Jobs are displayed with a Status – Finished, Cancelled, In Process (Running), etc…

SPRO. We have referenced the SPRO transaction elsewhere in this document-noting that configuration is a task belonging to the project's SAP consultants. One last point of interest for the SAP Operator about SPRO is that each section of the configuration guide is accompanied by its own documentation section. This documentation is a good source of reference information, especially in regards to Org Structures and Master Data requirements.

Function	Transaction
Access to SAP Implementation Management Guide (IMG) Customization Tool of SAP.	SPRO

Example: Display the SPRO documentation for the Sales Organization structure.

Info Required.
✓ N/A.

Note: Access to SPRO will be restricted in DEV, QA and Production clients.

1

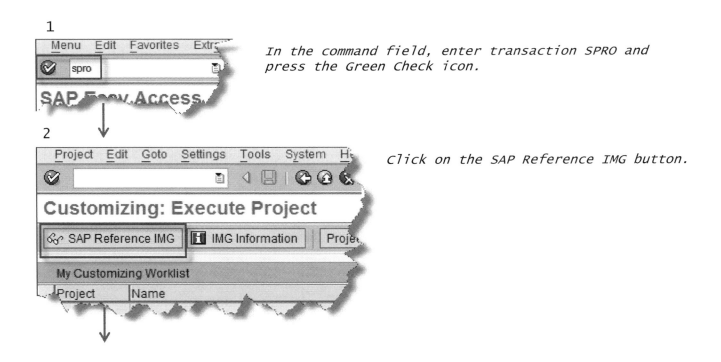

In the command field, enter transaction SPRO and press the Green Check icon.

2

Click on the SAP Reference IMG button.

3

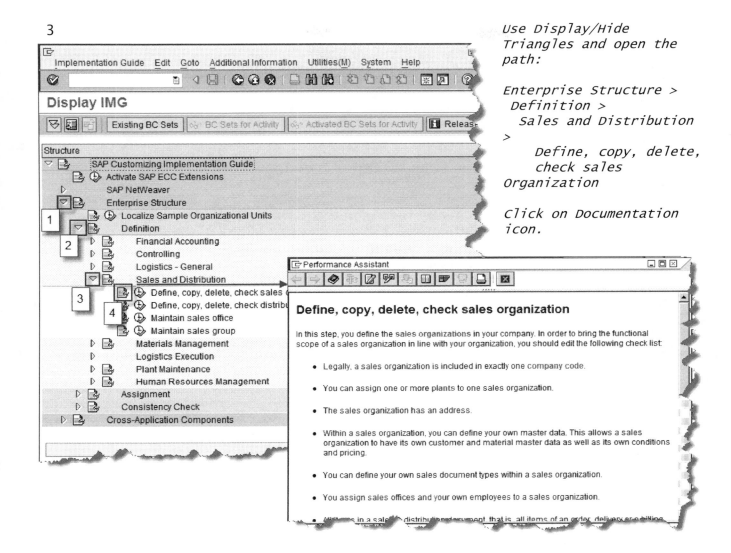

Use Display/Hide
Triangles and open the
path:

Enterprise Structure >
Definition >
Sales and Distribution
>
Define, copy, delete,
check sales
Organization

Click on Documentation
icon.

Table Display & Maintenance Transactions. We provide an overview of three transactions in this section. One of the transactions referenced here, the SE16N table viewer, was previously described in the Org Structure and Master Data section of this document.

Function	Transaction
Display a Table	SE16N
Maintain a Z Table	SM30
Build a Query	SQVI

SE16N. The table viewer transaction is useful in expecting Master Data in the early stages of a project – especially after it has been loaded into a system for verification and validation. A list of select Master Data tables can be found in the Appendix.

1

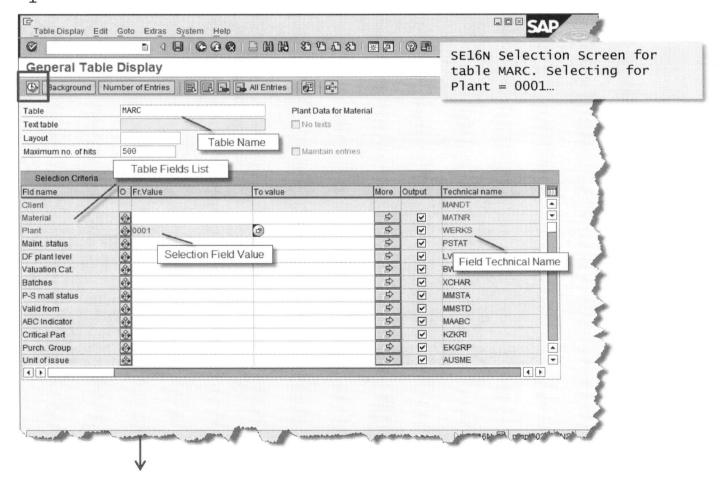

SE16N Display.

2

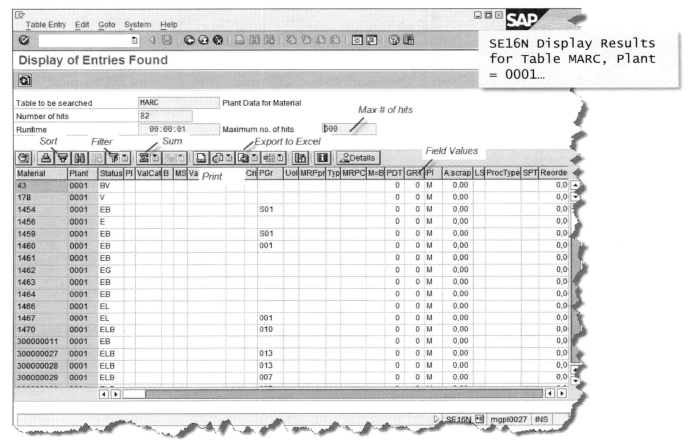

SE16N Display Results for Table MARC, Plant = 0001...

Display of Entries Found

Table to be searched	MARC	Plant Data for Material
Number of hits	82	
Runtime	00:00:01	Maximum no. of hits	500

Max # of hits

Sort   Filter   Sum   Export to Excel   Field Values   Print   Details

Material	Plant	Status	Pl	ValCat	B	MS	Va	Cri	PGr	Uol	MRPpr	Typ	MRPC	M=B	PDT	GR	PI	A.scrap	LS	ProcType	SPT	Reorde
43	0001	BV													0	0	M	0,00				0,0
178	0001	V													0	0	M	0,00				0,0
1454	0001	EB							S01						0	0	M	0,00				0,0
1456	0001	E													0	0	M	0,00				0,0
1459	0001	EB							S01						0	0	M	0,00				0,0
1460	0001	EB							001						0	0	M	0,00				0,0
1461	0001	EB													0	0	M	0,00				0,0
1462	0001	EG													0	0	M	0,00				0,0
1463	0001	EB													0	0	M	0,00				0,0
1464	0001	EB													0	0	M	0,00				0,0
1466	0001	EL													0	0	M	0,00				0,0
1467	0001	EL							001						0	0	M	0,00				0,0
1470	0001	ELB							010						0	0	M	0,00				0,0
300000011	0001	EB													0	0	M	0,00				0,0
300000027	0001	ELB							013						0	0	M	0,00				0,0
300000028	0001	ELB							013						0	0	M	0,00				0,0
300000029	0001	ELB							007						0	0	M	0,00				0,0

SE16N   mgpl0027   INS

SM30. This is Maintenance table viewer transaction and it is used only when values stored in a table must be changed. Normally this is not required (or allowed), because the table itself would be maintained and updated by a transaction or transaction series. In certain cases though, and especially in the early stages of a project, SM30 may be used by the project team in performing maintenance or updates of custom Z-tables. Remember, Z-Tables are tables specific to an SAP customer project, and are not part of the standard SAP.

1

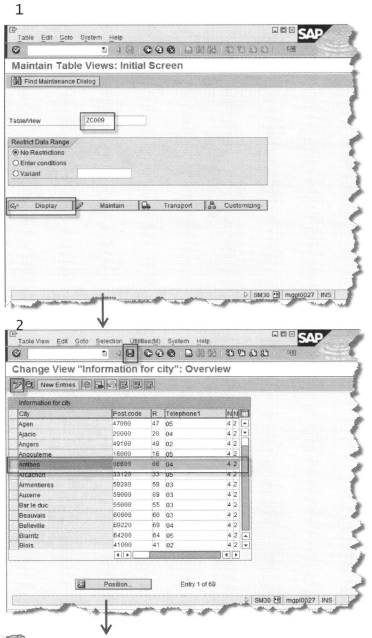

SM30 selecting for a Z Table...

SM30 in change mode...

SQVI. SAP provides a Table Query Builder transaction named SQVI that is useful in building custom reports for quick data validation, analysis or exception reporting functions. This transaction is normally used by SAP consultants, but many projects over time will provide business personnel with access to the transaction. We do not provide a full treatment of SQVI here – but provided below is a screen series of the tool that would be used to create a simple query / join of two tables.

1

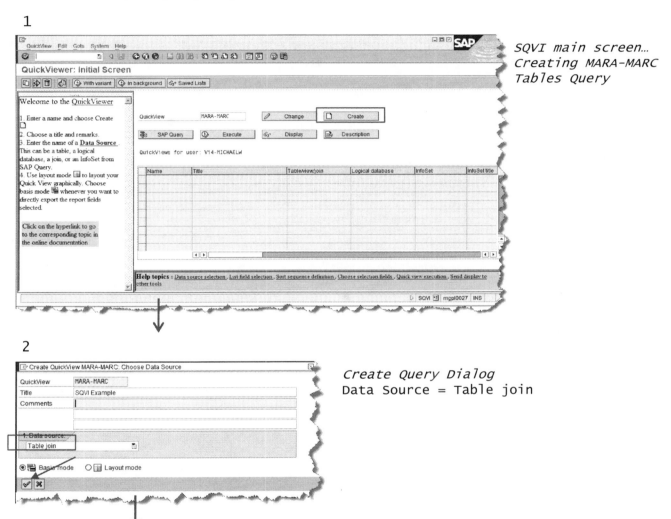

SQVI main screen...
Creating MARA-MARC
Tables Query

Create Query Dialog
Data Source = Table join

3

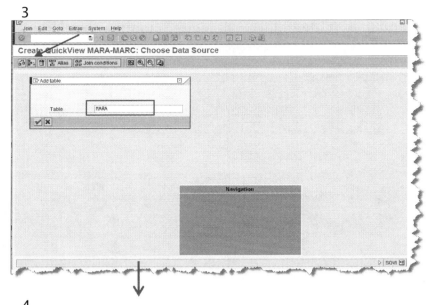

Data Source Viewer
Selecting for first table,
MARA...

4

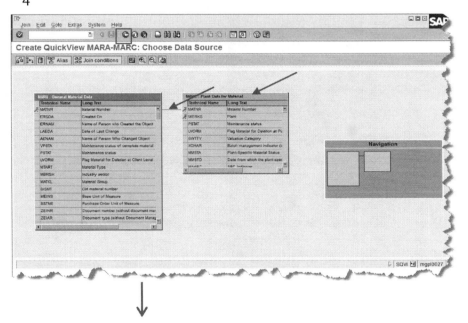

Data Source Viewer
with second table, MARC *added...*

SQVI automatically proposes a join...

5

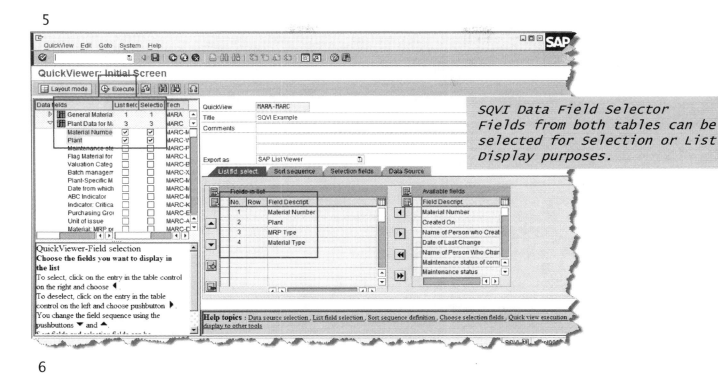

*SQVI Data Field Selector
Fields from both tables can be
selected for Selection or List
Display purposes.*

6

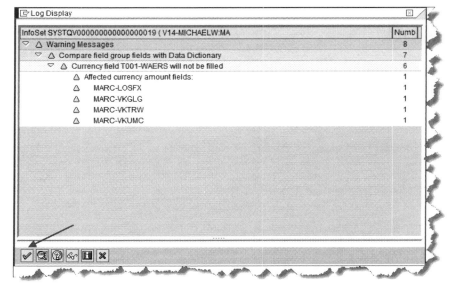

*SQVI Field Warning
Message*

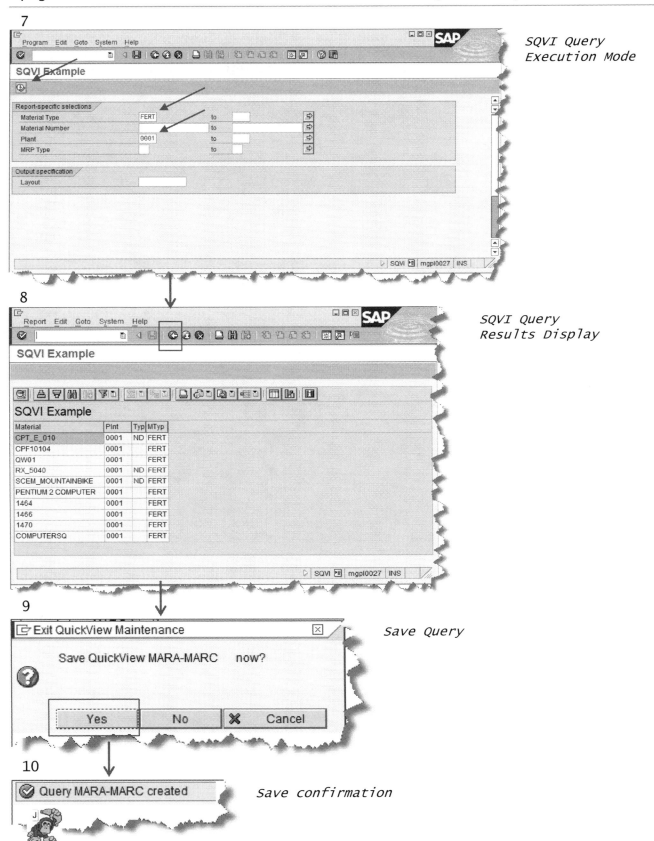

7 SQVI Query Execution Mode

8 SQVI Query Results Display

9 Save Query

10 Save confirmation

SP01. Print Output is managed with the SP01 transaction. SP01 enables report re-printing and re-direction of reports already printed to different printers defined in the system. SAP printing works around the concept of a *Print Spool Request.* SP01 manages these requests and works in all cases save one: this is the case where the user has selected a *Delete Spool Immediately after the Printing* option. In this case, the Spool request is deleted immediately after a successful printing – and is not available for use on SP01.

Function	Transaction
Print Output Management	SP01

Example: Display a User's Print Spool Requests

Info Required.
✓ User ID

1

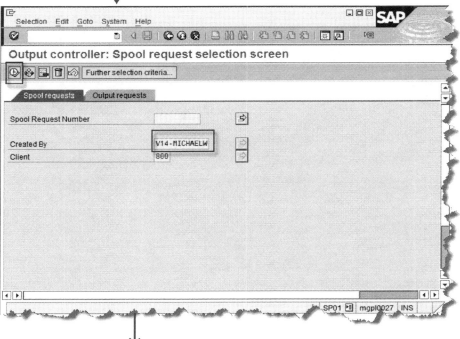

Enter SP01 and press the enter key

Enter user ID and click on the Execute button.

3

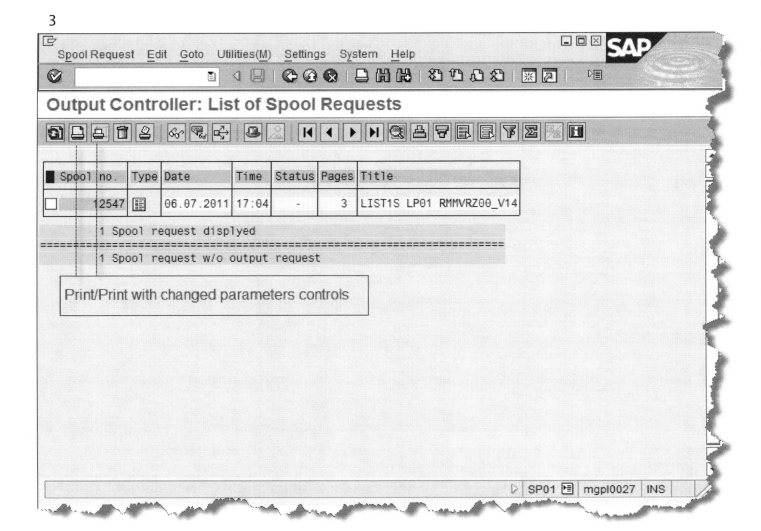

Print/Print with changed parameters controls

Display User/User Security. We look at three transactions in this area:

✓ **SOBN01** to find a user name – useful when trying to determine who made the last change to a master or transactional data record.

✓ **SU01D** to view a User Profile – useful when troubleshooting security authorization issues.

✓ **S_BCE_68001399** a report, also useful in troubleshooting User Security problems.

Function	Transaction
Display a User	SU01D
Find a User	SOBN01
Review User Security Roles	S_BCE_68001399

SU01D.
Info Required.
✓ User ID.

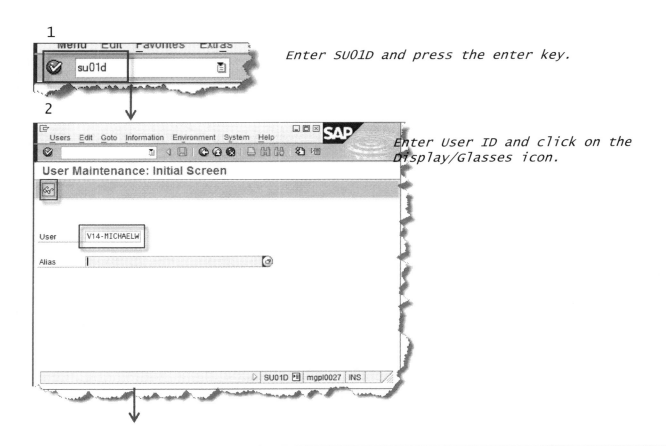

1   Enter SU01D and press the enter key.

2   Enter User ID and click on the Display/Glasses icon.

3

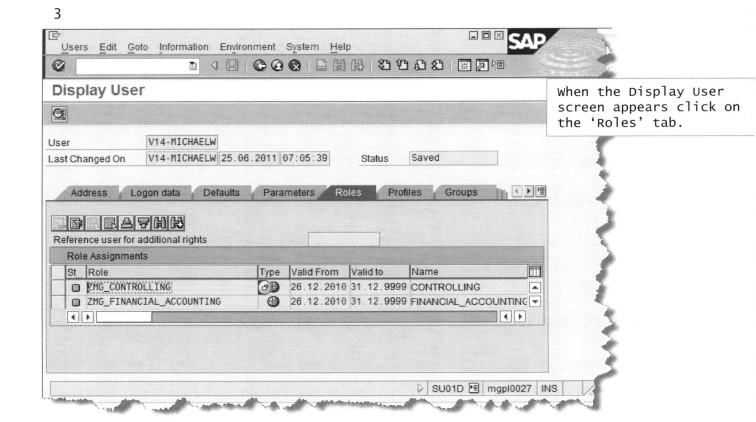

when the Display User screen appears click on the 'Roles' tab.

SOBN01. Find a user.

Info Required.
✓ User ID.

Enter transaction SOBN01 and press the enter key.

Enter User ID and click on the Execute icon.

The Address data maintained for the User in SAP is displayed.

S_BCE_68001399. Display User Roles.

Info Required.
✓   User ID.

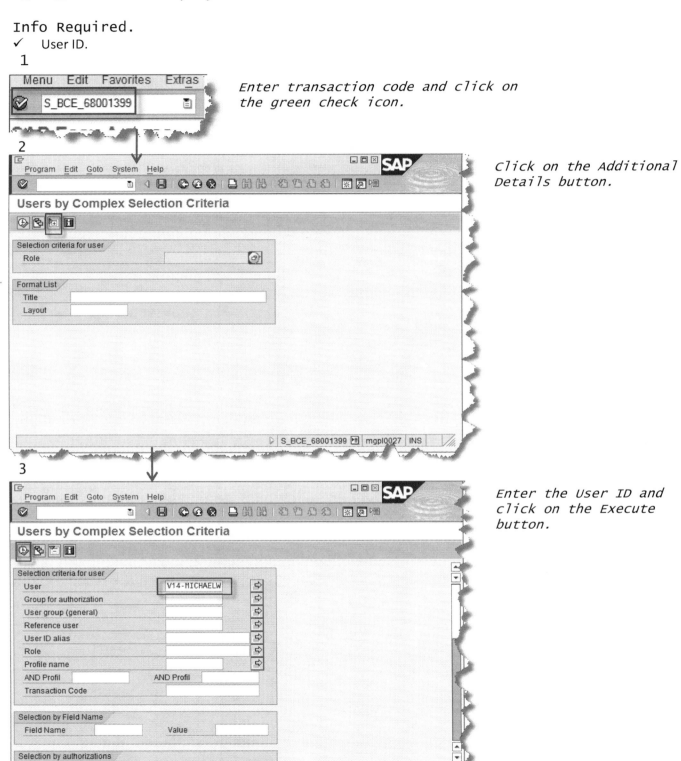

1

Enter transaction code and click on the green check icon.

2

Click on the Additional Details button.

3

Enter the User ID and click on the Execute button.

S_BCE_68001399 Report.

4

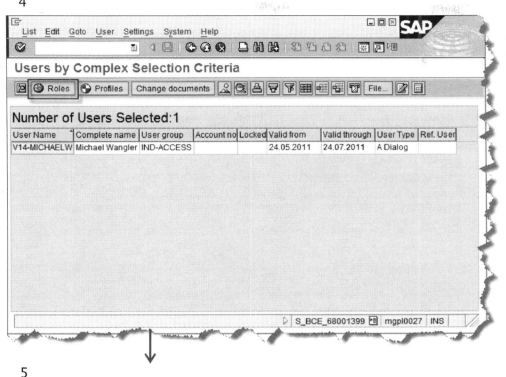

Click on the Roles button.

5

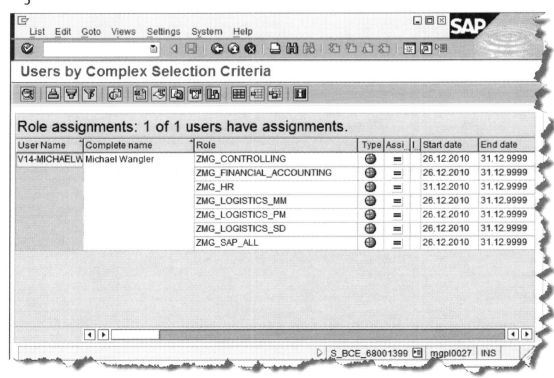

All the roles for the User ID are displayed.

The Language of SAP
An 'ITSA' Table Summary

As we use the term, Itsa can mean - it's a
transaction (user executable program)...
term (or concept)...
table (database table — where data is stored)...

The Language of SAP
SAP ECC Transactions, Tables, Parameters & Concepts Summary

#	Item	It's a…	Section	Area	Notes
1	Application Server	Concept	2-Operator Interface	SAPGUI	Component of the SAP Client-Server system between the SAPGUI on a PC or laptop and the database - it manages access to SAP business data.
2	AUFK	Table	3-Map	Org Str & Mstr Data	(Production) Order Master Data .
3	BUK	Parameter ID	2-Operator Interface	Users Parameters	Company Code Parameter ID. Set in User Profile - Parameters tab.
4	CA01	Transaction	3-Map	Org Str & Mstr Data	Create a Routing.
5	CA02	Transaction	3-Map	Org Str & Mstr Data	Change a Routing.
6	CA03	Transaction	3-Map	Org Str & Mstr Data	Display a Routing.
7	CEWB	Transaction	3-Map	Org Str & Mstr Data	Engineering Workbench.
8	CK11N	Transaction	3-Map	Org Str & Mstr Data	Create a Material Standard Cost.
9	CK24	Transaction	3-Map	Org Str & Mstr Data	Mark/Release a Material Cost.
10	CO01	Transaction	3-Map	MRP & Prod Plng	Create A Production Order.
11	CO02	Transaction	3-Map	MRP & Prod Plng	Change A Production Order.
12	CO03	Transaction	3-Map	MRP & Prod Plng	Display A Production Order.
13	CO06	Transaction	3-Map	Sales Order Entry	Availability Processing.
14	CO09	Transaction	3-Map	Sales Order Entry	Availability Overview.
15	CO11N	Transaction	3-Map	MRP & Prod Plng	Production Order Confirmation.
16	CO13	Transaction	3-Map	MRP & Prod Plng	Production Order Confirmation - Reversal.
17	CO14	Transaction	3-Map	MRP & Prod Plng	Production Order Confirmation Display.

#	Item	It's a...	Section	Area	Notes
18	CO24	Transaction	3-Map	MRP & Prod Plng	Missing Parts Information System.
19	CO41	Transaction	3-Map	MRP & Prod Plng	Collective Conversion of Planned Orders.
20	COHV	Transaction	3-Map	MRP & Prod Plng	Mass Processing Production Orders.
21	COMAC	Transaction	3-Map	MRP & Prod Plng	Collective Availability Check.
22	COOIS	Transaction	3-Map	MRP & Prod Plng	Production Order Information System.
23	CR03	Transaction	3-Map	Org Str & Mstr Data	Display Work Center
24	CS01	Transaction	3-Map	Org Str & Mstr Data	Create a Bill of Material.
25	CS02	Transaction	3-Map	Org Str & Mstr Data	Change a Bill of Material.
26	CS03	Transaction	3-Map	Org Str & Mstr Data	Display a Bill of Material.
27	CS13	Transaction	3-Map	Org Str & Mstr Data	BOM Multilevel Display.
28	CS15	Transaction	3-Map	Org Str & Mstr Data	BOM Where Used List.
29	DD02VV	Table	3-Map	Org Str & Mstr Data	List of Tables (useful to find tables).
30	DD03M	Table	3-Map	Org Str & Mstr Data	List of Fields (useful to find a list of tables for a field) .
31	DGR	Parameter ID	2-Operator Interface	Operator Interface	MRP Controller Parameter ID. Set in User Profile - Parameters tab.
32	Download-ing SAP Data	Concept	2-Operator Interface	Operator Interface	SAP data (report, tables, field values) can be downloaded into excel or other formats thru: System/List/Save/Local files where available. Field level data can be downloaded by right clicking and clicking on download.
33	EKG	Parameter ID	2-Operator Interface	Operator Interface	Purchasing Group Parameter ID. Set in User Profile - Parameters tab.

#	Item	Itsa...	Section	Area	Notes
34	EKKO	Table	3-Map	Org Str & Mstr Data	Purchasing Document Header.
35	EKO	Parameter ID	2-Operator Interface	Operator Interface	Purchasing Organization Parameter ID. Set in User Profile - Parameters tab.
36	EKPO	Table	3-Map	Org Str & Mstr Data	Purchasing Document Line Item.
37	Enter Key Function in SAP	Concept	2-Operator Interface	SAPGUI	Performs a Screen Level Data Integrity Check - prevents moving to next screen until required data is provided.
38	Executing a Transaction	Concept	2-Operator Interface	Transactions	Transactions can be executed by double clicking on them in the Favorites or Standard SAP Menus; or by entering them in the Command Field and pressing the enter key.
39	Extras > Settings > Display Technical Names	Control	2-Operator Interface	Window Controls	This setting causes the Transaction Code to be displayed in in all SAP and User Favorites Menus.
40	F1, F4, F8 Function Key Controls	Concept	2-Operator Interface		F1 = Help; F4 = List Selections; F8 = Execute.
41	Field Level Help	Concept	2-Operator Interface	Field Help	Click on F1 once the field has been highlighted to display the description of the field.
42	Field Level Selection Dialog Operations	Concept	2-Operator Interface	Field Selections	Click on F4 to select pre-defined values for a field where available.
43	Finding a Transaction Program Name	Concept	2-Operator Interface	Transactions	When inside a transaction click on the status bar on the bottom right of the screen and select the option Program.
44	Finding Transactions with Find / Find Again icons	Concept	2-Operator Interface	Transactions	Click on the Binoculars and type in the transaction name and then click the arrow or press enter. Make sure both options "in technical names" &"in texts" are selected. Use the binoculars + icon to find the next options that matches your entry.

#	Item	It's a...	Section	Area	Notes
45	Green Check Icon function	Control	2-Operator Interface	Window Controls	Performs the same function as the enter key - checks for screen data integrity - and advances to next screen if all checks are complete/without error.
46	LIKP	Table	3-Map	Org Str & Mstr Data	Delivery Header.
47	LIPS	Table	3-Map	Org Str & Mstr Data	Delivery Item.
48	MAPL	Table	3-Map	Org Str & Mstr Data	Task List to Materials (Materials Routings).
49	MARA	Table	3-Map	Org Str & Mstr Data	Material Master General Data.
50	MARC	Table	3-Map	Org Str & Mstr Data	Material Plant Data.
51	MARD	Table	3-Map	Org Str & Mstr Data	Stock Storage Location/Plant.
52	MAST	Table	3-Map	Org Str & Mstr Data	Material BOM Link.
53	MB51	Transaction	3-Map	MRP & Prod Plng	Goods Movements for a Material.
54	MB52	Transaction	3-Map	MRP & Prod Plng	Inventory for a Material.
55	MCSI	Transaction	3-Map	Deliveries & Billing	Sales Order Information System.
56	MD01	Transaction	3-Map	MRP & Prod Plng	Plant Level MRP.
57	MD04	Transaction	3-Map	MRP & Prod Plng	Planning Situation for a Material.
58	ME11	Transaction	3-Map	Org Str & Mstr Data	Create a Purchasing Info Record (PIR).
59	ME12	Transaction	3-Map	Org Str & Mstr Data	Change a PIR.
60	ME13	Transaction	3-Map	Org Str & Mstr Data	Display a PIR.
61	ME1M	Transaction	3-Map	Org Str & Mstr Data	List PIRs.
62	ME21N	Transaction	3-Map	Purchasing & Rcvng	Create a Purchase Order.
63	ME28	Transaction	3-Map	Purchasing & Rcvng	Release a Purchase Order.
64	ME2M	Transaction	3-Map	Purchasing & Rcvng	List Purchase Orders Report.

#	Item	Itsa...	Section	Area	Notes
65	ME57	Transaction	3-Map	Purchasing & Rcvng	Assign Source of Supply to a Purchase Req.
66	ME5A	Transaction	3-Map	Purchasing & Rcvng	List Purchase Requisitions Report.
67	MIGO_GI	Transaction	3-Map	Purchasing & Rcvng	Issue parts to a Production Order
68	MIGO_GR	Transaction	3-Map	Purchasing & Rcvng	Receive in Materials from a Purchase Order.
69	MM01	Transaction	3-Map	Org Str & Mstr Data	Create a Material Master.
70	MM02	Transaction	3-Map	Org Str & Mstr Data	Change a Material Master.
71	MM03	Transaction	3-Map	Org Str & Mstr Data	Display a Material Master.
72	MM60	Transaction	3-Map	Org Str & Mstr Data	List Material Masters Report.
73	MMBE	Transaction	3-Map	MRP & Prod Plng	Material Inventory.
74	NDR	Parameter ID	2-Operator Interface	Operator Interface	MM Printing Parameter ID.
75	Opening/Closing Windows/ Transactions	Concept	2-Operator Interface	Transactions	With new session control or using "/o" in the command line to generate a new session.
76	Printing in SAP	Concept	2-Operator Interface	Printing	Click on Customize Local Layout icon (hint: it's the rainbow colored box) and then click on the option "Hard Copy" to print.
77	Production Order Defined	Concept	1-FAQS	SAP is Orders	
78	Production Order Doc Flow	Concept	1-FAQS	SAP is Orders	
79	Purchase Order Defined	Concept	1-FAQS	SAP is Orders	
80	Purchase Order Doc Flow	Concept	1-FAQS	SAP is Orders	
81	S_BCE_68001399	Transaction	3-Map	Sys Mngmt & Security	

#	Item	It's a...	Section	Area	Notes
82	Sales Order Defined	Concept	1-FAQS	SAP is Orders	
83	Sales Order Doc Flow	Concept	1-FAQS	SAP is Orders	
84	Sandbox	Concept	2-Operator Interface	Operator Interface Basics	
85	SAP Create/Stop Session Controls	Control	2-Operator Interface	Window Controls	Running SAP transaction can be stopped by click the triangle /rectangle icon available on the top left corner of the screen and selecting Stop Transaction. Similarly sessions can be created by selecting Create Session.
86	SAP Main Menu Icons	Control	2-Operator Interface	Window Controls	
87	SAP Menu Folder Structure	Control	2-Operator Interface	Window Controls	
88	SAP System Icons	Control	2-Operator Interface	Window Controls	
89	SAP System Properties	Concept	2-Op Interface	SAPGUI	
90	SAPGUI	Concept	2-Operator Interface	SAPGUI	
91	SAPLOGON.INI	Concept	2-Operator Interface	SAPGUI	
92	SE10	Transaction	3-Map	Sys Mngmt & Security	Displays a Transport.
93	SE16N	Transaction	3-Map	Sys Mngmt & Security	Displays a Table.
94	SE38N	Transaction	3-Map	Sys Mngmt & Security	Displays a Program.
95	SM12	Transaction	3-Map	Sys Mngmt & Security	Displays Table Locks.

#	Item	It's a...	Section	Area	Notes
96	SM30	Transaction	3-Map	Sys Mngmt & Security	Maintains table entries.
97	SM37	Transaction	3-Map	Sys Mngmt & Security	Displays a Job.
98	SOBN01	Transaction	3-Map	Sys Mngmt & Security	Find a User.
99	SP01	Transaction	3-Map	Sys Mngmt & Security	Display Print Spooler Requests.
100	SPA	Parameter ID	2-Operator Interface	Operator Interface	Division Parameter ID. Set in User Profile - Parameters tab.
101	SPRO	Transaction	3-Map	Sys Mngmt & Security	Displays IMG.
102	SQVI	Transaction	3-Map	Sys Mngmt & Security	Query Builder.
103	ST22	Transaction	3-Map	Sys Mngmt & Security	Displays ABAP Run Time Errors.
104	STPO	Table	3-Map	Org Str & Mstr Data	BOM Item.
105	SU01D	Transaction	3-Map	Sys Mngmt & Security	Displays a User.
106	System ID	Concept	2-Operator Interface	SAPGUI	
107	System Menu Line function	Control	2-Operator Interface	Window Controls	
108	System Message Types	Control	2-2-Operator Interface	Window Controls	
109	System Notifications Area	Control	2-Operator Interface	Window Controls	
110	System Number	Concept	2-Operator Interface	SAPGUI	
111	System Status Bar Control Area	Control	2-Operator Interface	Window Controls	

#	Item	It's a...	Section	Area	Notes
112	T024E	Table	3-Map	Org Str & Mstr Data	Purchasing Org - Company Code.
113	T024W	Table	3-Map	Org Str & Mstr Data	Plant - Purchasing Org.
114	Tab Key function in SAP	Concept	2-Operator Interface	SAPGUI	
115	Transaction Command Field function	Control	2-Operator Interface	Window Controls	
116	Transaction Command Field Hide/Unhide Controls	Control	2-Operator Interface	Window Controls	
117	Transaction Command Field History	Control	2-Operator Interface	Window Controls	
118	Transaction Help	Concept	2-Operator Interface	Transactions	
119	Transaction Types - Action vs. Reporting	Concept	2-Operator Interface	Transactions	
120	Transaction Types - Custom vs. Standard	Concept	2-Operator Interface	Transactions	
121	TSTCT	Table	3-Map	Org Str & Mstr Data	List of Transaction Codes.
122	User Favorites	Control	2-Op Interface	Window Controls	
123	User Parameters	Concept	2-Op Interface	Users Parameters	
124	V.00	Transaction	3-Map	Sales Order Entry	Incomplete Sales Orders.
125	V_MAT_ROUT_BOM	Table	3-Map	Org Str & Mstr Data	Materials Routings & BOMs.
126	V_T001	Table	3-Map	Org Str & Mstr Data	List of Company Codes.

#	Item	Itsa...	Section	Area	Notes
127	V_T001K_LK	Table	3-Map	Org Str & Mstr Data	Assignment of Plants to Company Codes.
128	V_T001L	Table	3-Map	Org Str & Mstr Data	List of Storage Locations.
129	V_T001W	Table	3-Map	Org Str & Mstr Data	List of Plants.
130	V_T024E	Table	3-Map	Org Str & Mstr Data	List of Purchasing Orgs.
131	V_TVKO	Table	3-Map	Org Str & Mstr Data	List of Sales Orgs .
132	V_TVKO_LK	Table	3-Map	Org Str & Mstr Data	Assignments Co Codes to Sales Orgs.
133	VA01	Transaction	3-Map	Sales Order Entry	Create a Sales Order.
134	VA02	Transaction	3-Map	Sales Order Entry	Change a Sales Order.
135	VA03	Transaction	3-Map	Sales Order Entry	Display a Sales Order.
136	VA05	Transaction	3-Map	Sales Order Entry	List Sales Orders.
137	VA11	Transaction	3-Map	Sales Order Entry	Create an Inquiry.
138	VA12	Transaction	3-Map	Sales Order Entry	Change an Inquiry.
139	VA13	Transaction	3-Map	Sales Order Entry	Display an Inquiry.
140	VA21	Transaction	3-Map	Sales Order Entry	Create a Quotation.
141	VA22	Transaction	3-Map	Sales Order Entry	Change a Quotation.
142	VA23	Transaction	3-Map	Sales Order Entry	Display a Quotation.
143	VA25	Transaction	3-Map	Sales Order Entry	List Quotation.
144	VBAK	Table	3-Map	Org Str & Mstr Data	Sales Document Header.
145	VBAP	Table	3-Map	Org Str & Mstr Data	Sales Document Line Item.

#	Item	It's a...	Section	Area	Notes
146	VF01	Transaction	3-Map	Deliveries & Billing	Create a Billing Document.
147	VF04	Transaction	3-Map	Deliveries & Billing	Deliveries without a Billing Document
148	VK11	Transaction	3-Map	Org Str & Mstr Data	Create a Pricing Record.
149	VK12	Transaction	3-Map	Org Str & Mstr Data	Change a Pricing Record.
150	VK13	Transaction	3-Map	Org Str & Mstr Data	Display a Pricing Record.
151	VKB	Parameter ID	2-Operator Interface	Users Parameters	Sales Office Parameter ID. Set in User Profile - Parameters tab.
152	VKG	Parameter ID	2-Operator Interface	Users Parameters	Sales Group Parameter ID. Set in User Profile - Parameters tab.
153	VKO	Parameter ID	2-Operator Interface	Users Parameters	Sales Organization Parameter ID. Set in User Profile - Parameters tab.
154	VL01N	Transaction	3-Map	Deliveries & Billing	Create a Delivery.
155	VL02N	Transaction	3-Map	Deliveries & Billing	Change a Delivery.
156	VL03N	Transaction	3-Map	Deliveries & Billing	Display a Delivery.
157	VL06O	Transaction	3-Map	Deliveries & Billing	Delivery Monitor
158	VL10A	Transaction	3-Map	Deliveries & Billing	Create Deliveries - Sales Orders
159	VL10B	Transaction	3-Map	Deliveries & Billing	Create Deliveries - Purchase Orders
160	VL10G	Transaction	3-Map	Deliveries & Billing	Create Deliveries - Sales & Purchase Orders
161	VTW	Parameter ID	2-Operator Interface	Operator Interface	Distribution Channel Parameter ID. Set in User Profile - Parameters tab.

#	Item	It's a...	Section	Area	Notes
162	Window Controls - Min, Max, Close	Control	2-Operator Interface	Window Controls	
163	WRK	Parameter ID	2-Operator Interface	Operator Interface	Plant Parameter ID. Set in User Profile - Parameters tab.
164	XD01	Transaction	3-Map	Org Str & Mstr Data	Create a Customer Master.
165	XD02	Transaction	3-Map	Org Str & Mstr Data	Change a Customer Master.
166	XD03	Transaction	3-Map	Org Str & Mstr Data	Display Customer Master.
167	XK01	Transaction	3-Map	Org Str & Mstr Data	Create a Vendor Master.
168	XK02	Transaction	3-Map	Org Str & Mstr Data	Change a Vendor Master.
169	XK03	Transaction	3-Map	Org Str & Mstr Data	Display Vendor Master.

Materials related

Material Master	
Display	MM03
Change	MM02
Create	MM01
List	MM60
Delete	MM06

Bill of Material	
Display	CS03
Change	CS02
Create	CS01
List	CEWB
ML BOM Display	CS13
Where Used	CS15

Routing	
Display	CA03
Change	CA02
Create	CA01
Ds WrkCtr	CR03

MRP & Stock Situation	
MRP Pl Lvl	MD01
MRP Sl/ML	MD02
Stock Sit'n	MD04
Inventory	MMBE
Inventory	MB52
Gds Mov	MB51

Production Planning	
Prd Ord Mass Prc	COHV
Col Cnv Pl Ords	CO41
Prd Ord Info Sys	COOIS
Col Avail Check	COMAC
Missing Parts	CO24
Goods Issues	MIGO_GI
Prd Ord Cnfirm	CO11N
Prd Ord Cnf/Ds	CO14
Prd Ord Cnf/Can	CO13
Prd Ord Display	CO03
Prd Ord Change	CO02
Prd Ord Create	CO01

Sales related

Customer Master	
Display	XD03
Change	XD02
Create	XD01

Inquiries	
Display	VA13
Change	VA12
Create	VA11

Quotations	
Display	VA23
Change	VA22
Create	VA21
List	VA25

Sales Orders	
Display	VA03
Change	VA02
Create	VA01
List	VA05
Incomplete	V.00

Pricing Records	
Display	VK13
Change	VK12
Create	VK11

Availability	
Av Ovrvw	CO09
Bk Ord Prc	CO06

Deliveries	
Display	VL03N
Change	VL02N
Create	VL01N
Monitor	VL06O
Coll D/SO	VL10A
Coll D/PO	VL10B
Coll D/O	VL10G

Billing / Rptng	
Create	VF01
D w/o Inv	VF04
Sls Rptng	MCSI

Purchasing related

Vendor Master	
Display	XK03
Change	XK02
Create	XK01

Purch Info Rec	
Display	ME13
Change	ME12
Create	ME11
List	ME1M

Purchasing & Rcvg	
List PReqs	ME5A
Src PReqs	ME57
Create PO	ME21N
Rel PO	ME28
List PO	ME2M
PO GR	MIGO_GR

Costing	
Create	CK11N
Mk/Rel	CK24

Config, System & Security related

Systems Management	
Programs	SE38N
Transports	SE10
Table Locks	SM12
Runtime Errors	ST22
Jobs	SM37
IMG	SPRO
Display User	SU01D
Find User	SOBN01
User Sec Roles	S_BCE_68001399
Print Mngmt	SP01
Display Table	SE16N
Maint. Table	SM30
Build Query	SQVI

Topic	Page
ABAP Related Transactions	233
Adding a New System to SAP Logon Pad	30
Availability Check	153
Bills of Material (BOMs)	121
CA03, Display Routing	130
Client Server Concept	24
CO06, Back Order Processing	155
CO09, Material Availability	154
CO11N, Confirmation	191
CO13, Cancel Order Confirmation	194
CO14, Display Confirmations	193
CO24, Missing Parts Report	187
CO41, Mass Processing	181
COGI, Production Order Errors	195
COHV, Mass Processing	178
Collective Planned Order Processing Strategy	175
COMAC, Missing Parts Update	185
Company Codes	78
Configuration Overview	21
COOIS, Order Reporting	183
Copy/Paste example VA05 and COHV	177
CS03, Display BOM	123
Customer Master	142
Display User Info/User Security Transactions	250
Easy Access Window	38
Easy Access Window – User Favorites	37
ECC Order Process Flows	20
Exporting Data to Excel	60
Field Level Help Example	50
Field Level Selections	54
Finding a transaction	44
Finished Goods Planning with COHV	176
First Forty' List	67
Green Check and Command Field	34
Help Functions	47
IMG Configuration Tool (SPRO)	22
Initial Logon and Change Password Dialog	31
Inquiries	148
Internal vs. External Procurement	212
Key SAP Tables	89
Logon Pad	29
Main Menu – Logistics key areas	39
Main Menu Icons	36
Main Menu Window Controls	32
Maintaining User Favorites	66
Map Area 2B: Deliveries and Billing	158
Master vs. Transactional data	23
Material Costing	140
Material Master Data Types a Summary	92
Material Master Example Views	93
Material Master Key Fields	110
Material Master Views Concept Diagram	94
Material Master Views Examples	97
Material Master Views Summary	95
Material Masters in BOMs, Routings & PIRs	91
MB51, Material Movements	206
MB52, Stock Report	208

Topic	Page
MD01, Run MRP at Plant Level	197
MD02, Single Item / Multilevel MRP	199
MD04, Display Stock Situation	201
ME1M, Display PIR Report	137
ME21N, Create Purchase Order	222
ME28, Release Purchase Order	224
ME2M, List Purchase Orders	227
ME53N, Display Requisition	218
ME57, Process Requisitions	219
ME5A, List Requisitions	216
MIGO_GI, Goods Issues	189
MIGO_GR, Receive PO Materials	229
MM01, Create Material Master	118
MM02, Change Material Master	116
MM03, Display Material Master	113
MMBE, Stock Overview	205
MRP Concept: What happens when MRP runs	171
MRP, Production & Inventory Summary	170
Opening & Closing Windows	52
Org Structures Overview	74
Outside Processing	214
Plants	79
Pricing	144
Printing	58
Procurement Cycle and Types	211
Procurement Scenarios	215
Production Order Basics	173
Purchasing Info Records	136
Purchasing Organizations	83
Quotations	149
Routings	127
Sales Order Incompleteness Procedure	156
Sales Orders	150
Sales Orders: Additional Key Concepts	152
Sales Organizations	82
Sales Reporting	167
Sandbox, defined	28
SAP AG	16
SE16N Table Viewer	87
Security Overview	25
Setting User Parameters	62
SM37, Background Jobs	237
SPO1, Printing	248
SPRO	84, 239
Starting a transaction	46
Storage Locations	81
Subcontracting	213
System Icons	35
System Menu Line and Display Technical Names	33
System Notification & Status Bar	40
Table Viewer Transactions	241
The SAP Client	77
V.00, Incomplete Sales Documents	157
Vendor Master	134
VF01-VF04, Billing	165
VL01N, Create delivery	160
VL060, Outbound Delivery Monitor	162
VL10X, Create Deliveries	161
VT01N-VT03N, Shipments	163
Window and Controls	41

Made in United States
Troutdale, OR
09/28/2023

13254235R00148